CO 1 02 1766

GW01336276

Req
D.Fin
6.9.82
(hesnot
no honoury).
22. MAR. 1983

C395870

BOOKSTORE LOAN

COUNTY COUNCIL OF DURHAM
COUNTY LIBRARY

The latest date entered on the date label or card is the date by which book must be returned, and fines will be charged if the book is kept after this date.

Prospects for
British
Librarianship

Other books by K. C. Harrison

First steps in librarianship
Libraries in Britain
Libraries in Scandinavia
Public relations for librarians
The library and the community
Facts at your fingertips
Public libraries today

A Library Association Centenary Volume

Prospects for British Librarianship

Edited by K C Harrison

The Library Association/London

First published by
The Library Association
7 Ridgmount Street
London WC1E 7AE. 1976

ISBN 0 85365 009 8

© The editor and contributors, 1976

Cataloguing-in-publication data:

Prospects for British librarianship.
  Index.
  ISBN 0-85365-009-8
  1. Harrison, Kenneth Cecil
  2. Library Association
  020'.941 Z791
  Library science
  Libraries – Great Britain

Design: Graham Bishop
Index: Elisabeth Ingham
Set in 11 on 12 pt Garamond 156
on Fyneprint paper

Made and printed in Great Britain by
Unwin Brothers Limited
The Gresham Press
Old Woking, Surrey

Contents

Contributors vii

Introduction — K. C. Harrison ix

Chapter

1. The Library Association from within — R. P. Hilliard 1
2. A member's view of The Library Association — Neil A. Simpson 13
3. The future of library and information studies — P. Havard-Williams 29
4. Training future librarians — G. B. Eynon 43
5. The future management pattern for libraries — Gileon Holroyd 57
6. The role of government in library development — Ross Shimmon 71
7. The future of library techniques — Rollo G. Woods 89
8. Libraries as media centres — Norman Beswick 108
9. The library in the cultural framework — Brian Arnold and Bob Usherwood 126
10. Libraries and their users — Barry Totterdell 140
11. The book trade and libraries — Brian H. Baumfield and Clive Bingley 152
12. International directions — J. S. Parker 169
13. Hospital libraries and service to the handicapped
    1. The multidisciplinary professional library in the hospital — Jenny Wade 186

11	Library services for hospital patients, prisoners and housebound readers	Brian Cooper	195
14	Future library co-operation and the British Library	Jean M. Plaister	202
15	The academic librarian of the future	James Thompson	216
16	The special librarian of the future	M. N. Patten	230
17	The public librarian of the future	Melvyn Barnes	245
18	The school and youth librarian of the future	Jennifer Shepherd	262
19	Design of library buildings of the future	J. M. Orr	275
	Index		287

Contributors

Brian C. Arnold, ALA
Senior Assistant Librarian, Stevenage Central Library.

Melvyn Barnes, DMA, ALA, AMBIM, MILGA
Borough Librarian and Arts Officer, The Royal Borough of Kensington and Chelsea.

Brian H. Baumfield, FLA, FRSA, MBIM
Borough Librarian and Curator, London Borough of Brent.

Norman W. Beswick, MA, FLA
Lecturer, Department of Library and Information Studies, Loughborough University of Technology.

Clive Bingley
Editor of *New Library World* and Director of Clive Bingley Ltd, Publishers.

Brian Cooper, BSC(ECON), ALA
Librarian, Rampton Hospital, Notts.

G. B. Eynon, MA, ALA
Assistant City Librarian (Administration, Research and Development), Westminster City Libraries.

K. C. Harrison, MBE, FLA
City Librarian, Westminster City Libraries.

Professor P. Havard-Williams, MA, DIPED, ALA, FLAI, ANZLA
Head of Department of Library and Information Studies, Loughborough University of Technology.

R. P. Hilliard, BSC(ECON), FCA
Secretary, The Library Association.

Miss Gileon Holroyd, BA, FLA, ACDIPED
Senior Lecturer, School of Librarianship, The Polytechnic of North London.

J. M. Orr, MA, FLA
Head of School of Librarianship, Robert Gordon's Institute of Technology.

J. S. Parker, ALA
Research Assistant, College of Librarianship Wales

M. N. Patten, ALA
Head of Technical Information Systems, British Steel Corporation.

Miss Jean M. Plaister, BSC(ECON), FLA
Director, LASER.

Miss Jennifer Shepherd, ALA
Assistant County Librarian, Services to Education and Young People,
Leicestershire Libraries and Information Service.

Ross Shimmon, FLA
Services Librarian, Preston Polytechnic.

Neil A. Simpson, MA, ALA
Assistant Chief Librarian, Operational Services Tameside Libraries and Arts.

James Thompson, BA, FLA
Librarian, University of Reading.

Barry Totterdell, FLA
Deputy Chief Librarian, London Borough of Croydon.

R. C. Usherwood, ALA
Senior Assistant Director (Libraries), Directorate of Amenity Services, London Borough of Lambeth.

Miss J. R. Wade, ALA
Deputy Librarian, Clinical Research Centre, Harrow.

R. G. Woods, MA, ALA
Deputy Librarian, University of Southampton.

Introduction

As early as 1971 the Library Association began to think about marking its centenary in 1977 and appointed what was then a Centenary Celebrations Working Party. As time went on, and as the Working Party became more involved in preparations for 1977, it was strengthened numerically and was given the additional responsibility of planning the Centenary Conference programme. In this way the Working Party was elevated to become the Centenary Celebrations Sub-Committee of the Executive.

From its very first meeting, the Working Party recommended the publication in book form of a history of the Library Association, and Dr W. A. Munford was invited to undertake this task. At a later stage it was agreed to ask Professor Wilfred Saunders to prepare a completely new edition of the book *Librarianship in Britain today*, which had been originally published in 1967. Since Dr Munford's book would be a record of the past achievements, not forgetting the shortcomings, of the Association, and since Professor Saunders' compilation would be attempting to mirror the present state of the art of librarianship, it soon became obvious that a third and companion volume should be prepared as a tribute to the Association, on its 100th birthday, with the task of attempting to look into the future of the Association, of the profession, and of librarians. This idea was accepted by the Council and this, then, is that volume.

It is hoped that the three books, Munford, Saunders and this one, will between them mark the Library Association centenary in a permanent and fitting manner, and that they will be sought after not only by libraries all over the world, but also by many members who will want to add them to their personal shelves.

From the outset the attempt was made to form a team of contributors who, in the main, were going to be concerned with the future development of librarianship in Britain and with the future progress of the Library Association. I am very grateful to all the contributors for their ready acceptance of the assignments given to them, and for the energy and imagination with which they have tackled their varied topics. I would also thank Bruce Coward and Edward Dudley for their helpful comments.

I tried not to burden the contributors with too much advice. After pointing out that the volume would supplement those of Munford and Saunders, I simply asked writers to prognosticate on the future of their special subject as they themselves saw it. No advice was given on how far they should attempt to look ahead. Opinion varies so much as to the practicability of this – some say twenty-five years is the absolute limit, others say ten or five years, some as little as two – so it was left to each contributor to set his or her own limits to the forecast. It is interesting to note that quite a few of the writers have looked towards the year 2000, or in some cases 2001, and this perhaps is a not unnatural trend now that we are firmly in the last quarter of the twentieth century.

Contributors were aware of each other's existence and assignments, and there has been some consultation between them where it was thought overlaps might occur. Such consultation has been minimal, yet despite this it is fascinating to read the volume as a whole and to discover how different writers have sometimes arrived at the same conclusions via varied routes, and also to see how, despite many different approaches and some obvious clashes of opinion, the volume presents a coherent whole.

It is heartening for all of us, whatever our ages and stages of professional development, that so many experts appear to agree on at least one thing – that there *is* a future for libraries and librarians.

Reading the ensuing chapters, one comes across many intriguing glimpses of the future as seen through the eyes of the contributors. Gileon Holroyd, for example, looking at the possibilities of library management in the future, foresees the need for what she calls *agents-bibliothécaires*, a corps of roving librarians or trouble-shooters who will act in a consultant or free-lance capacity. Central government, she avers, will encourage this and may even provide roving librarians directly.

Teamwork will more than ever be the keynote of library management. Gileon Holroyd stresses this by pointing out that there will be less scope in the future for a dominant personality as chief, and this is underscored by Gordon Eynon who asserts that 'the days of the vertical hierarchies are over'. Eynon also indicates that there will be a gradual shift from supervisory

Introduction

training to management development, and it must be heartening to all Association people to find him concluding with the words 'the Association's role in all this must be central'.

Neil Simpson wants the Association to cater for the library technician, and he also feels that the LA should have an exemplary information service for its members. He takes a close look at the future possibilities of the LA's branches and groups, and he wants the Association to be less arrogant in its attitude towards foreign library qualifications.

Ross Shimmon's assignment was to examine the role of government in library development and, in looking at the importance of accurate and up-to-date statistics, he suggests that the British Library rather than the Department of Education and Science might be a better agency for their collection. He emphasises the need for current standards in all fields of library science and he wants the British library schools to become more involved in research. As for inspections from the DES, Shimmon suggests the 'visiting fireman' approach – a curious parallel with Gileon Holroyd's conception of roving consultant librarians.

Dealing with the future of library techniques, R. G. Woods has opportunities of which he makes full use. Starting from some existing techniques such as Viewdata, Ceefax and Postfax, which are still relatively in their infancy, he develops his theme towards the possibilities of the year 2001. In the world he describes, 'learned journals, scientific reports and research monographs would simply cease to be published'. Yet he concludes by saying that someone will still have to guide users through the maze of available information, and that person will still fundamentally be a librarian.

Norman Beswick examines the implications for future librarians of the development of media resources. He convinces us, if we needed convincing, that there is a librarianship dimension to audio-visual media because they are essentially information sources. He predicts that the use of audio-visual media will surely increase, but asserts that there need be no threat in this. Barry Totterdell calls for much more research into user needs, and for the establishment of experimental libraries in which traditional ideas might be thrown out of the window in favour of new ideas of outreach 'deliberately setting out to attract non-users and then to monitor success in doing so'.

In their conversation piece, Clive Bingley the publisher and Brian Baumfield the librarian look at the possible future for the book trade and libraries. Books, they conclude, will continue to be the chief medium of communication in the foreseeable future, and although the immediate prospects for the trade are gloomy (they always are!), the distant views, they feel, are good. Hope springs eternal! But much rethinking will be essential, they agree, on the part of booksellers, publishers and librarians.

James Thompson, Michael Patten, Melvyn Barnes and others who write about librarians of the future in varied fields of activity, are all naturally concerned about education, training and qualifications. They all endeavour to define the needs of future users of the various kinds of libraries, and then try to assess how many professional librarians will be wanted to serve these users, what kind of librarians they will need to be, and what special experience and qualifications they will require. Michael Patten may end his contribution with an epitaph, but a perusal of his conclusions will not be found to be too depressing.

Jennifer Shepherd visualises much change in the role of the school librarians, and indeed in the whole relationship between school libraries and youth work within the public libraries. She comments on the increasing sophistication of young library users, implying that this itself must force new attitudes upon school and youth librarians.

Pondering over library design in the future, James Orr suggests a kind of psychological game called 'brain-storming' in which a group of interested people are put together for an informal discussion. Airing their views in this way, Orr believes that out of the recorded, edited dialogue many useful new ideas may emerge. He, too, stresses the needs of the user and insists that library buildings of tomorrow must be tailor-made for their clientèles.

Other contributors to this volume have put forward their individual concepts of future development. Was the idea of larger local government units really right, or will there be some unscrambling in the future? What will be the effect on public libraries if this happens? When shall we see, if ever, co-ordinated programmes for libraries in hospitals and in prisons? Are we moving towards the integration of public libraries with those of polytechnics in their areas? Will school libraries and children's

Introduction

public libraries ever combine? What of the influence of the British Library? Will this ever-growing Colossus stride dictatorially over librarianship in Britain? Will the influence of the Library Association continue to grow, or is it about to go into a decline?

These, and very many other intriguing questions, are posed in this volume, and some answers are proffered. I hope that enough has been said to whet the appetites of readers and to urge them to explore the chapters with the detailed attention they deserve. Many of the contributors make the point that outside events, economic and political, may well disturb the equilibrium of library progress, but we must all hope that the last quarter of this century can be lived in peace and increasing prosperity. If such conditions can be achieved, this volume proves that we have the right calibre of professionals equipped to lead British librarianship and the Library Association in the future.

One thing seems certain. This book will be perused well into the twenty-first century. After man reached the moon, we all went back to the works of Jules Verne and H. G. Wells if only to see where they went wrong. The future of librarianship in Britain may well work out quite differently from the ideas put forward today, but my contributors have made courageous attempts to visualise it, and they will always be given credit for that.

It only remains for me, on behalf of the contributors and myself, to offer this volume to the Library Association with congratulations on its 100th birthday. We thank the Association for what it has done for us and its thousands of other members, past and present. With this tribute goes every good wish for the future development, growth, progress and influence of the Library Association.

K. C. Harrison

Editor
Chairman, Centenary
Celebrations Sub-Committee

January 1976

Chapter One

The Library Association from Within

R P Hilliard

Over the decade to 1974, and perhaps the last two decades, the profession enjoyed an enormous expansion in the resources applied to library and information work and an enhancement in the general awareness of the importance of this work in an advanced economy and increasingly technological society. Similarly the Association has enjoyed an expansion of personal membership, by 55% in that last decade alone, and has been instrumental in securing the development of the provision for education for the profession to a level undreamt of even in 1964. The number of chartered librarians has doubled and the resources made available for research and development increased substantially. These few examples could be multiplied many times, but the facts of the general pattern are self-evident and unlikely to be questioned. Although the development of the profession and the Association have been part of and dependent upon economic growth and wider trends within society, they have also been closely and directly interrelated and, in particular, the strength of the Association as a representative focus for the profession has provided a foundation on which many of the claims for the expansion of resources to services provided by the profession could be based.

More recently there has been experienced a significant revision of the bland assumption, previously predominant, that we live in an era of continuing economic development. Probably, at least in the medium term, growth will continue to be the dynamic of the advanced economy but there seems little doubt that the current period of economic difficulty will result in changes which will, for some years, influence the way in which society in general will plan for the future and will review plans for development.

One of these changes, signs of which existed before the implications of the current recession became apparent (in response to an increased awareness of the importance of the services of the profession and the resources being applied to them), will be in the planning and allocation of resources to library and information work. In these circumstances it becomes of even greater importance that the profession is capable of offering a cohesive, coherent and authoritative view on all matters of professional concern in discussions of these concerns, and capable of influencing decisions. This implies that the question of the development of the Association must be of considerable importance to the profession.

Of the areas of concern reflected by the chapter-headings in this book that of the development of the Association is the one in which the profession itself has had and will continue to have the most determining influence. It is the one area in which the profession can substantially decide both the level of resources which will be made available and, through the collective control of the application of those resources, the programmes to which they are applied. The Association will not be immune from other influences and limitations upon its development, but the basic pattern of and motive for change will come from the membership and, even if only partially achieved, will reflect the priority which the profession places upon its ability to have an influential voice as a profession on matters of professional concern.

Even within the acknowledged constraints upon its development – for example, the organisation of governmental interests in library and information work, the control of research funds, the general availability of resources – which will limit the determining influence of the profession, the fact remains that the Association does, should and will very largely take the form and priorities required of it by the profession and will reflect the priorities established by the profession. And in that context it is both pertinent and impertinent for a non-librarian Secretary to write about that future development.

Pertinent because for the reasons suggested above, coupled with the fact of the Centenary, there is unlikely to be a more appropriate time to consider that development. Impertinent because there is little formal policy on which to base even an outline programme of development; it is not practical to rely on indications from the past too heavily, and neither is it practical to look to existing stated policies or even to the reports of the Working Party on Association Services (which completed its work in 1975) for guidance on the view of the profession on the development of the Association. Perhaps the profession has been too busy in recent years in developing library and information services, for nowhere does it appear that significant attention has been given to a consideration of this development in a way which lends itself to projection over even a five or ten-year period. The absence of a policy creates an opportunity to suggest some lines of development: perhaps it is an opportunity which should have been resisted.

In considering the activities of any professional body it is helpful to visualise two main concerns. The first is the concern to provide a framework for the development of the *individual* professional: the second, the concern to influence the creation of the social framework within which the *profession* as a whole can develop. (It is taken for granted, for the purpose here, that the professions are and are believed to be 'a good thing' and act in the interest of society generally.) It is rarely possible to state that any specific activity belongs exclusively to either one of these concerns, but is usually practical to state of some activities that in the short-term they are primarily directed towards one or other concern. The education interests and activities of the Association at the pre-qualifying level are directed both towards the training of the individual and, simultaneously, towards seeking the provision of the institutional framework which will ensure that entrants of the appropriate calibre will continue to be attracted to the profession and be trained in a manner which will ensure the future development of the profession. At some levels, for example the assessing of examination results for a particular year, the Association is particularly concerned about individual performance: at others, for instance concern for the formulation of standards for provision in departments or schools of librarianship or the consideration with ABLISS of particular lines of development, the concern is more with the development of the framework for the profession as a whole. But the two concerns are so closely interrelated and interwoven that they are often not easily distinguished, and neither should they be.

In the case of the development of standards of provision for library services, the standards are primarily aimed at securing on a national basis policies which will eventually make possible the provision of services to an acceptable professional standard; the same standards will also be used, in some specific cases, to support the efforts of individual professionals to secure development of a particular service, and often as a consequence the development of the individual professional interests within that service. The standards clearly straddle both concerns, as do the Association's concerns with post-qualification education, salary levels and conditions of service, research and development, and indeed most others. However, if we review the present situation of the priorities and apparent philosophy of the Association, the main emphasis of its activities in recent years has lain in the area of its concern for the development of the individual professional rather than, in the broad sense, that of representing the interests of the profession as a whole in the decision-making framework. This statement has to be made with caution, and can be challenged with a number of specific instances in which effective 'political' representation has been made; it must also be recognised that the institutional structure within which most jobs in the profession are placed makes difficult the identification of the Association's role.

It is worth noting that prior to 1961 voting rights were held by the representatives of institutional members: the decision to become a professional association on a pattern common to most other professional bodies of note meant that these voting rights were withdrawn. To some extent it appears to have been assumed at that time that the corollary of that change was a change to the emphasis referred to above, by virtue of which comes an increased concern with individual professional development and a diminished concern for the institutional, and consequently the social and political, aspect relating to the professional environment. Interestingly the name of The Library Association still reflects the pre-1961 situation rather than the presently existing one. The main development in the policies to be anticipated in future years will probably reflect a greater emphasis on the 'profession as a whole' approach, resulting from a reassessment of the range of concerns appropriate to a professional body representing a profession for which the major proportion of resource level and provision is decided either directly or indirectly by central government and its agencies.

The increased specialisation of a modern advanced society creates vast areas of ignorance of the detail of one man's dependence upon, and interdependence with, others. The profession has not in the past attacked with vigour the problems of presenting to the wider public an explanation of the importance and potential of its concerns and the significance of the resources at its disposal. The approach of the Association to this area of public relations has reflected the traditional view of the effectiveness of the professions through skilled application of the quiet voice of authority, and there can be little doubt that this approach has been successful, both in general and specifically in the affairs of the Association over a long period of time. But now it is less easy to be convinced that the quiet voice of authority will not, in the informational noise of our society, be drowned by the stentorian efforts of those with perhaps less claim to be heard. This aspect of the conduct of the Association's affairs, and the setting of its priorities, is closely tied to the need to ensure effective representation. Public relations, and particularly the question of direct and continuous political representation and lobbying, is very much part of the reason for the existence of a representative association and in the economic situation which now threatens, or worse, its importance becomes more highlighted.

This changing situation will enforce upon the Association the need to consider its order of priorities and this will probably have the result of a much greater emphasis being placed upon efforts to ensure effective political representation. In the past the major efforts of the profession would appear to have been directed internally: the need now is to direct the effort towards the creation of a climate within the social framework in which there can exist a fuller understanding of the contribution being made by the profession and the extent of the further potential contribution. Because of the peculiarly intangible nature of many of the services with which the profession is concerned this is a difficult task, and certainly it will not be done effectively unless it is given a much greater priority by the profession.

As the Association and the profession have moved from strength to strength over the years, the members' requirements and expectations of their professional body must have changed substantially. A number of responses to these changing requirements have developed, amongst them the policy encouraging the creation of specialist groups and sections. But other responses, which might have been appropriate but perhaps more expensive, have not been made. This is particularly apparent from an examination of the Association's payroll, and an assessment of the availability within the Secretariat of programme personnel with recognised professional expertise in areas of concern to the profession.

The current situation is that a professional staff of seven is available to deal with the whole range of activities which now constitute the practice of librarianship. There undoubtedly exists the need for the Association to help formulate and co-ordinate the views of members of the profession on a wide range of matters and to ensure that effective representation is given to those views both within and outside the profession. The existing structure is weak in the provision it makes for this. It is pertinent to note that one of the main areas in which the Association in the recent past has formulated policies and seen them bear fruit has been that of professional education: the results achieved were achieved not through the existence of a group or section, formally organised to support an informed interest in education for the profession, but through the recognition of the importance of the matter and its priority and consequently the provision on the Secretariat of a staff member specifically charged with responsibility for the development of educational provision. The achievements, and they are substantial, were largely the result of a fruitful combination of committees and committee chairmen well served by a specific member of staff within a concerned Secretariat and wide general debate within the profession. Education has a high priority in the affairs of any professional association, and it cannot be expected that the quality of attention offered to that concern can be duplicated over too wide a field. But it is possible to list a number of areas in which it is apparent that the strength of the representations which the profession is able to make is seriously limited by the unavailability of staff time to service the formulation and presentation of the considered viewpoint of the profession.

School libraries, youth libraries, hospital services, some aspects of academic library provision, and modern information techniques are examples of areas in which the degree of involvement of the profession is indicated by the support given by members to groups and sections; but the overall effectiveness of the interest is limited in part by the extent to which the efforts of the members, voluntary efforts, can be given effective representation on a wider platform through the existing structure. This need can probably only be supplied, other than in very exceptional circumstances, by having within the staffing of the Association personnel with the responsibility for servicing interests in a particular professional area, and who might in time develop the expertise and authority to act as a representative of the profession on particular matters. There is suggested the need to develop the staffing structure to create opportunity for the employment of the professional specialist to a much greater extent than presently provided for.

It is envisaged that such a person would be responsible for working closely with the relevant group or section, where there is one, on the development of policies, leaving questions of administration entirely to the members, as is the present practice. The staff member, together with the group, would be responsible for bringing before the appropriate central committee detailed policy recommendations and would have some responsibility for seeking their implementation. Those who have experience of the workings of the Association will be aware that this would involve, in most cases, a basic change in the relationship between the Secretariat and the voluntary efforts made by members. But there are cases in which this system of working has been adopted successfully over a period of years and has led to effective representation of the profession's viewpoint, for example in the international field of cataloguing. The only objection which can be raised to a development of the staffing in this way is the financial one: certainly there would be considerable benefit to members if additional resources for programme staff could be made available and any consequent increase in purely administrative staff would be minimal and, effectively, would ensure better value for money already being spent on administration. The groups would benefit from the knowledge that they had available the support of the Secretariat and more direct assistance in policy formulation and, once policies were adopted by the Association, the promulgation and active pursuit of those policies. In its turn, the Association would gain from the greater support of its members, and the enhanced authority which will arise from a greater range of policy coverage. The strengthening of the Secretariat would be of considerable benefit to the whole of the membership; it is possible to identify a number of areas in which a strong lead from the Association at the appropriate time would be of great value to the profession.

The emphasis placed above on the development of the Secretariat makes necessary some consideration of the balance between the members' role and that of the staff. Inherent in the staffing suggestion would be a change in the relationship between groups and branches and the central policy bodies and administration. The existing pattern appears to be largely based, in practice, on an almost 'federal' approach rather than on recognition of the unity of the profession. Tensions will always exist within a profession as judgments differ as to where the real professional practice or advantage lies or on the importance of certain emphases, but the recognition of a common basic set of priorities and a strong community of interest is essential to the development of the professional outlook and approach. It has been argued that this profession is so diverse that no community of interest exists, and therefore no basis for professionalism. The argument fails to recognise both the range of concerns common to all segments of the profession and the volume of resources required to ensure representation of an authoritative professional viewpoint, which can only be made available through the collective efforts of many individuals.

Librarianship is not a numerically strong profession, and can ill afford not to co-ordinate the available energies and resources. In part the existing degree of independence enjoyed by branches and groups is a result of deliberate staffing policies developed from the shortage of resources, past and present: staff time for direct involvement in the affairs and concerns of branches and groups has not been available, and these bodies have been free to organise their affairs and finances with the central administration becoming involved only in rare moments of difficulty or crisis, usually financial. This limited control from the centre, given that the Council has the ultimate responsibility for the affairs of the Association, has disadvantages, but the disadvantages of central control would be greater and certainly it would be more expensive of costly administrative time and effort. It would be unwise to anticipate any real change in the administrative and financial arrangements, but what would be beneficial is the development of a much greater use of the availability of the expertise offered voluntarily by the development of closer contact and consultation between branches and groups and the central administration. Regardless of any improvement in staffing levels, mechanisms must be developed to ensure improvements in the degree of contact and the sense of unity within the profession.

Currently the groups are seen mainly to serve the individual professional interests of members – providing a focus for sharing information and professional concern in the context of a specialism. Whilst not exclusively the case, the tendency has been for the groups not to be seen as having a concern with the broader policies of the profession and even, in some cases, with the policy considerations affecting the particular specialism of a group. This has been reflected formally in the absence of staff links with branches and groups in most cases, the lack of any direct representation of the groups on Council, the attitude to the creation of groups and the absence of any categorisation of them in their diversity, and the lack of any serious expectation that groups and branches will be the source of significant policy recommendations. There are groups whose role can be expected, appropriately, not to develop beyond the provision of a forum for mutually-shared professional interest in a defined area of concern (Library history, for example). But it should be expected that certain groups will be concerned to encourage the Association towards more active consideration of policy recommendations relating to their particular area of concern, and the active promulgation of professional viewpoints.

Some impetus towards this change of emphasis has been provided by the recent provision of representation for certain of the groups on the standing committees of Council and by indications that the central administration does positively welcome the input of policy proposals from branches and groups. But it is difficult to see that the best advantage will be secured before more formal links are developed. A combination of the efforts of the specialist groups and sections with the efforts of some additional specialist professional staff should lead to the enhancement of the policy approach of the Association, the formulation of programmes of action for the professional body and clear statements of professional priority.

The development of a more strongly policy-based approach over a wider professional field will also imply a change in emphasis of the concerns of the Council. It will mean that the Council and, more particularly, its standing committees will become less concerned with the detail of administration and policy. This is reflected in the committee structure introduced in 1976 as a result of the proposals put forward by the Working Party on Association Services. The extent to which this will have achieved an adequate, efficient and economical devolution of authority between Council, its standing committees and the Secretariat has yet to be fully established.

The concentration upon the need to identify, formulate and promulgate professional policy might be taken to indicate a failure of the Association in this area in the past, and to some extent this is the case although the considerable work carried out over the years on the development of policies which have substantially influenced the levels of provision of library and information services in most institutional areas of concern to the profession must not be lost sight of. The need for a heightened emphasis in these areas arises in response to the dramatic change in the pattern of institutional provision within which the profession is now in the main required to function.

It is not possible to examine the changes in detail, but what is readily apparent is that at least three major changes in particular have altered the environment within which the work of the Association is conducted. The development of the British Library as the intended 'hub' of the provision of library services in the United Kingdom, the creation of a statutory responsibility for the Secretary of State for Education to oversee the provision of certain services and the development of proper institutional provision for academic education for the profession, represent a combination of change which radically affects the place of the Association and the need of the profession for effective representation. During the same period the change in the general perception of the scope and significance of the profession and an increased awareness that it is an integral and far-reaching aspect of the complex whole which constitutes information and communication, and a wider appreciation of the significance of information for our society have also made necessary a reappraisal of the way in which the Association is to serve the profession and the range of concerns which it must encompass. There are two facets to this concern. The first is that of the existing institutional representation of the profession: for several years it has been one of the concerns of the Association to provide the initiative towards greater cooperation and mutual co-ordination of the various bodies active in representing in one area or another the views of professionals. There are those who argue that representation is more effective when made by a number of smaller bodies singing the same, or very similar, tunes when called upon, for instance, to give evidence to a committee of enquiry. Whether or not the harmonies created in this way are attractive to the listener is an open question, but in the view of the Association more effective representation would result from the presentation by a single representative voice of an agreed professional view which has first been established by consultation within the profession. The second facet is that of the scope of the Association, and whether the range of membership is sufficiently broad, given the developments which have taken place in recent years in communications technology.

In recent discussions an informal group defined a need for a reformulation of the Association's objectives, on a wider basis, to include promotion of the maximum availability and utilisation of documentary and other sources of information for the public advantage, in terms of information, education and recreation. This, it was thought, could imply a broader-based programme, more actively concerned with community information and intelligence activities, and a departure from the traditional 'value-free' concept of information which has underlined much professional practice in the past. The broader base could reflect the more widely defined concepts of information and communication in modern society and relate librarianship more closely to these developments. Development of the Association in this way offers exciting possibilities. The act of will necessary to widen the horizons to reflect more accurately and acutely the changing pattern of societal expectations will be difficult to achieve, and offers a serious challenge to the Association.

Chapter Two

A Member's View of The Library Association

Neil A Simpson

The Library Association and the Profession
Over the years there have been many learned disputes over whether librarianship is a profession. In the main, these disputes have served to illustrate the different interpretations of the word 'profession' held by the writers. Avoiding this interesting but somewhat sterile side issue, what of the relationship between the Library Association and this profession, craft or calling known as librarianship? Even if there are doubts about the classification of the occupation – and some about its name – can it be said that the Library Association at least embraces it all? Well, no, because after all there are Aslib, the Institute of Information Scientists, the Circle of State Librarians, Librarians for Social Change, the Art Libraries Society and others.

Of course, there is some overlap between the memberships of all these organisations and the Library Association. This is only to be expected of an organisation in which there are public librarians, university librarians, special librarians, school librarians, librarians in national libraries; there are medical librarians, law librarians, music librarians, art librarians, information scientists, hospital librarians, local history librarians, reference librarians and resource centre managers; there are cataloguers, serial librarians, mobile librarians, children's librarians, audio-visual librarians, stock editors and film librarians; there are librarians specialising in computers, personnel, training, administration, research, display and public relations. The list ends here because of fear of boredom for the reader, not because it is complete. For example, no mention has

13

been made of those who teach librarianship, a group prominent in the affairs of the profession and the Association.

Can anything bring all this together? What is there in common? All these people are concerned in some way or other with the collection, storage and use of recorded information and the recorded products of the imagination. This, surely, is the basis for any concern to unite. A member should gain a sense of identity with other members of his profession. This sense of identity is of particular importance to those working in smaller libraries who have little or no regular contact with fellow professionals in their daily work. Following on from this initial desire to come together, there comes the wish to speak with a single, authoritative voice on matters of concern to the profession. In this way, the professional association assumes a representational role, offering advice to government and other outside bodies, devising standards of provision and encouraging research and technical development.

The tendency for the profession to splinter, to divide itself up like one of its own classification systems, is not a new one. Ernest Savage wrote of it in 1952:

Whether other professions have a disjunctive urge I do not know, but certainly librarianship favours tabernacular sectionalism, an absorbing passion for one's creed, and almost a hatred of others' creeds.[1]

The luxury of such behaviour cannot be afforded in such a small profession when the philosophies and practices which unite us are stronger than our individual specialities and interests. The interdependence of all kinds of libraries, public and academic, industrial and national, has been demonstrated in the complex national – and international – network of interloan arrangements and in co-operation in cataloguing, classification and other matters. This interdependence is not a theoretical abstraction but a practical reality, and libraries and librarians of all kinds can only gain from supporting one another. The Library Association contains librarians of all kinds and it is the largest organisation concerned with libraries. These two facts have enabled it to bring pressure to bear on the appropriate authorities to bring in legislation, to produce official reports, recommendations and standards, examples of which are the Public Libraries Act, the Parry Report, the British Library and Standards for Libraries in Colleges of Education.

The future of the Library Association is bound up with the future of the profession. From reading the professional press it sometimes seems that the librarians of the future will either be white-coated technocrats tending their electronic gadgetry or community activists providing the information ammunition for social revolution – and all of them graduates, of course.

Whether it is liked or not, the profession is becoming a graduate one, partly due to academic inflation and partly to the continuing upward pressure of education in the community. For the librarian should be well-educated and knowledgeable, not for the prestige of the profession, but because it is necessary for his work. The 'graduate profession issue' is one which has generated much heat and many words in the professional journals over the last few years and it would be wrong to say that the transition will be a quick or easy one. Nevertheless, it is coming and there is very little that the profession can do to prevent it even if it wishes to do so.

It seems highly likely that in future librarianship will be split into at least three levels:

i   The professional, highly qualified librarian
ii   The qualified library technician or intermediate professional
iii The unqualified library assistant

Such a situation already exists in university libraries in which the middle level is occupied by non-graduate chartered librarians. In public libraries there is a tendency towards the creation of posts of senior library assistant which are filled by experienced assistants who may have no formal qualifications or, in some cases, the rather unsatisfactory Library Assistants' Certificate. Staff without formal library qualifications have filled important posts in special libraries for many years. This suggested new level would lie somewhere between that of the present non-graduate chartered librarian and the senior (unqualified) library assistant and would involve formal training and qualification. At present, on the one hand there are too many chartered librarians who are being under-used and, on the other hand, there are too many able assistants who are not allowed to realise their full potential or are underpaid for it if they are.

What the Library Association has to consider is whether it is to cater for the library technician. To exclude such people will probably mean a reduction in numbers of the Association and the creation of a new and possibly larger organisation in librarianship, because this new grouping will undoubtedly wish to have a voice, to belong to an organisation. Of course, it is open to anyone to join the Library Association, but only chartered librarians have a controlling voice in its affairs. The advent of a new three-tier arrangement would require the Association to consider again the question of differing classes of membership. If this were done, it would be in keeping with the traditions of the Association to ensure that it is possible to move from one class of membership to a higher.

There are three further developments in the profession which are likely to affect the Association:

i   The development of school libraries
ii   The British Library
iii The increasing number of experts in other fields working in a library context

The emphasis on student-centred learning, on resource-based work in schools is causing increasing attention to be paid to the assembly, storage and control of these resources, to what, in fact, the profession would call a library. However, other people have decided to call them resource centres and it seems that, for better or worse, this term is here to stay; it is even used by the Library Association itself. This use of a different name, combined with the fact that much use is made of non-book materials, has led to the idea that resource centres are not the concern of librarians. Fortunately the profession has come alive to the dangers inherent in this approach and it seems likely that in the long term they will be controlled by librarians.

A Member's View of The Library Association

Of course, it is not only in the use of non-book materials that the value of a trained librarian is not always recognised in a school context; most schools do not yet have a trained librarian on the staff either in a full or a part-time capacity. The reasons for this sad state of affairs are many and complex, but again, there are encouraging signs. Many of the new local authorities are recognising the importance of a good, professionally run school library service and, once the advantages of such a service become clear, it is likely that development will accelerate. The increased possibilities of dual qualifications in librarianship and teaching due to the development of courses in London, Leeds, Loughborough and elsewhere lead to a hope that the schools will at last recognise the importance of library resources in the learning process. At the same time it must be said that there is a cloud on the near horizon in the shape of the current financial situation which may lead to cuts in educational expenditure. It is to be hoped that this will only cause a delay in the gradual improvement in school libraries.

If the above predictions prove to be true, and it becomes the rule rather than the exception to have a librarian in at least every secondary school, this will have a big impact on the professional association as there are 6000 secondary schools and 27,000 primary schools in the country. What kind of impact this will be is impossible to predict but it is interesting to note that it will increase greatly the proportion of members of the profession employed in educational establishments. However, if past experience is any guide it is unlikely that all these 'educational/academic' librarians will speak with one voice; university, polytechnic, college and school librarians will probably continue to go their separate ways. The point is that even if they do go their separate way the school librarians will form a significant group.

It is already clear that the British Library will have a big influence on the profession and the Association. While it is true that the British Library is founded upon existing libraries, there is no doubt that the new whole is more important – as well as greater – than the sum of its old constituent parts. Furthermore, some parts of the British Library – notably the British Museum

Library – have played little or no part in the affairs of the Library Association in the immediate past. However, the people in charge of the new organisation are more committed to the professional association and to a professional librarian's approach to the problems of the national library. The British Library is concerned with all libraries and information services in the country and with research in librarianship.

Its influence will be immense and it is vital that its officers should play their part in the Library Association and that the Association should be recognised by the British Library as the voice of librarianship in the country as a whole.

The British Library is a government institution and it is not the only sign of increasing central government control over libraries. Not only are there the Library Advisory Councils and the Department of Education and Science's Library Advisers but most of the larger libraries in the country are financed directly or indirectly by central government. It is important that the profession be organised to influence decisions, to urge reforms and to suggest new departures in dealings with these national agencies.

The non-librarian expert working in libraries is already with us – in administration, in computers, in social work, in design, in subject or language specialisation – and this trend seems likely to continue. While it is no doubt desirable that such people should also be qualified in librarianship, this is neither practical nor necessary in most cases. Nevertheless, they should be encouraged to join the Library Association – and some do – because of their close involvement in library work. Their influence in the Association is likely to remain peripheral, but it would make sense for the Association to make use of their expertise whenever occasion arises.

One of the most important aspects of the work of a professional association is the provision of information and advice for prospective entrants to the profession. The Library Association does provide careers advice and information but more positive action is required. The provision of such advice in schools, colleges and universities is now highly organised by individual organisations and by professional bodies. If the right people are to be attracted into librarianship and the wrong people warned away, it is of great importance that a real effort is made to provide good, attractive yet truthful information and advice. The first aim should be to redesign the literature to make it more attractive and up to date. Many librarians up and down the country do good work in providing careers information. They could be assisted by a regular flow of information for intending librarians on salary levels, qualifications, courses and the like. The Library Association could contact careers officers to offer talks, slide shows and films. The importance of this work should not be underestimated because on the quality and availability of this advice depends the future of the profession.

The Library Association and the individual
'What does the Library Association do for me?' This is the cry which recurs in the professional press and on the lips of many librarians. Of course, the obvious reply, made many times, is 'What do you do for the Library Association, your Association?' Though a little trite, the response is a fair one. However, the original question, while perhaps unfair or ill-considered, is an indication of a problem. For many members, the Library Association is a somewhat vague body to which they pay subscriptions and which is run by paid officials – too highly paid, they would probably add – and bureaucratic committees of chief librarians and others more or less in their dotage.

Brave efforts have been made over the last few years by the Secretariat and, to a lesser extent, by Library Association Councillors, to change this image. However, it still persists, even among activists in groups and branches who often refer to the Library Association as if it were some autonomous and faintly hostile external body instead of the parent organisation.

Like all such institutions, the Library Association is the subject of frequent and somewhat lazy, generalised attacks by its own members. One hears that it is dull, does nothing, wastes money, is too much London based. Of course, at times it probably is guilty of all of those things because no organisation is perfect.

Prospects for British Librarianship

Although it is important that the Secretariat and the activists in the Association should do all they can to counter such an image, they will not eliminate such attitudes. It seems to be a necessary function of a professional organisation for its members to be able to grumble about it. Certainly, the Library Association is not alone in this; other professional organisations, otherwise very different, also seem to fulfil this function.

It is an illusion to think that the professional association will ever be led by other than its senior members; this is how it is in every sphere of life – even in the Association of Assistant Librarians. This does not have to mean that these people are senile, complacent or devoid of original ideas. Nevertheless, the dangers are there and it is important that the establishment be constantly prodded, questioned and, when necessary, criticised. This has to be done by the branches and groups, by the professional press and by the individual member.

The branches could be, and sometimes are, an important aspect of the Library Association. The suggestion by the Working Party on Association Services that the branches be abolished and that the subdivision of the Association should be by occupational and interest groupings, although defeated for the moment, is likely to be repeated and, unless the branches really come to life, there is a danger that it will be successful.

The branch is the level at which the essential unity of the profession should be emphasised. The central organisation is concerned with overall policy, the representational role in the national context, and central services to members. The branches should concern themselves more with the individual librarian as a person requiring both professional and social contact with fellow workers.

The Association should provide a means of contact with others in the profession, both those working in the same field and those working in others. It should do this on the formal level of exchange of information and ideas and also on the informal social level. It is important that the process should not be a

A Member's View of The Library Association

solemn and arid one. The profession should not always take itself too seriously.

New members, or members moving into a new area, should be contacted direct by the branch, to welcome them and make them aware of the activities of the branch and of the groups in the area. Such action will help the individual member to make contact with others at what is often a difficult and sometimes a lonely time, and is likely to help in creating the kind of atmosphere in which more people will play an active part in the affairs of the Association.

The groups of the Library Association can, with the notable and massive exception of the AAL, be divided into two categories:

i   The type of library, e.g. the Public Libraries Group
ii Special interest groups, e.g. Cataloguing and Indexing.

Are there too many of them? They certainly seem to bear witness to the 'disjunctive urge' mentioned by Savage. On the one hand, it is useful for people of like interests to join together; on the other hand there is the danger of a narrow blinkered outlook. On the whole, though, diversity is to be welcomed provided that all members are willing to subscribe to the proposal that they are all librarians first and librarians specialising in a particular area second.

The groups do important and useful work in their own fields, and they involve many members of the Association. The adoption of a new structure for the Secretariat and the committees of Council is intended to assist the groups to relate their work more directly to that of the central organisation and enable the Council to make more direct use of the expertise available within the groups. This should lead to some breakdown in the feeling of detachment from the centre referred to above. That this problem is recognised by the Council is clear from the recommendation of the Working Party on Association Services that

> ... specific encouragement should be given to Groups and sections of the Association to bring forward detailed policy recommendations to

relevant standing committees: we believe that for some Groups this encouragement will lead to a re-definition of their role in professional matters and, it is to be hoped, a strengthening in the interest of the members in the work of the Groups.[2]

The groups are also to be allowed to nominate limited numbers of people as members of certain committees of Council. This is a fairly modest innovation and is unlikely to end the pressures for direct representation on Council. The Working Party should have considered more closely the idea of a Council composed entirely of representatives of branches or groups instead of nationally or locally elected Councillors or of a mixture of the two – a fine British compromise. There is much to be said for some such direct representation. Apart from the advantage of linking the branch and group structure more closely with the central organisation, the Councillors would have someone to whom they were directly accountable, to whom they would have to report back. This direct accountability would help to ensure that the Councillors were active, not passive like all too many at present. Another advantage would be to the ordinary members of the Association who are, at present, called on to vote for candidates as Councillors, most of whom they know little about, with the consequence that the 'establishment' is reinforced by those few who trouble to vote electing the people whose names they have heard even though they may know nothing of their views. A Council composed mainly of representatives of branches or groups would not eliminate this but it should reduce it because there is likely to be more knowledge of individuals within a branch or group.

It is too early to say yet what effect the Public Libraries Group will have on the Association as a whole but the creation of this new and very large group at a time when more influence is being given to the groups should help to reduce the disporportionate time spent by the Council and its committees on public library matters, a situation which has been in part caused by the absence of such a group, in part by the excessive influence of public librarians in the affairs of the Association.

Reference has already been made to the largest group, the

A Member's View of The Library Association

Association of Assistant Librarians, which includes nearly two-thirds of the membership of the Library Association as a whole. Its origins as a separate Association have led to its present strange position as an Association within the Association with its own President, National Council and other trappings of independence. The AAL does involve the less senior members of the profession but it also mirrors the Library Association in that it is usually led by its most senior people. In recent years it has been characterised at national level by an apparently more 'liberal' approach, by an emphasis on the social aspects of librarianship but, paradoxically, it has taken a fairly middle of the road and occasionally even a reactionary attitude in the affairs of the Library Association. The AAL has, like the Library Association generally, been conducting some soul-searching about its own raison d'être and it has come up with a pleasingly pragmatic approach:

> It can be claimed that in an ideal situation The Library Association would carry out all the functions that the AAL performs at present, and that providing the LA would do this efficiently and effectively, there would be no need for the AAL to remain in existence. In our view this ideal situation does not obtain at present, and we do not consider that it will come about without a fundamental change in the attitudes and activities of the LA.[3]

It is worth noting that this report again treats the Library Association as if it were an entirely separate body although this is perhaps more understandable in the case of the AAL than for the other groups. All the same, it is possible to argue that the Library Association *is* carrying out the functions mentioned through the agency of the AAL.

The AAL seems likely to continue for the foreseeable future but it must always avoid complacency and the temptation to rest on its image as a ginger group without providing some actual ginger. An organisation whose existence is difficult to defend on theoretical grounds cannot afford to stagnate.

It is worth noting here that the AAL provides the only means by which students of librarianship gain a voice in the central affairs of the Library Association. It is important that the librarians of the future be given a chance to air their views, particularly at a time when the withdrawal of the Association from its direct role in professional education raises the danger of divorcing the students even more from its affairs.

The professional press is facing an uncertain future. The *Library Association Record* has been altered, under new editorship, and how this will develop is still uncertain. Of particular concern, however, are the difficulties being experienced by the branches and groups who publish journals. Currently the most affected is the *YLG News* although the largest and oldest, *The Assistant Librarian,* has also had financial difficulties. In fact, the difficulties are almost wholly financial, caused by rapid inflation leading to increased printing and distribution costs at a time when the Library Association feels unable to increase capitation allowances to the groups. Ways must be found to enable the continued publication of such threatened periodicals, not on the grounds that all existing publications must continue forever, but because those mentioned are important parts of the communications network of librarianship.

The Library Association rightly 'tries to ensure that no work which librarians need goes unpublished because commercial success is doubtful'. This is a proper aim for a professional association but it is one which requires finance. One of the most satisfactory ways in which to achieve this is by the publication of profitable books which will support the unprofitable but necessary publications. In the last few years there have probably been too few of these really profitable publications and the Association has missed some opportunities through a lack of a clearly defined policy on publications combined with a very conservative attitude. The appointment of a new publications manager together with changes in the committee structure give hope that this situation will change. For the individual member, it is important that the criterion which is applied to publications of dubious commercial value is that of usefulness to the profession not that of esoteric academic rarity and prestige.

The number of visits to this country by librarians from overseas does not decrease and the Association obviously has a useful role to play in ensuring that these visitors meet British librarians and that they are helped in planning visits to the libraries which will be of most interest to them. There is a natural desire on the part of all such visitors to come to London and, of course, there are many important libraries to be seen in London, but it is desirable that foreign librarians should visit other parts of the country.

When such a group is visiting any part of the country, the local branch should be informed and it should attempt to provide a means of contact and exchange of information with the librarians of the area. Although the Association has rejected the idea of an international relations office, it is to be hoped that the designation of an officer of the Secretariat to take an overall view of international relations will lead to more co-ordination in this field and to more contacts being made.

For British librarians who wish to work or visit abroad individually or in groups, the Library Association should provide information on the library situation in the country to be visited, educational qualifications, salary levels and general organisation together with addresses and contacts to be made. This work is at present hardly undertaken at all or, where it is, it is done in a haphazard manner. The only regular study tours arranged within the Association are those undertaken by the AAL which, working entirely through its honorary officers, has built up a network of contacts with other countries. However, this work requires more resources if it is to be developed, as the International and Comparative Librarianship Group has been arguing for some time. In fact, much could be achieved by the central Secretariat in the way of assembly of information and of contacts without a great deal of expenditure, a fact which should commend such developments to the Council.

Another aspect of international relations may prove to have far-reaching consequences for the Association. Britain's entry to the European Community will mean that the Library Association will have to consider again the question of recognition of European qualifications. Freedom of movement between member states has been established and work permits are no longer required. It is the declared intention of the Community to work towards mutual recognition of qualifications for professionals. On present trends and on the general evidence of the slow pace of Community bureaucracy, it is likely that it will be some years before the moment of decision on this question but the widely differing approaches to library qualifications at present to be found mean that there will be great difficulty in achieving the final aim. At the same time, perhaps the Association should be a little less arrogant in its approach to some foreign qualifications. It should explore the possibility of introducing some form of examination in knowledge of British librarianship which, when passed by holders of certain designated foreign qualifications, would enable the holder to have his qualification recognised by the Library Association.

There are members who feel that the Library Association should become a trade union or, alternatively, that a trade union for librarians should be formed. The Association is not allowed by its Charter to act as a trade union and it is doubtful whether that is desirable or even whether it is desirable to have any trade union exclusively for librarians. The formation of a craft union would be completely against the trend of modern trade union practice which is to favour industrial unions. There are two powerful reasons why librarians should not form a union of their own: these are numerical strength and the organisational structure of libraries. With only 22,000 members, such a union would be in a very weak bargaining position in the trade union movement as a whole and, of course, the number of members working within any one of the different 'industries' of which libraries are part is even smaller. With very few exceptions, libraries form part of larger organisations whether they be local authorities, universities, colleges, industrial firms or research institutes. The librarians in these organisations share common salary structures and conditions of service with the other workers in the organisation and it is with them that they should join for collective bargaining purposes.

This is not to say that the Association has no part to play in the discussion of salaries and conditions of service for librarians. In fact, it does play a part in advising, persuading and assisting unions and employers, in co-ordinating information on libraries of all kinds and in setting standards. This is important and useful work and must continue. A corollary of this is the provision of information and advice to individual members on salaries and conditions of service, an aspect of the Association's work which may well be expanded in future.

The information service to members should be developed, strengthened and extended. A start has already been made but more needs to be done. The Library Association should have an exemplary information service for its members. That it has not had this in the past has been due mainly to a lack of resources which probably in turn reflected the comparatively low priority given to it. However, this has led to the situation in which members have not made full use of the service, in some cases because they had tried it and found it wanting, in some because they were unaware of the service.

The organisational structure of the Library Association is considered in the preceding chapter. Although the structure is important, even more important than the detail is that it should be open to change. Any organisation should be organic, able to grow and adapt to new circumstances and not to fossilise. The Association has shown considerable ability to adapt to major changes over the last twenty years, notably in the growth of the library schools and its withdrawal from its direct educational role. Much has been said and written in recent years, and many deliberations have been held over the Association's objectives and structure. It is now time to settle on a particular structure and to try it, retaining sufficient flexibility to be able to change again wherever it is thought necessary.

This flexibility should be combined with more informality and freedom in the relationships among all parts of the Association. It is a fault of institutions that they tend to take themselves too seriously. The Library Association, as it approaches its centenary, should have the confidence to take a relaxed attitude to its own affairs.

Two possible visions of the future of the Association can be imagined. One is that which has been indicated above of an Association representing a united profession, with a more active membership and an open and flexible approach to the conduct of its affairs, including within it various categories of members. The other is of a reduced Association of a highly qualified élite, one among a number of organisations in the field of librarianship, clinging to an esoteric concept of professional purity. Librarianship is a practical, pragmatic and open profession; its professional association should reflect those qualities.

In describing the activities and services of the Association and in suggesting trends and new departures, the enormous assumption is made that there will be sufficient finance available for it to continue to develop. In the present financial state of the country, this assumption may be without secure foundation. Nevertheless, it is important to decide on the ends at which the Association should be aiming. It is for the membership to will the means once it has decided on the ends. There is an understandable reluctance to pay ever-increasing subscriptions but the members cannot expect services to continue, far less to expand, while subscriptions stand still in an inflationary economy.

It may well be, then, that the developments predicted here will be delayed or even that some present services will be curtailed. This does not alter the desirability of providing such services, nor does it preclude their provision in the longer term.

References in text

1. Savage, E. A. *A librarian's memories*. Grafton, 1952, p. 128.
2. Restructuring the Association. *Libr. Ass. Rec.* 77 (10) October 1975, Supp. 2.
3. Pluse, J. M. The AAL's working parties and the future. *Assistant Librarian*, 68 (2) February 1975, 23-24.

Chapter Three

The Future of Library & Information Studies

P Havard-Williams

In the forties or fifties, anyone who took library or information science education really seriously would have advised a graduate student to go to the United States, and take an MA, MSC, or MLS at a good accredited school such as Illinois, Chicago or California. It is true that there was the school at University College London, but this was primarily for those with a humanities degree, and perhaps mainly catered for those with particular interests in palaeography or historical bibliography. Certainly, the scientist had to look elsewhere. In the last twelve years the picture has changed. The small struggling schools in the technical colleges in the fifties have become forces to be reckoned with: schools with two or four or even six staff have become schools with ten or twenty or even forty staff, and with a corresponding increase in the number of students. This is a transformation for which the Library Association was responsible, with its insistence on an entrance standard equivalent to minimum university requirements, and full-time education. Greater numbers of staff, and the development of libraries of every kind with, consequently, an increasing number of qualified staff, together with the development of new thought in and attitudes to library and information studies produced a new literature. The stimulus of the Paris Conference on Cataloguing Principles, and such groups as the Classification Research Group, provided starting points for their investigation, while the stimulus of computer development and of the improvement in audio-visual materials and reprography provided yet another departure point for the extension of information education into new fields.

Prospects for British Librarianship

The conceptual development in library and information studies was accompanied by organisational change. In the forties and fifties, all library and information schools were teaching to the syllabus of the Library Association, while the examining continued to be done by practising librarians who did not always see eye to eye with the teachers. The restraints of the Library Association syllabus were considered to be a stranglehold by many in the schools, but in fact it held the schools to high standards, and allowed them to grow towards the new opportunities of the sixties.

The sixties will be remembered as a remarkable decade in British library education. In the early sixties the new library and information education syllabus of the Library Association was being prepared with the cooperation not only of practising librarians interested in the subject but also with a significant contribution from teachers of librarianship. Approaches were made to universities to establish new departments of library studies. The year 1964 was crucial. In that year the first students were received at the Postgraduate School of Librarianship at Sheffield University, the College of Librarianship Wales was established at Aberystwyth, and Northern Ireland saw – as the result of a recommendation of a Library Association Committee, and the generosity of a substantial grant from the Leverhulme Trustees – the foundation of the School of Library Studies at Queen's University Belfast.

This was also the year of the implementation of the new Library Association syllabus and the year of the beginning of the Council for National Academic Awards. Each of these events had a particular significance for the future of library and information education in the United Kingdom. The Library Association syllabus itself had the seeds of greater freedom for library schools by the very number of its options: this, together with the standards for internal examining, gave possibilities for the future. The Council for National Academic Awards at first turned its attention to modern traditional subjects, but at the same time gave notice that it would be prepared to consider innovatory syllabuses. The establishment of the postgraduate school at Sheffield broke the monopoly of London University, and made the foundation of future university schools easier. The school at Queen's University Belfast had a syllabus not only for postgraduate students, but also for two-year non-graduate students. This introduced the notion of internal examining and an internal syllabus for two-year students, and helped the Library Association to accept an internal syllabus and examination in what were to become the polytechnics. The College of Librarianship Wales showed what could be done in an institution wholly devoted to the study of librarianship and information science, particularly when it could be closely associated with a university institution, with facilities for establishing its own degrees. The schools mentioned so far, together with the School of Librarianship at the then North-Western Polytechnic, London, made one further major contribution: each of them, particularly that at Sheffield, developed significant research programmes, which not only influenced the practice of librarianship and information work, but also contributed to the teaching programmes of the Schools, and drew out fundamental questions of principle and practice, transforming the subject into something a great deal more than the descriptive content it had had in the earlier period.

The development of the non-university schools was further helped by the establishment of the polytechnics. The most forward-looking of these soon looked to the development of overall standards in research, teaching and library provision comparable with, if different from, those of universities. 'Schools of librarianship' became 'departments of library and information studies', and sometimes additionally took archive studies under their wing. They were able to propose, in due course, degree courses to the Council of National Academic Awards, the first to be approved being those of Leeds in 1968, which were a BA in library studies and a BSC in information studies. Two other developments should not be ignored. One was the establishment of a degree with librarianship as the principal subject at Strathclyde University, in 1967, and that of an honours degree (BA or BSC) in 1968 at the Loughborough University of Technology in association with the School of Librarianship, Loughborough Technical College. In the same year, the same institutions introduced an MA in librarianship, which for extraneous reasons was discontinued after two years, but which set the pattern for the introduction of a master's degree instead of a diploma as a postgraduate qualification. The establishment of a master's degree was assisted by the more general development of master's degree syllabuses as 'conversion courses' for graduates with degrees in subjects other than those of the master's degree. Sheffield University introduced an MA in librarianship in 1968 and an MSC in Information Studies in the same year. The first PHD in library or information studies was awarded at Loughborough University in 1973.

As at 1976, there are then possibilities of training as a professional librarian ranging from a two-year course to a PHD, with an enormous variety of BA/BSC/BLIB courses, in which library studies can be studied as one subject of a joint honours course (Wales); as a major or minor subject in an honours or pass degree (Strathclyde); as a major subject with ancillaries in an honours degree (Polytechnic of North London); and as a main subject with subsidiary subjects – which can include anything from chemical engineering to religious studies and from economics or social studies to Russian – for an honours or general degree. Loughborough University, with the most recent department of library and information studies, also offers a joint honours degree in education and library studies which will enable successful graduates to qualify both as librarians and teachers.

If this is the *status quo*, where will future developments lie? Any development of library and information studies must depend on the development of the profession itself. This has been transformed in the past twenty years, **a** by a greater social awareness, evidenced by the greater concern of academic libraries for overall provision for their readers and in public libraries by the expansion of services for the disadvantaged, **b** by the development of library technology, in the field of mechanisation, non-book media and reprography, **c** by the application of management principles and techniques to libraries and information centres, **d** by the development of educational theory, resulting in an emphasis on learning, rather than teaching and thus an enhanced role for the school library and resource centre, and **e** by the development of the subject itself. Another important factor is the contribution of two major international conferences which between them cover the field of information science and librarianship; these are the UNISIST Conference and the Intergovernmental Conference on the Overall Planning of National Documentation, Library and Archives Infrastructures, held in 1974 at Unesco in Paris. The overall conclusion one must draw from these two conferences is that a world system of information services for science and technology is a feasible objective and that this needs to be supported by national information systems, to be built on broadly based government supported schemes concerned with documentation, library and archive services, which must be conceived of as 'national information systems' (NATIS). There are, of course, inconsistencies in this view, since national information systems are concerned with documentation, library and archive services in all subject fields, while UNISIST is primarily concerned with science and technology. Indeed there is a danger that methods appropriate to science and technology will swamp information work in other fields where different methods are required. For the future in Great Britain, the overall view in the field of information – including documentation, libraries and archives – must take account of both these world systems recommended by Unesco, which itself is currently trying to reconcile the objectives of the two projects.

The first consequence of this view is that education for the information field broadly viewed must be conceived as a whole. While one cannot offer the same basic syllabus for archivists and information specialists, the various choices offered must arise from a common 'stem'. Secondly, with the required enhancement of qualification and status which is required by broad systems of information organisation, librarians, like information specialists and archivists, will have to have subject specialisms which will bear upon their work in addition to their education in library studies. In the long term, therefore, library studies, like information science and archive studies, must become postgraduate in character, and there must be a means for graduate and 'two-year' students to enhance their studies. Thirdly, with the continued development of the subject, postgraduate courses will eventually become of two years' duration, as they are in Canada and in some schools in the United States, thus increasing the possibility that all initial postgraduate courses in the United Kingdom will be masters' degrees. A period of two years' duration is already required by the Council of National Academic Awards for a postgraduate 'conversion' course in a second subject. With the downgrading of secondary education already in progress, it may well be that for senior posts in ten or twenty years' time, a master's degree in the librarian's first subject of study will be needed in addition to one in librarianship, information or archive studies, as is frequently found already in the United States.

Fourthly, there will be a need for 'higher' master's degrees, by thesis or advanced course, possibly taught on a modular basis – i.e. several sections of the course may be taken successively and in any order – to accommodate *inter alia* the needs of part-time students. Fifth and last, advanced study in addition to a thesis may well be an alternative to the present PHD by thesis alone. This will give an opportunity for practising librarians to develop their knowledge of new specialisms in the information field, and also to study the broader consequences of information provision as a whole in an increasingly complex society. It will be particularly useful to the leaders of the profession in countries where information services are very much in the development phase.

The core curriculum devised by a Unesco committee of experts in 1974 and included in my *Planning information manpower* and amended in my paper to the IFLA Section on Library Schools in 1975 still has some interest: it is set out in Table 3.1.

This illustrates the problem of quantity, and the necessity for the eventual development of two-year postgraduate courses. It also illustrates the problems of information science *versus* library studies *versus* archive studies. It is probable that, as the result of the impetus given by NATIS to the development of National Information Infrastructures, the lines of demarcation will become blurred. The sociology of information, for instance, is as important now to librarians as it is to information scientists.

The Future of Library Studies

Table 3.1 *A core curriculum in documentation, library and archives studies*

Courses	Information Science	Library Studies	Archives Studies
Foundations (Masonry)	Sociology of information History of science Scientific communication Theory of communication Research methods	Library in society Library legislation History of libraries and library education User research Research methods	Economic ⎫ Legal ⎬ history Social ⎭ Genealogy, heraldry Research methods
Materials	Various formats – reports, documents data (ideas) Information services	Various formats – books, serials, new media Reference sources Bibliographical tools History of book arts	Various formats – manuscripts, maps letters Registers, inventories, etc. Bibliographical tools
Methods	Indexing, contents analysis Documentary languages Storage and retrieval Data organisation Information dissemination Systems analysis	Indexing, contents analysis Reader services Organisation of knowledge Reference processes Systems analysis Preservation and restoration	Registry systems Palaeography Museum techniques Records management Library techniques Preservation and restoration
Management	Management and administration Personnel Systems organisation and planning Legal aspects	Management and administration Personnel Systems organisation and planning Type of library operation Legal aspects	Management and administration Personnel Systems organization Type of archives operation Legal aspects
Mechanisation	Computer and reprographic technology	Computer and reprographic technology	Computer and reprographic technology
Men	Educating the user	Educating the user	Educating the user

35

Bibliographical tools are as important to the information scientist as they are to the librarian. The increased requirement for information that is characteristic of the informed society – 'A national information policy reflecting the needs of all sectors of the community . . .' – and the nature of archive material is such – in the enormous documentary output of government departments and agencies, and indeed non-government agencies – that the dividing line between contemporary and archive material is likely to become blurred too. Archive copies even of fiction are being kept in reserves the problems of which are not being faced, and in which archival principles as well as librarianship are involved. Library education to take care of such problems will need to be broader based, with support from the study of sociology, education and history. It will need, therefore, to have some reference also to archive practice and information science, and these in turn will have to have some reference to library studies and either information science or archive studies. Students' specialisations in these fields will often also have some reference to the studies in their first degree.

The practical requirements for training will also become more demanding. A two-year course will provide the opportunity to give students more directed experience in one of the shorter vacations each year together with an extended period in the long vacation between the two academic sessions. Directed experience in activities like community librarianship, or in practical information work, where the 'book work' is not the primary element, would greatly enhance present library education and training.

It might well be that an integrated master's degree of five years' duration might be an alternative, on the model of the five-year degree in architecture. The difficulty about information studies is that they are really amalgams of other subjects – bibliography, computer studies, management. They are also dependent on studies in education, sociology, science and technology, the arts and the humanities. Though library and information studies have developed out of all recognition in the last twenty years, and will continue to develop, the subject has yet to find its own 'integrity': hence one can expect the 'core' to change. It is probable that it will become more numerical in conception, but that in the light of a similar tendency in secondary education remedial work will have to be done in the literary field – 'world literature' might be an optional, even obligatory, paper whilst literary expression in report writing and verbal expression in public speaking exercises, for instance, will be necessary adjuncts. A typical two-year postgraduate master's course might look like the example set out in Table 3.2.

Table 3.2   *Future two-year postgraduate master's course.*

Year One

Term 1: Documents and information in society (survey).
Recent history of libraries, archives and information services in relation to government, educational services, industry, etc.
Theory and practice of communication:
a. in science
b. in society
Systems analysis.
Introduction to indexing and bibliography

Term 2: Organisation of knowledge

Bibliographical tools.
Various formats – books, serials, news media, reports, data, mss. maps, letters, etc.

Term 3: As above.

Term 4: Reference processes.

Contents analysis; indexing.
Documentary languages.
Storage and retrieval systems.
Data organisation.
Information dissemination.

Term 5: Management and administration.

Types of library/information/archives operation.
Systems organisation.

Term 6: Special subjects.

Not only is there a difficulty about the subject of information studies as a subject but there is the problem of information/library/archive work. This is a service to a service – information is a service to research, management, technology, economical development, etc., as is librarianship or archive work. The relation between information work or librarianship to its subject matter is therefore a special one, if its contribution is at a sufficiently high level – at a level in fact at which it will be necessary to employ an expensive specialist. This is an argument in fact against any five-year integrated programme, and in support of continued postgraduate education in the field, with a first degree in another subject.

The number of information specialists of this kind with managerial responsibilities will be limited. There will be, however, numbers of posts for intermediate professionals who will be concerned with cataloguing, readers' services and acquisition work. These will follow a more elementary form of the core curriculum in one field only – information *or* library *or* archive studies – either in a three-year course for a degree or a two-year course for a diploma in higher education. There should be a means of qualifying as a full professional for those with these qualifications.

If a master's degree will be necessary for managerial positions in the information field, there will be pressures for advanced qualifications, partly because of the desire to advance knowledge in the field, partly to advance in terms of career prospects in an increasingly competitive world. These degrees will take one of two forms: one will be the traditional form of a thesis or dissertation; the second will be by course, probably on a modular basis. That is to say, the degree will be made up of, say, six or four 'units', each one of which may be taken separately and in any order. With the development of the subject, it will become easier to provide advanced courses of this kind, which are already being provided at Leeds, London, Loughborough and Sheffield. These degrees can be either at master's or doctor's level.

The notion of advanced course degrees at master's level is not

The Future of Library Studies

uncommon in the United Kingdom. The idea of a PH D by course is almost unknown in the United Kingdom, though it is common in the United States, where the dissertation is submitted in 'partial requirement' for the degree, and a number of advanced courses have to be completed before the submission of the thesis. A possible scheme might be as in Table 3.3.

Table 3.3   *Possible scheme for PH D course.*

Master's programme *First year*

Doctoral programme *Second year*

1. Three of:
i. Sociology – communication in society.
ii. Psychology of communication.
iii. Communication and the mass media.
iv. History of science and technology.
v. Educational psychology and sociology of education.

2. Two of:
i. Information studies and computer appreciation.
ii. Non-book materials.
iii. Reprography.
iv. Resource centres.
v. Archive organisation and records management.
vi. Library infrastructures.

3. Seminar on educational principles in the field of information (libraries, archives, information services).

4. Quantitative methods.

Education in a practical field like information can hardly be divorced from training. As education develops and becomes more theoretically orientated, professional training will become more important. While professional education will aim to prepare its candidates for professional problems twenty years ahead – not indeed to train for specific problems but for problem-solving in general – candidates will still need to start work on finishing their degree, and will need to have real experience with real people. The application of theory is also important. The role of the professional association will therefore continue to develop. Professional membership will be a greater hurdle. Managerial capability will be judged several years after qualifying. Hence, while the 'associateship' will continue to be awarded a year or two after the final examination, real professional membership – either 'Member' (as the engineering institutions) or 'Fellow' (thus finding a new role for the present dying Fellowship) – will be awarded only after evidence is shown of real managerial ability and professional knowledge based on extensive or intensive experience. The associateship will include either experienced intermediate professionals or recently qualified full professionals on two separate registers.

While it is easy to offer 'prophecies' on the development of professional education in terms of curriculum development, it is not so easy to forecast the orientation of new objectives. The general emphasis on information, computer studies, community librarianship and services to education is likely to continue. If Britain is a proletarian democracy by the early 2000s, these tendencies will be accelerated, and the non-vocational aspects of the subject – 'reading for pleasure' – will be minimised. The emphasis on the book will be correspondingly reduced, though the importance of the inside of books for information workers will paradoxically increase since information will need to be packaged. Data-banks will be integral to the work of librarians, while specialisation in community work will offer another channel of activity. The development of the professional will be such that 'information specialist' will be the title of the full professional, while 'librarian' will remain the description of the intermediate professional. The future of libraries and librarians lies in their integration in the broad world of information as defined by the NATIS conference – any future development of education must take account of this.

There is one field which librarians have neglected: the commercial world of publishing and bookselling. The emphasis on knowledge of the *insides* of books, rather than lists of

The Future of Library Studies

bibliographies, and the overall concern with information in society will also develop a more realistic attitude to the book trade, and to non-book media. The study of the history of the book trade, contemporary bookselling and publishing will need to be placed more centrally in the training of those who will work in the field of books in public and academic libraries. Already information scientists are greatly concerned with the publishing of journals, their editing, their economics, their use. A similar concern for books needs to be shown by librarians. It may well be that the education of publishers and booksellers, developed to a standard similar to that required in some continental countries, will take place in departments of library and information studies. The whole world of books, journals, reports and microforms needs to be carefully analysed so that the processes of communication are fully understood. We have, with the emphasis on management and technology, tended to ignore the traditional materials of communication. The future will compensate for this neglect.

Finally, departments of library and information studies will need to broaden their scope and provide education not only for information officers and librarians, but also for users. Indeed the whole concept of the activity of departments will change to the fulfilment of a broader role of concern with information transfer and the organisation of the materials of communication. User studies will progress in the light of greater economic pressures on information agencies, and the connection between information provision and information reception will be considerably tightened. It would not be too fanciful to think not of Departments of Library and Information Studies but of Departments of Information Transfer and Communication Materials in which what are now known as information studies, archive studies, library studies, communication and the mass media, and public relations information work are gathered 'under one roof' providing an education for the practitioners in these fields, and more generalised service teaching for other disciplines and departments. This 'generalisation' – in terms of the consumers – will be important in developing the profession, making it look outwards to users, and not inward to techniques. Such a department will need extensive laboratories with on-line computer facilities, bibliographical collections, collections of trade and report literature, microforms, slides, disco and video-tapes with appropriate consols for operation by classes, individually and by self-instruction. Communication studies will not only be the specialised domains they are, but will be part of the new general education of the future.

Chapter Four

Training Future Librarians

G B Eynon

Even in these uncertain times it would be fainthearted not to foresee a change in training's functional, unemotive Martha-like image, and the way becoming clearer for a translation into action of the growing awareness of its essential contribution to all forms of library service. The obligation to train and the right to be trained will be enshrined in a future Bill of Rights.

Professional literature is rich in testimony of this awareness. In his presidential address to the Public Libraries Conference 1974, Eric Clough linked staff training, 'the more important', with effective management and staff recruitment, as the triple agents to realise his theme 'Making librarians work'. The Librarian of Reading University quotes P. D. Morrison in support of his belief that libraries themselves should provide 'rich in-service education for experienced librarians'.[1] Elizabeth Mack of Aslib sees the realisation of the kind of environment in which assistants at all levels exercise imagination and enterprise 'can be brought about by the continuance of an in-training programme'.[2] Completing the magic circle, Professor Saunders believes that the library supports the schools by 'giving the essential and complementary in-service experience'.[3] Awareness then is abroad but Eric Clough sounded a warning note with a reference in his address to the lip-service that is paid to training which echoed a similar sentiment expressed over a quarter of a century earlier by E. V. Corbett, addressing a conference on the problems of staffing and staff training, when he was obliged to confess that 'while lip-service is given to the value and necessity of training, in actual fact very little or none at all is given'. Mr Corbett's concern at that time was to ensure that the newly established library schools should flourish but his words embraced in-service training then and are regrettably relevant to many library systems at the present moment. Nevertheless, the anticipated impact of the kaleidoscope of social, economic, technological, political and educational changes allows a reassertion of confidence. Although wary of oversell and propheteering, it is not unreasonable to assume that training will be present in many of the other contributions in this volume.

The vocabulary or jargon of change and forecasting provide a starting point in considering the nature of the challenge librarians or information workers will face and the implications for their education and training. Transience, diversity, mobility, systems, interface, multi-disciplinary, networks, are a few of the symbols used to describe the science fiction dream become automated reality. One pale mouth'd prophet, having regard for the problem of programming systems and the major impact of the radical broadening of the communication spectrum from print to sound and image, points to the implication for the background and cultural experience of the public who require information and knowledge. Leaving aside for a moment the consequences for the selection and education of future librarians, the organisational response will result in larger cost-conscious systems, interdependent and interlocked into networks.

What, then, of our future librarians who will have to face the reality of an ever-accelerating rate of change and be required to meet the more and more urgent demands for greater accessibility and comprehensive provision? Their education and training must reflect this situation, providing the means for the release of their potential in this brave new world and reinforcing and safeguarding the current trend to a user-orientated service. The push-buttons and screens will and should multiply but the needs of the user, actual and potential, will still have to be actively sought out and creatively interpreted.

A recent editorial in *The Times Educational Supplement*, reflecting on the results of a schools competition, 'Europe 2000', concluded that they supported those who want to introduce future studies in the school curricula not just as an end of term aside but as a main focus for thinking about the world. Alvin Tofler in *Future shock* has traced the lines of change which lead in personal, educational and work terms, to the new free form world of kinetic organisations based on the principle of adhocracy, whose objectives and methods will be conceived in the future rather than the past. Professional education will have the responsibility for creating the necessary learning situation for producing people who are flexible, adaptable, capable of critical judgement and educated to face and discern the patterns of future change. This ongoing process will bring in its wake expectations which will have to be satisfied within the work situation by the application of a number of management skills, one of which is training.

How library schools meet their commitment bears directly on the training function. If James Thompson's diagnosis of the needs of the academic library user is correct, then fewer, more in-depth educated, professionals will be required, which means that responsibility for technical training will shift to the employer. Guy Garrison believes that the wider assertion of public libraries as service centred and people orientated, will mean a more imaginative and innovative approach in and beyond the library school.[4] H. Schur's analysis of the requirements for education and training of future information specialists will mean that library schools will have to pay greater attention to more theoretical topics at the expense of some practical training, which can 'in most advanced countries be obtained by training in employment'.[5] The responsibility of the library school, therefore, will be to build up a body of principles, a hierarchy of theories, Peter Jordan has called it, to be applied to particular work situations. There are also consequential implications for practical training both before and during courses. The emphasis of an education in general principles, concerned with library philosophy, communication and learning processes, objectives and attitudes, and the inculcating of a critical questioning approach, helps to define potential training needs. These needs will also be refined by the rate of technological change, developments of new knowledge and techniques, as well as the requirement to provide for a wide and increasing range of specialisations. All this reinforces how essential it will be to integrate more closely the ways in which the educational and training needs of future librarians are met.

In part an answer to the questions 'why train?' and 'what training?' will be given by a consideration of the objectives of library schools and the programmes they evolve. Also important to the training functions is the concept of a training continuum, that future librarians will be a product of an evolving, adapting, continuous process. The profession, acting through the Library Association, must ensure the necessary working situation in which this will obtain. The individual has, of course, an important part to play. H. William Axford, studying the effective allocation of resources, writes that

> All members of the library faculty are called upon to be managers – managers of the most important resource at their disposal – their own time and talents. In other words it is the library administrator's responsibility to create a professional working environment. It is the individual faculty member's responsibility to exploit it to the best of his or her ability.[6]

The Library Association in its list of professional and non-professional duties has also emphasised the continuing obligation placed on staff for self development.

The coming together of professional, educational and individual needs in the work situation completes the eternal triangle. F. Herzberg believes mental health is and will become increasingly the core issue of our times, so that if for no other reason it will be a matter of enlightened self interest to fulfil what he sees as

> ... the primary function of any organisation whether religious, political or industrial ... to implement the needs for man to enjoy a meaningful existence.[7]

This imperative has assumed at the time of writing a very practical sense of urgency. From all sides come prophecies of apocalyptic economic doom giving rise to exhortations to husband ever more carefully the most precious resource

Training Future Librarians

available to any organisation – staff. Public expenditure funds a large measure of library service and while it is cast in the role of villain, in what promises to be a long running drama, there will be a continuing premium on staff management. Staff account for between 40–60% of most libraries' costs and clearly training, along with other management skills, will have an increasingly important part to play in maximising the creative use of this resource.

Even without the transition from a period of growth to retrenchment, conditions already exist and pressures can be anticipated which will oblige a more extensive and systematic attention being paid to staff selection, deployment and training. Local government is still adjusting to the greatly increased size of authorities and looking at ways of overcoming problems of communication and co-ordination. There has been the concurrent impact of the corporate approach to the provision of services in terms of interrelated programme areas with team policy making and decision taking. The team concept, of course, extends beyond the public library scene, since groupings of bands of co-equals, including specialists, non-librarians as well as librarians, has been postulated for the future of academic library staffing. And a complex of inter-disciplinary specialisations has been described by H. Schur as fundamental if future information needs are to be met.

At the same time as organisations become larger, with more diversified, loosely structured and mobile staff establishments, there emerges another future theme – that of togetherness. There will be a number of reasons for the development of systems and networks, all aspects of the necessity of realising the full potential of resources. A common ground for commentators of the library scene now and in the future is the need for libraries to develop a heightened sense of cost-consciousness. This will receive impetus in the need to make further patterns of information systems and system networks commercially viable. Even in less economically orientated areas of library provision, there will be an increasingly urgent need for research and training in techniques of evaluation, performance measures, cost benefit and cost effective analysis. Staff, their deployment, training and development will be an integral part in all this.

What Richard Emery has said of communication is equally true of staff training, with which it is closely linked, that it is not a secondary or derived aspect of management but is central to organisational activity.[8] The aims of training are identified with the aims of the organisation, which the work of Maslow, Herzberg and others teach, must tie in with the needs of the individual. Training is concerned with the opening up, the 'unfreezing' of creative talent. C. D. Ellis has enumerated the cost of not training, 'high labour turnover, low morale and failure to respond to changes in environment',[9] with the consequent result of poor and inefficient service to the user. Ellis says 'training means the organisation of learning opportunities and the provision of resources to enable effectively motivated people to learn quickly and well'; to learn is understood here to mean to gain knowledge, skill or ability. The participation and involvement of all staff in the training function as a continuous process is acknowledged as essential. So too is its close relationship with other elements of management. By improving the quality of the work situation and paying attention to individual's needs, training makes job prospects more rewarding, which has an impact on the selection process and this in turn can reduce training needs. Operating alongside training should and will increasingly be a systematic process of staff assessment, which ties in with the wider question of library evaluation. Enmeshed in all, is the responsibility for providing job satisfaction, an opportunity to enjoy a sense of achievement and pride. J. L. Schofield writes that

Any library service, whether public, academic or special, is labour intensive and therefore job satisfaction and the satisfaction of psychological needs are of the utmost importance because manpower is the most expensive resource in libraries.[10]

What training should be given turns on the needs as expressed by the interrelated parts of the training triangle composed of the professional, individual and work situation. These will be made explicit and co-ordinated by an analysis in preparation of the organisation's training audit.

Some indicators have already been given by looking at training in relation to professional education, but librarians in future would do well to look at developments in other fields, particularly industry, for guidance in working out a framework within which a systematic training process may be evolved which is capable of analysing problems while allowing for consideration of alternative approaches and providing terms of reference for evaluation. This process, as Lorna Paulin has said, 'needs constant re-thinking and re-designing to fit changing needs.'[11] The requirement for a formal structure of training will increase as library organisations get larger and care must be taken not to overlook important training adjuncts such as the provision of staff libraries, with study accommodation and facilities, to ensure staff have the opportunity for self-learning and time for reading both professional and local community material.

Implicit in this approach is that future organisations within which libraries operate will be seeking to apply D. M. McGregor's Theory Y to library management and thereby aiming to create an environment 'consistent with maintaining the objectives of an organisation', in which

> an employee is given the maximum opportunity for self-determination and is subject to the minimum amount of obvious authority. . . . His innate desire to be creative, useful, respected and superior should be encouraged rather than thwarted.[12]

Library management in the future will be concerned with the ever more delicate task of balancing authority and freedom. The trend will be away from management by control to management by objectives, arrived at in an open system of participative consultation at all levels.

The days of the vertical hierarchies are numbered and the movement is away from the Galbraithian idea of organisation as being more important than people. The approach of Management Review Analysis Programmes, being carried out in North American university libraries at present, emphasises a group dynamics approach aimed at bringing internal changes necessary to make the library service more responsive to the needs of present and future users, and is dependent on an open consultative working situation. The team and project task approach involved carries enormous educational and training opportunities. Some observers, like H. W. Axford, see a danger of creating a confusion of administrative infrastructures, engaged in what Lawrence Clark Powell has described as a 'kind of library incest, an activity which takes librarians from the fertile intercourse with library users into sterile intercourse with each other' – a forceful reminder that management as a whole and training in particular must relate all that it does to the client.

Whatever the style and structure of the organisation, training must come to be accepted as an integral part of the total management complex. It is represented in the continuing study of staff resources that is manpower planning. It is one factor in controlling performance with subsequent benefit to the individual and community. Training will not only be seen as a necessary part of the realisation of the principle of accountability, but also provide a channel for communicating and confirming the librarian's management credibility.

The starting point in a systems approach to training is an examination of the aims and objectives of the service expressed in terms of the needs of the community or organisation served. A training audit will take these as its terms of reference in analysing the work to be done, establishing the expected performance levels, the characteristics of the staff involved, the resources available and the methods and evaluation procedures to be adopted. The emphasis will be on objectives and performance achievement, since this is the core of training problems, the bridging of the gap between actual and potential performance. There is a clear link between training, selection, job analysis and evaluation, and staff assessment.

As an aside, before looking at possible particular areas of training provision, it will be assumed that the needs of non-professional staff will be properly looked after since it is on these that the realisation of the service objectives will depend to a large degree. All organisations have an obligation in terms of self-realisation to every member of staff, and as in future the lines defining professional and non-professional duties come to be drawn increasingly sharply, the dependence on the well-being of support staff will be critical. Staffing trends in all types of library services will see an increase in this group, possessing their own well defined promotion career structure. The public relations value of front line managers and their staff has always been vital, and forms a necessary part of the training continuum. W. J. Murison's observation on this value extends to all kinds of library 'that courtesy in public service will cover to the user's satisfaction a multitude of shortcomings arising from reduced resources'.[13]

Central to all effective in-service training is *induction* for staff at all levels. It is the start of the process that marries the requirements of the individual to those of the organisation in the service of the client. New entrants will be assisted to fit into the daily life of the organisation and understand their part in it. Industrial sociologists who, with psychologists, may well be employed in future by the governing bodies of libraries, describe induction as a specific and important example of the socialisation of the individual to the expectations of management. For librarians this process of identification, which is a continuing one, is assisted by the presence of what Jesse Shera has described as the 'irreducible minimum of the vocational'. There are as many approaches to induction programmes, their timing and content, as there are types of library services or indeed librarians, but the overall objective will be common – the meaningful involvement and participation of staff combined with the confirming and sustaining of their motivation.

Induction training, in whatever form, will be given against the background of on-the-job or skills training, and the aim of the two programmes will be to improve performance and test aptitudes. Analysis is also the starting point of skills training, a difficult process since it involves identifying specific stimuli and relevant responses. In a future world of expanding and increasingly complex technology, the emphasis on this area of training will increase. In addition all libraries will be faced with the question of instruction of library users. It has already been mentioned that more of the weight of technical training will move from the library school to work situations, not only in the field of technology but in traditional skills of cataloguing and bibliographical searching. Newer skills will become important in the cost-conscious world of information provision, where selling and marketing techniques will form part of training programmes.

An underlying assumption in considering training future librarians must be that there will grow a much closer co-operation between library school and library than exists at present in formulating training policies and programmes. This stands out particularly clearly when considering the place of practical experience in education and training, either as a pre-library-school requirement or as a planned part of the library school course.

There are those who see pre-library-school experience coming increasingly to the fore as a result of the demand and supply of library school places. Others see it as desirable for its own sake, agreeing with the Library Association's statement on in-service training that

A student's ability to benefit from the education he will receive at library school will depend to a large extent upon the background and attitudes to the profession he has acquired as a result of his training.[14]

Another report has since highlighted the indifferent mix of present arrangements for pre-school training and stressed that some provision is very desirable and that, particularly in the case of direct entrants to library schools, 'the student should not start the formal library school course without such preparation'.[15] Close co-operation between library school and library employer is essential if substance is to be given to this recommendation.

The merits of a practical period as a planned part of the library school course have also been widely and continuously debated which perhaps at least indicates agreement that some experience is necessary. Patricia Knapp is in no doubt as to the part the carefully planned and administered field work experience plays by helping to bridge the gap between the ideal and real and so reducing the possibility of trauma at the taking up of the first professional appointment. What is essential is not only to define terms, but more importantly to clarify the relationship between practice and principle in the teaching and learning process and demonstrating how experience aids instruction.

The training programmes for newly qualified professionals will continue the period of adjustment from the school of theory to the world of actuality. This will be the critical time when ideals and ideas should be harnessed, when needs, constraints, responsibilities and potential of individual and organisation are made explicit. At first the emphasis, following induction, will be on supervisory training for the overseeing of staff in operational areas, with sessions reinforcing the courses of inter-personal relationships and communications received at library school. Where the team approach to staff deployment is adopted, account will have to be taken of the effects of the loss of group identity and high turnover of relationships, as well as the increased level of delegation for which training allowance must be made.

A sense of involvement and the reassurance of being able to influence service effectiveness will come in part from the opportunity to apply recently acquired research attitudes and techniques. The loosely structured interdisciplinary teams of the future will at different times during career development provide for the setting up of project and task programmes, tailored to meet individual needs and interests as well as specific problem areas of the service. The team deployments in some authority library systems at present, and the potential of MRAP-type approaches, provide ready frameworks for this.

Training programmes must provide for specialisation in subject areas which will be grafted on to the professional education received to date. This, and an increasing involvement in management techniques, such as computer application, cost techniques and personnel, will be provided for by both internal and external courses. Training will be the agent enabling the individual to respond and prepare for change as well as providing preparation for promotion and opportunities for job enrichment. There will be a gradual shift of emphasis from supervisory training to management development. The latter must take into account not only the supervisory element but also a vital new ingredient which becomes more and more dynamic the higher one climbs up the managerial ladder. This is an area where first consideration must be with individual growth, a more educational concern than the job description or terminal behaviour analysis of other areas of training.

New staff structures will involve shifts in power relationships and decision making processes and contain the seeds of psychological pressure and tension. Management development must take account of this as well as adjusting to the pressures resulting from a world of rapid economic, political, technical and organisational change, with all that this implies for the market world of the individuals and groups to be served. This level of training must be insightful, giving the senior managers a better understanding of themselves and their functions in order that they may disseminate and sustain a sense of creative possibility throughout the service structure. In management development it is the teaching process that is more important than content, and according to occasion and need, there will be an intermix of the wide range of methods available, of lectures, group seminars, tutorials, case studies, projects, T-groups and role playing. Where applicable, internships and sabbaticals of varying periods will be employed.

Training, in whatever form, along with all other library activities will be called upon to justify itself in terms of benefits bestowed against costs incurred. This will again link training into the total measurement and evaluation process, reinforcing its part in the overall management structure and identifying it with the service aims and objectives. Supervisory and skills training in a systems approach, in as far as it is performance orientated, will be more amenable to evaluation. The more difficult area is in development where the emphasis is educational, with no terminal behaviour specified. But C. D. Ellis stresses the point that, if training is to be accepted as a work and service enhancing necessity and not an optional extra to be cut back at the first breath of economic frost, then a value must be put on its benefits, in social as well as financial terms.

Training Future Librarians

Responsibility for establishing and meeting the training needs of future librarians in the work situation rests with the organisation as a whole and with every individual member of it. This responsibility will only be realised and met in a meaningful and continuous way when all are educated in the part they must play. This condition satisfied, there must be a focal point, a co-ordinator, well qualified in both librarianship and personnel management, who analyses problems in training terms and has direct responsibility at a senior level for the training function. The organisational framework of training will vary considerably between library services but for public libraries there are signs that the latest round of local government reorganisation, under the tutelage of Bains and embracing the concept of corporate management, is seeing the emergence of centralised training departments. For libraries there are both the danger of opting out of training responsibilities and the potential advantages of maximising expertise and facilities. There are implications in this development, particularly during a period of financial constraint, for the provision by the profession of certain categories of external short courses. On the political front the process of devolution may bring closer to realisation the idea of area training boards providing a network of training facilities for a whole range of libraries.

The organisation for training and the scope for it to become part of the future patterns of co-ordination and co-operation, will be encouraged by the advances in technology and telecommunications. The use of computer aided instruction, satellite and direct dialling link-ups will make for not only regional co-operation but also the internationalisation of training resources. And the technological, audio-visual world of tomorrow will extend the range of possible training methods to be matched in a variety of permutations to the different staff groupings. Traditional methods will be reinforced by greater use of film, closed circuit television and computer.

The Association's role in all this must be central. Responsibility for and involvement in the training of future librarians is part of its mainstream obligation for maintaining high professional standards. A positive and active lead must be given in creating the conditions necessary for co-ordination and co-operation between all parties in the provision of systematic training policies and suitable facilities. The British Library grant to the Association, made in August 1975, for the study of management training, will hopefully have developed into an ongoing programme of research covering the whole spectrum of training and formulated in terms of future needs. Finally, since tomorrow's world will be no place for the timid, unimaginative, well-mannered introvert, the Association's initiative on career advice and recruitment, which bears directly on training, will assume a new dynamic.

References in text

1. Thompson, J. *Library power*. Bingley, 1974. pp. 20-21.
2. Mack, E. *In-training in information and special library units*. Aslib, 1974.
3. Saunders, W. L. *Professional education: some challenges for the next decade*. In *Essays on Information and Libraries*. ed. K. Barr and M. Line. Bingley, 1974.
4. Garrison, G. Library education and the public library. *Libr. J.* 95 (9) September 1970, 2763-2767.
5. Schur, H. *Education and training for information specialists for the 1970s*. Sheffield, University of Sheffield Postgraduate School of Librarianship and Information Service, 1972.
6. Axford, H. W. The inter-relations of structure, governance and effective resource utilization in academic libraries. *Libr. Trends*, 23, April 1975, 567.
7. Herzberg, F. *Work and the nature of man*. Staples Press, 1968.
8. Emery, R. *Staff communication in libraries*. Bingley, 1975.
9. Talbot, J. R. and Ellis, C. D. *Analysis and costing of company training*. Gower Press, 1969.
10. Schofield, J. L. Job evaluation, job analysis, job satisfaction and resistance to change. *Libr. Ass. Rec.*, 77 (10) October 1975, 241-243.
11. Paulin, L. V. In-service training. *Library Association, Annual Conference. Reference, Special and Information Section, 1964*, pp. 9-15.
12. McGregor, D. M. *The human side of enterprise*. McGraw, 1960.
13. Murison, W. J. Images and real people. *New Libr. Wld*, 76 (10) October 1975, 200-201.
14. Library Association. Report of the sub-committee on in-service training. *Lib. Ass. Rec.*, 64 (5) May 1962, 171-175.
15. Department of Education and Science. *The supply and training of librarians. Report*. HMSO, 1968. pp. 38-39.

Chapter Five

The Future Management Pattern for Libraries

Gileon Holroyd

In the crystal ball lent by my local media resources centre, there are two future management patterns for libraries. One is pleasantly familiar: an apparently realistic picture of the near future with a mixture of libraries as before. Small and large libraries continue with cloudy but detectable relationships between them. The management arrangements for the small library are simple though not always easy, just as they are now. Local authority libraries demonstrate similar relationships with their elected policy makers as happens now, or as Savage[1] described thirty years ago. But beyond this picture of familiar variety, there is one that is much more diffuse and turbulent. The gazer can discriminate strands of development, and a few clots, rather than a neat pattern.

Amateur librarians
One strand in the more distant picture consists of small libraries. Some of these have been developed by single individuals for their own use during their leisure and work. Some of the collections are as rich and as cherished as the 'gentleman's libraries' that have been admired for so long. The collectors are perhaps more highly respected as library owners than as amateur librarians, though they may have one of only two principles of library arrangement. These are to find an item by remembering where one put it – or else buy another – or by inventing a personal classification scheme, which is a useful way of clarifying one's own mind about personal interests, but may be less useful to others. In a future where everybody has been

taught, and most people have learnt, about libraries in school and college, the standard of amateur librarianship will be much improved. We shall have persuaded people that skilled handling of one's personal cultural and information stores is an important matter, requiring the least cumbersome and most effective methods of organisation and retrieval. No thinking person will himself, let alone suppose that professional librarians might, generate an excessive array of indexes, forms and prohibitions before taking out a single item for use.

It is arguable that the perfect library is possible, provided that it is designed to serve only one user. When a second person shares the service, the arrangement of materials is compromised and queuing problems set in. Duplication of materials for the second person does mitigate some of the deficiency, but the single focus of perfection no longer exists. It is possible now for all sorts of people to have their perfect libraries – if they lead a simple life in every respect – or if they spend a high proportion of their own time and money on it. In the future there will be much more emphasis on perfect library services at the points where the biggest national decisions are made. Some of these perfect services will consist of a single sheet distilled from public and confidential information, dropped into the executive handbag as he leaves for work.

For the small library shared among a few users, the future pattern will be more complicated. We have plenty of these little libraries already, but no thorough way of knowing where they are, short of regular inspection of virtually every non-domestic and even domestic premise in the country. Some of the people who have these small office or workshop libraries at present emphatically reject the idea of assistance in handling their material. A variety of limitations may affect the collections, such as one individual's desire to 'control' the information in the library, an assumption that the library should be made out of materials received rather than materials required, a feeling that any management of the collection is impossible until someone is employed to apply to it the impressive techniques seen in universities or public libraries serving half a million people, or the limitation of an awareness that using more information may

The Future Management Pattern

involve doing more work. For whatever cause, the following quotation illustrates the results:

It was hoped to visit other architects' libraries, but approaches to them were not well received. One large firm when approached said that the librarian had left and had not been replaced, so the library was in disarray; another said that the practice was no longer doing the same work and that the library was too small to be of interest. An architect from the Scottish office of the first firm said that the northern library was of little use, because the material was always out on loan or not available when required. The general picture seemed to be one of small libraries in a disordered state which the firms would not like an outsider to see.[2]

Much more effective work will be done through the media and education to help youngsters to understand their use of ideas. Then adults such as these architects, who have enough need for a library to generate a starter, and enough acumen to know that it is not meeting their need, will have learnt enough already to identify what should be done about their disarrayed collections and by whom.

Such architects in the future will send for a roving librarian, who will help them to work out their library needs and show them how to meet these needs. Secretaries will not be involved in the solution because they will be much too expensive for junior duties, but a promising trainee architect may be favoured with this sort of responsibility. The main load of organising materials will be taken by external information services, supported in some specialised areas by a few surviving manual systems like that of the visiting 'librarians' who keep Barbour Indexes in a usable state. The fact that, even now, considerable external services coexist with these sad little libraries, shut away in shame from visitors, demonstrates that there must be a much greater use of roving, consultant, or free-lance librarians, and soon.

Agents-bibliothécaires
There are already a few consultant and free-lance librarians, undertaking a range of jobs from advising on the development of large systems to lending a hand with the indexing. Because

the gap between the need for information and the actual access to it is so obvious, a way will be found for people who cannot hire a whole librarian to borrow one for the tricky bits. This gap could be restated as the difference between what an experienced librarian can do for his own employer and what an external service can do for a client: whether the external service is a public library, Aslib, national information centre, industry or research organisation, chamber of commerce, small firms' information centre, government department selective service, automated SDI service, commercial news sheet or a friend in the City.

Roving librarians or *agents-bibliothécaires* will have the job of getting themselves accepted wherever there is a recurring need for information and library materials. They will help clients to work out their information flow, and will discuss ways of supporting it effectively and economically. They will be involved, as Alan Gilchrist[3] has already indicated, with management information intertwined with published data. The *agents* will arrange suitable external services for their clients, revise the existing information stores – probably discarding quantities of materials – set up simple systems for people about the office to maintain, and provide a list of necessary Telex numbers. The *agents* will have enough confidence in their ability to help, and enough awareness of the need for others to understand information use, to encourage the amateur librarians they meet instead of regretting their existence.

The crystal ball is not quite clear about how these roving librarians collect their pay. It will probably depend on their individual degree of specialisation and on the prevailing employers in their territory. Some roving librarians specialising in the educational sector will be employed by local authority education departments to help small and special schools, careers advisory services, firms providing educational materials, and young people's leisure centres. The librarians specialising in agricultural information will be knitted into the existing advisory services of the Ministry of Agriculture, Fisheries and Food, extended by its European links. Perhaps most of the roving librarians will be based on external information services,

The Future Management Pattern

which will in turn be based, through the British Library, on the international information network. The link between the *agents* and the external services will provide a more sensitive way of reporting back between users and centre, as well as providing more varied activities for external service librarians.

There may be certain areas in which the roving librarians find a need to be fee-charging independents, particularly where there may be an adversary relation between a private person and central or local government. In this way, tax advisers are independent of the Inland Revenue, patent agents are independent of the Patent Office, and surveyors in private practice are usually independent of local authority building surveyors. On the other hand, neighbourhood advice centres and social services departments have already found ways of containing legitimate adversaries within the embrace of a local authority.

It is clear that central government will have taken an influential interest in the functions of roving librarians. It will be providing funds through the British Library for development of external services and assessment of further needs. Central government will 'encourage' local authority roving services, and will provide some roving services directly through its own departments.

The potential directions for future government involvement in libraries are more fully discussed in Chapter Six of this volume. However, in relation to roving librarians, there is a restraint on over-centralisation of information services directly under central government control, just as there has been restraint on over-centralisation of police. 'Knowledge is power' has been inscribed on enough Carnegie library doorsteps and Marxist newspapers to be recognised as a problem as well as an axiom. Central government is excellently placed to arrange for co-ordination of library information services, but if it were to control individual services too closely its offerings would undoubtedly meet suspicion and rejection.

Large libraries
So far, the crystal has shown signs of being a 'scientific'

forecaster. It has detected small developing activities in areas of need, and has extrapolated them into a larger feature. However, one does need a crystal to decide whether extrapolation is wise. There are risks with the technique, as illustrated in Cockburn's now famous warning:

Thus world population, and also the available labour force in industrial countries, is doubling every 50 years. The gross national product is doubling every 20 years and so are the number of major scientific discoveries. The whole scientific and engineering establishment, including for instance numbers of graduates, membership of learned societies and scientific publications, is doubling every 15 years. The money spent on applied research is doubling every 7 years, and so also is the demand for electronics and aviation. If all these processes were to continue unchecked we should certainly be heading for catastrophe. Within about 100 years every one of us would be a scientist, the entire national output would be absorbed in research, and we should be spending most of our lives airborne at 40,000 feet.[4]

In surveying the present scene of libraries already large – those of extensive local authorities, hyperpolytechnics and megaministries, and now the discreetly massive British Library – to extrapolate much further growth of the existing large library institutions is to ignore the disadvantages of size.[5] The problem of the library becoming imperfect with more than one user becomes steadily more acute with the larger library. This is primarily because of distance: the distance between the reader and the centre of larger areas of government, and the distance between the front doorstep of the library and the various items he requires. A highly educated society, valuing variety of ideas, will produce a higher proportion of people who want the resources of a substantial library. Consequently, a total replacement of the public library service by a fleet of mobiles operated from Boston Spa is unlikely, especially as the topography of Britain and its rural road system will alter little. We shall of course have the technological competence to reduce the obstacle of distance through facsimile transmission and high speed transport, but there may not be enough money to develop such non-priority items in the present century. Arguments like these lean against the proposition that because libraries have got

The Future Management Pattern

big they will therefore get bigger. Yet one can note that librarians are steadily debugging their techniques of managing larger systems, and there will be no restraint on further enlargement for reasons of unmanageability. One can also note that there is a group of libraries to which the 'not much bigger' forecast might not apply. These are the libraries of central government departments. For some years, these libraries have been exploring their future pattern of relationships, but the present author is even less competent to speculate on what the outcome of these discussions may be.

In media opinion, rather than in forecasting, there are alternatives to extrapolation for a methodical crystal to use. One is the pendulum idea, the supposition for example that overpackaging must lead to oversalvaging and back again. Although smallness is currently fashionable, it is somewhat rarer for the institutions that maintain large libraries to fragment into little ones, or to be squeezed into becoming significantly smaller. Though we have seen in some counties and in Scotland that such things can happen, even Anthony Crosland has admitted on radio that local authorities could not be rescrambled again in the near future and still work. By the time institutional reorganisation has been digested, the pendulum may well have brought us back to espousing the economies of scale.

Another notion of predictable development is that of cycles – shared in their various ways by economists, biologists, astrologists and Shakespeare's history plays. One cycle that may well feature in the future of library organisation is that of formalised co-operation. Britain has just been growing out of co-operation as an austerity measure. In the United States co-operatives have started to blossom in the last decade, as a way of making better use of new resources. Newer techniques of information transfer make the mechanisms of international co-operatives more possible. This can be helpful to developing countries where libraries have special austerity problems. Newer understanding of how organisations work may also help the diverse and autonomous participants in co-operatives over some of the obstacles in the way of their effective collaboration.

Internal management patterns
Internal management of large libraries is taken here to be that practised within the domains of individual chief librarians. Most of these large libraries are under public administration, either directly as public libraries, or those of colleges, large schools, and government departments, or indirectly as the British Library, or those of universities and public corporations. This leaves only some large industrial chains of libraries in different divisions, as in ICI, and the University of Buckingham. These 'private' libraries confront their managers with basically similar stewardship problems to those of managers working with public funds.

The crystal shows a continuing clarity on the principle of accountability and a continuing cloudiness on how exactly this may be achieved – in services which do not lend themselves readily to measurement, but which do lend themselves to dual direction by officials and politicians. When libraries are more conspicuous in their consumption of public wealth, they will be more vulnerable to redirection at high political levels. An example of such redirection was the rather sudden announcement by Patrick Gordon Walker that the Bloomsbury site would not be used for extending the British Museum Library. A continuing example has been elaborated by Richard Marsh, for instance, in *Managing to survive*.[6] He argues that for an enterprise to be efficiently managed it must be quite clear who is accountable for what at every level. Yet he says that it is usual for transitory ministers to intervene in the policies implemented by permanent directors of such enterprises as British Rail. Consequently, the permanent managers cannot be fully accountable for policies they do not control, any more than the politicians are fully accountable for policies they do not last long enough to implement.

Local authority libraries have a considerable future as political footballs, especially in matches between local and regional councillors. There will be far more councillors able to be forceful and effective on individual local matters than on the broader scale of regional government. Complaints about the disparity between branch and central library services may thus reverberate indefinitely. Results obtained from sophisticated techniques of measurement will not only be a tool for the library manager, they will also be the stuff of controversy in the progress of 'open' government. If the controversy were to be seen as wholly destructive, then measurement techniques could remain at the primitive level of issue statistics, population and budget. However, if the library managers are confident of their position, they will develop methods of forecasting future use of materials, assessing future abilities of individual librarians, and of analysing the quality of their services. The results of any of these measurements may be freely discussed in news media. Individual librarians may have to decide publicly, for example, whether to go on acquiring materials from inexperienced authors, composers and artists, in the face of demonstrably low forecast usage figures; though in a locality where the authors' lobby is weak the librarians could find themselves directed by their employers to drop the least promising materials.

Such a problem as this illustrates the question of whether a democratic internal style of management is compatible with democratic external control. A public authority that is jealous of its power to make an impact on services may need a highly bureaucratic structure of officials to ensure that detailed control remains with elected representatives. A public authority that delegates most decisions to its officials in effect transfers the opportunity for democratic management – participative management is a more accurate term – to its employees.

When Likert[7] presented his conclusions on effective new patterns of management a decade and a half ago, he was convinced from his researches that a highly participative style produced much more effective organisational performance. The advantages of managing in a way that allows for general discussion of important decisions include better communication[8] and organisational cohesion. The disadvantages are partly reflected in Thomas and Ward's study[9] showing the very high proportion of time that library managers already give to the communicative processes, presumably of participative decision. However, managers of any enterprise at any time have only a limited choice of how autocratic or how participative they will be. If the organisation includes only people reared to autocracy, much training is needed to make participation acceptable. When the social norm is fairly participative, the only organisations that can effectively maintain a strong autocracy are those with powerful sanctions against the rebellious. Public employers are not likely to receive approval for operating such sanctions for non-emergency services, which most libraries will be. So how useful will ever more participation be in future library management?

The most visible effect will be to abolish dead-end jobs, such as those of some non-professional staff, in libraries. The division of library staff into professional and non-professional has been a necessary transitional phase to demonstrate what librarians can do besides using a date stamp. Some movement from this transitional phase is already evident in the opening of administrative careers for non-librarians working in libraries. It will also be appropriate for such staff to go into administrative posts in other departments of their authority. The evidence that we have so far from library assistant's certificate students is that many of them have too great a capacity to be 'trained down' to the mechanical jobs allocated to them in the Library Association's list of non-professional duties.[10] Since machines will not be available for all routine work, additional labour will be needed for the basics of library housekeeping. Depending on the population pattern in the locality, the 'junior' staff will be a more or less varied mixture of trainee librarians, part time parents, unsupported students, senior citizens, the moderately handicapped, school children on job experience, delinquents on community service, and *au pairs* liberated from the domestic sphere. For public libraries, a rich mixture of the above will help to demonstrate that the library is for everybody.

Meanwhile, the quality of library service experienced by the reader depends heavily on the attitude and sense of the 'junior' staff. To achieve a high quality of service with a high turnover of diverse staff makes very heavy demands on first line supervision. A strengthening of first line supervision will be a conspicuous feature of future library management. The people filling such roles will be junior managers (either professional or

The Future Management Pattern

non-professional librarians), but they will not be trainees. To have the authority to persuade and encourage their colleagues to a high standard of service, the first line managers must be seen to have considerable influence on decisions, and to achieve this in a participative context their recommendations will have to be good enough to command wide support. These managers will have a significant role in personnel policies as applied to the colleagues for whom they are responsible. The more senior managers in the libraries will discuss management style with the first line managers, but the effective choice of what constitutes good management for each unit will rest primarily with the first line supervisors.

Also operating from the library, there will be the specialists in different kinds of service – for special groups and special subjects. Many of these will be roving librarians, but some will have established spots in the library where readers can expect to find them consistently. This pattern will not be new. It is already well established in some counties and many academic libraries. However, the practice has not spread as rapidly as the literature might suggest. This is shown by Martin Walker's comment on the limited numbers of subject specialists in polytechnic libraries:

Our survey of all thirty polytechnics in Britain showed clearly that there are not enough subject specialists yet: only eight polytechnics of the twenty who returned the questionnaire reported having more than six specialists.[11]

There may be various reasons for slow progress. To release staff fully for specialist roles generates more demands on the library and increases the need for money. It may be found that the existing pay structure is not apparently compatible with a looser grouping of more independent professionals. The librarians may feel that their service will become fragmented as they see less and less of their roving colleagues. These inhibitions will be worse when we try to base roving librarians on groups of local libraries – such as public, college and university – instead of on just one library. Librarians have tended to bow to the view that the library must be imperfect when it is shared by more than one user – if that user is an institution rather than a person. Yet if the variety of demand from Open University and other unattached students develops, there may be less justification for limiting the use of roving librarians and publicly financed collections to specified clienteles.

The senior managers of large libraries have quite a task. Much of the choice of managerial style will be delegated to first line management. Much of the expensive labour force will be out and about developing the service in accordance with its own assorted ideals. The participative idea can be pushed so far that senior managers seem to have little room left to participate themselves, beyond perhaps receiving complaints, chairing numberless staff meetings, preparing bullet-proof budgets, and arguing for more resources. The 'public face' that was once the prerogative of the chief is already a team achievement. It seems inevitable that, the greater the sharing of such decision making as there is in libraries, the less scope there is for a dominant personality as chief. Still, some library systems are more admired than others, and not solely for architectural elegance or richness of stock. Some libraries are still known as 'good places to leave' because of the distinguished careers of former staff. The profession is as yet shy of identifying the admired qualities of senior management, but it will become better at such analysis in order to find ways to make these admired qualities more generally found. At present there is only a random chance of providing adequate training for senior management until we know what it is that makes some managements more effective than others.

We do have one clue, however, from the literature on leadership,[12] to suggest that in modern institutions leadership is as much a function of the people led as of the person doing the leading. In other words, the managed tend to get the management they deserve. Future senior library managers, finding themselves at the hub (in Dr Hookway's phrase) of a system of highly individualistic subject specialists, with a few senior management specialists in staffing, finance and public relations, for example, some powerful first line supervisors, and a highly unionised cadre of library assistants (NUPE rather than NALGO), may envy the National Health Service its traditional

The Future Management Pattern

authority structure, last heard of in the 1970s. To achieve unity of action and purpose, senior library managers will have few carrots and virtually no sticks. Their tools will be staff selection, communication and training. Some senior managers will give up hope of unity, and will accept a range of variation in service they do not approve of. Many subject specialists will prefer to vary their careers by switching to new subjects and new readership groups rather than apply for senior management posts.

There will remain a fundamental problem of all library management that the ability to make a contribution to the library will depend in part on the choice of action available. Industrial managers are giving some gloomy warnings on this topic:

Here, at last, I present a tentative definition of the word 'management' – for our times. It seems to me that in calmer times we could afford to imagine that management was a positive activity concerned with controlling environments. Although we cling to this kind of formulation in much of our management teaching, the fact is dawning on us that, in a time of uncontrollable environments, management is increasingly about reaction, and quick reaction at that.[13]

It is a future task to elucidate what there is for the library manager to react to, and what effects follow, internally and externally, when he or she does.

The social scientists are promising us a period of turbulence. Access to information will be important to people trying to cope with, or indeed to aggravate, the turbulence around them. All parts of the country's information and cultural resources are vulnerable to the strains inevitable in such a situation. The consequences for the remainder of the century are likely to lead to more varied staff structures, from scientific laboratory traditionalism to artistic anarchy; more varied techniques, from constantly obsolescent objectives to aggressive serendipity; more varied resources, from a congested home county to a sparse hillside. The future management pattern for libraries will become so demanding that library managers will acquire such subtle and sophisticated management skills as to make them the most sought after managers in the whole of public and industrial administration.

References in text

1. Savage, E. A. *The librarian and his committee.* Grafton, 1942.
2. Johnston, J. A survey of construction industry libraries. *Aslib Proc.,* 27 (10) October 1975, 401–413. (Quotation p. 403)
3. Gilchrist, A. Lectures at The Polytechnic of North London. Unpublished.
4. Cockburn, R. Science, defence and society: Trueman Memorial Lecture, February 1967. *Quoted in* Young, M., ed. *Forecasting and the social sciences.* Heinemann, 1968. p. 14.
5. These have been discussed on the scale of national economy in: Schumacher, E. F. *Small is beautiful: a study of economics as if people mattered.* Blond & Briggs, 1973.
6. Marsh, R. In place of profit. *In* Watkinson, H., *and others. Managing to survive.* BBC, 1975. pp. 13–18.
7. Likert, R. *New patterns of management.* McGraw-Hill, 1961.
8. This theme is developed in the context of librarianship by: Emery, R. *Staff communication in libraries.* Bingley, 1975.
9. Thomas, P., *and* Ward, V. *Where the time goes: librarians as managers, an exploratory survey.* Aslib, 1973. (Aslib occasional publication no. 12)
10. Library Association. *Professional and non-professional duties in libraries: a descriptive list.* LA, 1974.
11. Walker, M. Subject specialisation: introduction and survey. *In* Cowley, J., ed. *Libraries in higher education: the user approach to service.* Bingley, 1975. 106.
12. Bavelas, A. Leadership: man and function. *Reprinted in* Gibb, C. A., ed. *Leadership: selected readings.* Penguin, 1969.
13. Mant, A. The manager as professional. *Management Today,* September 1975, 58–61. (Quotation p. 61)
Also:
Stuttard, G. *Work is hell: an anatomy of workplace clichés.* Macdonald, 1969.
Thompson, J. *Library power: a new philosophy of librarianship.* Bingley, 1974.

Chapter Six

The Role of Government in Library Development

Ross Shimmon

Background
Government concern for libraries is a recent phenomenon in the UK, as Philip Sewell, Senior Library Adviser in the Department of Education and Science, has pointed out:

During the years 1966–70 ... we find for the first time a conscious acceptance on the part of government of the need for the overall co-ordination and development of library and information systems in Britain.[1]

Librarians would, no doubt, like to believe that this implies on the part of central government a growing realisation of the vital importance of library and information services to the educational, cultural, economic and political life of the country. There is, after all, strong evidence of the vital importance of some areas of library activity; had the literature been searched thoroughly at the design stages, perhaps the collapse of the Ferrybridge cooling towers and of the Ronan Point high-rise flats could have been avoided. It has also been suggested that $1\frac{1}{2}$ million dollars were lost in the US Apollo project because the literature on titanium was inadequately searched.[2] The general need for well-developed library and information services was well argued by an MP in these terms:

If anyone doubts the need for good library and reference facilities available to all, rich and poor, educated and uneducated, they might try a spell with an MP, preferable in a Northern constituency ... the entire democratic system requires a well-informed electorate.[3]

Government is certainly aware of the need for adequate scientific and technical information services; the scale of financial support given through OSTI – now the Research and Development Department of the British Library – in recent years [4] is witness to this. The OECD has added an international dimension to the pressures leading to government interest in libraries by strongly recommending that each member country establish a single focus for co-ordinating activity in the field of scientific and technical information. In fact, whether by accident or design or even a combination of both, 'by 1966 governmental concern for library and information systems was largely concentrated in the Department of Education and Science.' [5]

Another reason for this, perhaps belated, interest in libraries, on the part of government is an economic one. Libraries are increasingly expensive organisations and are financed mainly from the public purse. Their raw materials, books and other media, are expensive, unique items, required in large quantities. They are labour intensive organisations, requiring relatively expensive staff to acquire, store and exploit these raw materials and their parent organisations have invested in relatively sophisticated, and costly, buildings and equipment in recent years. Careful reading of a recent document produced for the Library Advisory Council for England [6] suggests that public funding of libraries and information systems of all kinds cannot be much less than £200 million a year at the present time. The old adage 'He who pays the piper calls the tune' is very relevant here; government must, in some way, ensure that value for public money is obtained and that it is spent in accordance with publicly acceptable priorities. Inflation and the general economic situation are of overriding importance to government and it is to be expected that, in the foreseeable future, its interest in this aspect of libraries will wax rather than wane.

Although tangible government support for libraries has occurred only recently, there has been considerable pressure over a long period of time from the profession and elsewhere for such support. Demands for government concern can in fact be traced back earlier than the 1849 Select Committee on Public Libraries. [7] Later the Adams report of 1917 to the Carnegie

The Role of Government

United Kingdom Trust,[8] the Kenyon Report of 1927[9] recommending, prophetically, Board of Education superintendence of public libraries, the McColvin Report of 1942[10] to the Library Association, the Roberts Report of 1957[11] leading *via* the Working Party Reports[12] to the 1964 Public Libraries and Museums Act, all, to some degree, added their weight to the claim for governmental concern for libraries. The Parry Report of 1967[13] to the University Grants Committee which ultimately, via the Dainton Committee's Report[14] led to the setting up of the British Library, continued the pressure. This development can only continue. It is inconceivable that any agency, other than central government, can provide the resources and co-ordinating role for the further development of library and information services in the UK, if only because at this stage in our history, government is necessarily concerned with all spheres of national, regional and local activity. How fast this development in library matters will continue, and in what directions, are the significant questions.

Political considerations
The direction of government involvement depends to a significant extent on the political climate of the country, perhaps more so now and in the future than in the past. Sharper differences in the attitudes of the two parties towards the provision of libraries have become apparent. The swift action in 1970 of the then newly-elected Conservative government in splitting the recently-formed Library and Information Systems Branch of DES back into two distinct parts, involving the 'return' of information systems interests to OSTI and the merging of library interests with concern for the arts to form the Arts and Libraries Branch under Lord Eccles, is but one piece of evidence. In the event, the formation of the Arts and Libraries Branch could be regarded as a trifle embarrassing in view of the conflicting interests of the two halves over the long-running Public Lending Right saga. Further evidence of the Conservative approach was the abandonment of OSTI's Documentation Processing Centre which had been established in Manchester 'to centralise computing capacity, peripheral equipment, programmes and expertise in support of experimental information projects'.[15]

The same government introduced museum charges (since revoked) and declared an intention to consider charges for public libraries, an intention several local authorities took seriously enough to investigate the technical possibilities; at least one, Leicestershire, published a report on the subject. This is not to suggest that a future Conservative government would set into reverse all the developments of recent years but, in opposition, the party is at present committed to a huge reduction in public expenditure and 'less government' which is often assumed to mean less 'interference' in the affairs of local government by central government. These two objectives may well be regarded as conflicting. Central funds now provide two-thirds of the income available to local authorities, inevitably resulting in greater rather than less supervision. The only apparent method of reversing this trend is to transfer the financing of some areas of activity from local to central government: that of teachers' salaries is an often-quoted possibility. In this connection, it is interesting to note that the average annual capital expenditure on new public library buildings during the last four years the closely supervised loan sanction scheme was in operation was £4·6m, while an average of £9·6m was spent annually in the first two years when local authorities were free to decide for themselves how to allocate non-key-sector capital investment.[16]

One indication of the ways some members, at least, of the Labour Party are thinking is contained in *The Arts: a discussion document for the Labour Movement*:

The aim of a Socialist policy for literature must be to make more books available to more people, both in quantity and in scope and to encourage people to write.[17]

Libraries feature occasionally in the document; for example,

libraries and bookshops must be made more attractive to potential users and the transition from school or children's library to the adult section must be made easier and more attractive.

But the recommendation with the greatest implication is:

The Role of Government

At present Government responsibility [for the arts] is divided between Ministries, which works against policy co-ordination and makes it more difficult for artists and the public to have their questions or problems answered quickly and satisfactorily. We therefore advocate the setting up of a separate Ministry for Arts, Communications and Entertainment which will have responsibility for the whole area of the arts....[18]

including, by implication, *public* libraries. The implementation of such a proposal could mean the final separation of the responsibility for public libraries from that for other kinds of libraries including academic libraries and the British Library, which would be a great pity in view of the way some of the barriers between different kinds of libraries have been coming down in recent years.

Apart from these ideas, and subject always to unforeseen crises and changes of direction, it might be expected that the emerging trends, to be treated more fully in the rest of the chapter, would continue in the event of the Labour Party retaining office. The possibility of the coming to power of other political groupings are beyond the scope of this chapter.

Finance

According to the Library Advisory Council Report referred to earlier[19], in 1972–73 public expenditure on libraries, i.e. public, national and academic, totalled approximately £150 million. These figures are, in fact, an underestimate; public library capital expenditure, expenditure on library premises and accommodation by universities, polytechnics, colleges of education and of further education were all excluded, as were certain other minor items. No account was taken of any expenditure on school libraries of any kind, nor of the libraries of government departments, research organisations, etc. Other figures in the same report suggest that public library expenditure has, in general, kept pace with other local government expenditure in recent years.[20] However, there is no doubt that in a period of unprecedented inflation, when central government is exhorting local authorities not to increase or even to cut back spending and when the local authorities are themselves under severe pressure from their own electorate to avoid large rate increases, public libraries are, and will increasingly be, extremely vulnerable. This is a situation where the provisions of the 1964 Public Libraries and Museums Act should come into play and, despite the often-criticised lack of 'teeth' in the Act, some of the more outrageous attempts by individual authorities to make disproportionate cuts in public library expenditure have been curbed by the efforts of the Library Advisers, much to the relief of the chief librarians involved.[21] In this respect, the Library Advisers act as guardians of the Act and of the 1962 Bourdillon Standards.[22] It is reasonable to expect this activity to be called for frequently in the near future. But there is an inherent difficulty: the government, in the shape of DES, is often accused of, on the one hand, instructing authorities to *reduce* spending and, on the other, preventing them from doing so or even encouraging them to improve specific aspects of services which often implies *more* expenditure. It was this dilemma which delayed some developments in DES interest in libraries during the sixties.

It is also fair to say that the Department has a tradition of treating its relationship with local authorities very cautiously, much more so than other Departments of State seem to, perhaps partly because of the unique position of Her Majesty's Inspectorate. It is interesting to note in this connection the newly established post of HMI (Libraries) in Scotland which puts the appointee in a rather different position from that of the DES Library Advisers. Their work in restraining excessive zeal on the part of local authorities in cutting expenditure on public libraries will continue to be hampered unless the Department becomes more decisive in its attitude. The impact of the Library Advisers in this, as in other aspects of their work, is reduced by the undue modesty and secrecy with which the DES has traditionally treated its library activities. Indeed, until recently, virtually the only public sign of activity has been a few paragraphs buried in the Department's annual reports. Both E. V. Corbett[23] and Lorna Paulin[24] have recently criticised this secrecy. It is to be hoped that the publication of the Library Information Series and of other reports will be continued and developed and that the often promised 'open' government will materialise at least as far as this minute corner of governmental activity is concerned. Further complications include the inscrutable language which is used for Rate Support Grant announcements and for other communications to local authorities. The support given by Arts and Libraries Branch staff to public librarians in fighting unfavourable interpretations of such documents will continue to be required unless their drafting and the local interpretation of them improve.

It seems likely that some tighter form of control of capital expenditure might be introduced in the near future. The loan sanction system which existed before 1971 ensured not only a ceiling to the total expenditure on new public library buildings in a given year, but also gave DES the opportunity to ensure a system of priorities was established and that the resources went to those with most need – within the limitations of subjective judgments. The Library Advisers were also able to assist with the preparation of plans in a large number of cases and to suggest improvements in siting, layout and in overall conformity with IFLA standards. A further very significant factor was the existence of a cost target: annoying to local authorities, and to chief librarians but it did ensure that no one received an unfair slice of the cake. A few extra pounds per square metre on a large central library project for expensive finishes, for example, might well be better spent instead on providing a number of branch libraries up and down the country. In the foreseeable future, the reintroduction of a similar scheme must be a distinct possibility.

The DES has much tighter control of capital expenditure in the public sector of further and higher education and the cutbacks announced for 1976/77 will probably mean that plans for a number of polytechnic libraries will be deferred or reduced in size. There have already been hints at reductions in standards in, for example, provision of reader places, as a result of occupation studies carried out by the Cambridge Library Management Research Unit. On the other hand, government, because of the system of quinquennial budgeting through the University Grants Committee (UGC), has had a rather looser control over capital expenditure in universities. The UGC has, however, recently set up a committee to consider the present capacity of university library accommodation and future needs. Some kind of loan sanction system might well be a possibility in this sector also.

A noticeable developing trend in all kinds of libraries is that expenditure on books and other materials is decreasing in proportion to the total budget. For example, in 1967–68 23% of the total expenditure on public libraries in England and Wales was spent on books, 48% on staff, and 'other' expenditure – premises, overheads, etc. – accounted for the remaining 29%, but by 1975/76 the (estimated) figures were 18% on books, 52% on staff and 30% on 'other'. This situation is also probably true of other kinds of libraries and reflects the relative vulnerability of the book fund compared with expenditure on staff and buildings. It is, of course, much easier to reduce bookfund estimates, with little immediate, visible effect than it is to save on staff or administrative costs. Is it within the area of competence of DES successfully to protect individual bookfunds in such circumstances? Cuts of this kind achieve little except deterioration in the service and poor morale among the staff. It would surely be better to devise ways of avoiding unnecessary waste of money, scrutinising new and existing services and of encouraging economy, self-help and initiative at the local level.[25] Rising staff costs probably reflect the success of librarians with the help of DES in achieving Bourdillon standards, but they also reflect one of the results of local government reorganisation in raising salary levels as new hierarchies were created.

Manpower
DES has, in recent years, been working towards a manpower forecasting model for librarianship and information science. The Bourdillon Report's recommendations for staffing[26] might be regarded as the first step in that direction. Work by A. C. Jones for the Library Advisory Councils in estimating the needs in the UK for librarians of different levels of qualification was contained in the Jessup Report on the Supply and Training of Librarians.[27] These calculations led to the imposition by DES of a limit to the expansion of output of the UK library schools. The Saunders/Schur Report of 1969[28] was a further step towards the construction of a manpower model. The Public Libraries

The Role of Government

Staffing Project undertaken by the Local Authorities' Management Services and Computer Committee (LAMSAC) was the most thorough, and expensive, investigation of the present and future needs for staff in public libraries. The Department's habitual delay in publication of the results of research projects has occurred in this case, thereby reducing the value of the statistical data if not of the report itself.

The *Census of staff in librarianship and information work in the UK, 1972*[29] was a further step towards the complete model. When it is completed, the Department will be in a strong position to attempt a balance between the supply of and demand for librarians. It is to be hoped that the Department will use this new tool rather less crudely than it has handled the situation arising from the revised manpower estimate for trained teachers. It is a possibility that, if, as has been suggested in many quarters, some element at least of education expenditure is taken away from local authorities, undergraduate student grants might well be administered centrally. In this event, DES would have a very strong influence on the numbers of students enrolling for courses in librarianship, as Post Graduate Bursaries are already in their hands. There would, of course, still be an 'independent' proportion of foreign students, those funding themselves or being sponsored by an employer, especially on post-graduate courses. But these form a relatively small proportion of the total.

If supply were expected to exceed demand, then reductions in student numbers would be a distinct possibility; this could have serious implications, especially to the smaller of the library schools. The fairly recent introduction and development of first degrees in librarianship with a potential market outside the strict confines of a career in libraries could be regarded as a complicating factor here. In any case, forecasting the need for librarians must be made problematical by the relatively small numbers involved and the resultant difficulty in identifying trends and, like everything else, by the imponderables of the economic future. The employment of librarians depends not on the birth rate nor on legislation – both of which significantly affect the demand for teachers – but on much less tangible factors such as the ability and willingness of local authorities and others to provide resources for the continued development of libraries. Additionally, different factors apply at different times to each of the major fields of librarianship: public, academic, national and special. No model can forecast these factors with precision. It must be hoped therefore that library schools do not find themselves in the same situation as that of colleges of education at the time of writing.

Inter-library co-operation
Since the arrival of P. H. Sewell as the first Library Adviser, DES has played a significant part in inter-library co-operation. Following the publication of the Baker Report[30] in 1962, it has supported the regional bureaux in a number of ways, notably the amalgamation of the London Union Catalogue with the South Eastern Region following the London local government reorganisation a decade ago, and the subsequent automation of the catalogue of the resultant organisation, the London and South East Region (LASER). The future pattern of inter-library co-operation has been in the melting pot while the wider issue of local government reorganisation in the whole of the UK was settled and while the formation of the British Library was being planned. The success of the former National Lending Library for Science and Technology (NLLST) in supplying journal articles, together with the amalgamation of NLLST with the National Central Library (NCL) to form the British Library Lending Division (BLLD), suggested to some that the significance of the regional bureaux and of local co-operative schemes might even decline; the recent partial abandonment of subject specialism is an indication of this. However, the increasing cost and decreasing efficiency of the postal service, together with the decision that BLLD must work towards an economic charge for loans and copies, has perhaps shifted the emphasis slightly back towards local and regional schemes of co-operation. As a result of proposals made by DES Advisers, libraries in Yorkshire have a system of inter-library transport linked with BLLD; the North Western Region has also been investigating the possibilities of such a scheme. The Local Government Operational Research Unit has also been studying the subject on a wider basis.[31]

The case for the stocks of libraries of all kinds in a given area

The Role of Government

being regarded as a 'pool' to be exploited for the benefit of any reader in that area was argued in the Parry Report.[32] Since then local inter-library co-operation has increased. Financial stringency in the future might well encourage librarians and their parent organisations to consider the wisdom of further rationalisation of acquisition policies, of subscriptions to, and holdings of, periodical titles, of joint computerisation projects and of the need for reciprocal arrangements for the interavailability of library services. DES has given these approaches its seal of approval in a circular[33] following publication of the report of the Sheffield co-operation project.[34]

What is needed, in addition, is a decision on the future national pattern of inter-library co-operation. In view of the high success rate of BLLD – according to its latest report 'it is estimated that BLLD is now dealing with three-quarters of all inter-library loan traffic in the UK. Eighty-three per cent of valid requests are satisfied from stock. . . .' – would it be wise to consider the abolition of the regional bureaux, at the same time encouraging local schemes of co-operation on the one hand, and ensuring sufficient funds for the further development of BLLD on the other? In other words, should one tier of the inter-library co-operative structure be abolished? Section 3 of the 1964 Public Libraries and Museums Act requires the Secretary of State to 'designate as library regions, areas together extending to the whole of England and Wales'. The uncertainties surrounding the successive bouts of local government reorganisation has delayed such a designation, but the time has now surely come to make the decision.

Statistics

Anyone who has attempted to prepare a case for committee, to write a paper or carry out a piece of research which requires some statistics of library provision in the UK, knows that there is urgent need for a comprehensive series of statistics of different kinds of libraries. Admittedly there have been some minor improvements in recent years: the contents and details of *Public library statistics*[35] have been tinkered with year by year – incidentally making comparisons difficult – but there has been no major successful effort to involve the profession in deciding how best to obtain the statistics that librarians, DES and research workers need as essential tools. In some areas of activity, for example, school libraries, there are still no statistics at all. A characteristic of library statistics is the plethora of bodies responsible for collecting and publishing. For example, statistics relating to public libraries are collected jointly by the Chartered Institute for Public Finance and Accountancy (CIPFA), formerly the Institute of Municipal Treasurers and Accountants (IMTA), and the Society of County Treasurers (SCT), in association with DES. They are published jointly by the two Institutes. But both the Library Association and the Association of London Chief Librarians collect and disseminate other statistics relating to public libraries, and, of course, the DES itself from time to time collects its own statistics on certain aspects of public libraries. The need, then, is for one agency to collect and publish a comprehensive series of *useful* statistics relating to all kinds of libraries. If neither the Arts and Libraries Branch nor the Statistics Branch of DES can cope with the task, perhaps the appropriate agency might well be the British Library?

Research

Arguably the biggest impact on UK library and information services in recent years has been made by OSTI and its successor, the British Library Research and Development Department. This is largely because of its ability to fund research and experimental projects and financially to support Aslib in its research activities. The specifically scientific and technical remit of OSTI did, however, effectively mean that public libraries, school libraries and some aspects of academic libraries were comparatively neglected as a subject of significant research and planned development. The Library Management Units at Lancaster and Cambridge Universities, for example, have in the main concentrated on the problems and needs of national and university libraries. The Arts and Libraries Branch of DES has been able to finance a few projects, notably the LAMSAC public libraries staffing project already mentioned and the survey which culminated in the report *Libraries and their use*.[36] The original intention behind this project was that it would be phase one of a comprehensive look at the design of public library buildings. It

The Role of Government

remains to be seen whether funds are forthcoming for the continuation of the completed study. It is disappointing, however, that DES architects have not been able to devote some of their time to looking at the design of library buildings, perhaps by collaborating with a local authority in the design of some actual libraries. It may, of course, be too late; the public library building boom was in the sixties and, barring an economic miracle it seems unlikely that this will be repeated in the foreseeable future. All the more reason, perhaps, for a radically different approach for the provision of accommodation for libraries? Future possibilities for research, now that OSTI is under the British Library umbrella and now that DES Arts and Libraries Branch is responsible for British Library's overall funding, may be that the relatively neglected sectors will be the subject of significant planned research and development. Public libraries, as one of these hitherto neglected areas do, after all, account for about 50% of the total public funding of libraries in the UK. In addition to the encouragement of development in the design of buildings, projects concerned with the experimental provision of particular services including a genuine community library would be especially welcome. How exciting it would be if DES were able to give a grant to a local authority to finance a High John type of experiment and to monitor the results.

A disappointing feature of recent research activity has been the relative lack of involvement of the library schools. The Polytechnic of North London has an impressive list and both Leeds Polytechnic and the College of Librarianship Wales have been successful in attracting outside funds. But only the Postgraduate School of Librarianship and Information Science at Sheffield University has carried out a significant number of major successful projects. It is to be regretted that neither of the Library Management Research Units was established within a library school. Many of the schools now have large teams of well-qualified staff and a stream of ongoing research would enable them to relate more satisfactorily with their colleagues 'in the field': there would also be undoubted consequent benefits to the learning situation. It is satisfying to note in this connection the recent setting up of the Centre for Research in User Studies at Sheffield University.

Another interesting development is the establishment of the Public Libraries Management Research Unit, headed by John Allred, at Leeds Polytechnic, possibly pre-empting the persistently rumoured intention of DES to fund such a unit. It is to be hoped that the next decade will, with the help of the British Library and DES, see continued development of research in our field together with a greater involvement on the part of the library schools.

Inspections
One activity of the Library Advisers which attracts a great deal of interest is their programme of 'inspections' of public libraries. Techniques for the evaluation of library services under the 1964 Public Libraries and Museums Act have developed considerably since the mid sixties and a number of accounts of some aspects of this work have been published.[37] Inspections arise in a number of ways; as a result of complaints from the public, from statistical and other evidence that an authority may not be providing 'a comprehensive and efficient service' or in response to a request from the authority itself. The evaluation may be concerned with a comparative study of a particular aspect of provision, with overall provision in a particular kind of area (e.g. rural areas), or simply with the public library service of a particular authority. It is generally felt that comparative studies of a particular aspect of provision and visits by invitation are more conducive to success and it is expected that these will be continued and that evaluative techniques will need to be developed still further. A recent example of a comparative study, concerned with provision in the rural areas of Devon and Cornwall, has been published by the two authorities,[38] and gives an indication of the kind of study undertaken. However, if, as seems likely, the financial position of local authorities continues to worsen, the 'visiting fireman' approach such as that reported to have been carried out in Buckinghamshire[39] may well become familiar (and welcome) to public librarians.

Standards
A co-ordinated system of DES-approved standards for all kinds of libraries seems at the moment to be a remote pipe-dream.

The Role of Government

There are in existence standards, of a kind, for most kinds of libraries, produced by a plethora of organisations but some are much more authoritative and up-to-date than others. One area that needs urgent attention is standards for provision of school libraries: perhaps the total lack of authoritative standards can be explained by the the sheer size of the task involved, the absence of accurate data and the need to maintain the delicate relationship with the Inspectorate. Health service and prison libraries also display tremendous disparity in provision. But here DES is involved only by consultation; the Departments responsible are Health and Social Security and the Home Office respectively. There does, however, seem to be a common factor in the approach of DES to all three types of library: namely the encouragement of public library authorities to provide, or at least participate in the provision of, school, health service and prison libraries on an agency basis. There is some dispute among librarians concerned whether this is, in fact, the best approach; or whether the education, health and prison services should instead be encouraged to develop their own library provision, leaving public libraries to concentrate on non-institutional provision, and to provide back-up support where necessary. The debate is likely to continue in the next few years. Meanwhile the need for well-researched, authoritative standards for provision continues to be felt.

Library Advisory Councils
It is difficult satisfactorily to separate the activities of the Library Advisory Councils from those of the Department. There is, however, a noticeable and welcome trend towards greater publicity of its activities; a number of articles on the work of the Councils have been published in the professional press [40] and some of their deliberations have resulted in publications. [41] It is hoped that this will continue. The English Council has shown particular interest in library services

to those who may be described as disadvantaged – whether by problems related to access (e.g. the housebound and the physically handicapped), by handicaps specifically related to reading or by the limitations or orientation of the existing services. [42]

It has set up a Working Party to 'identify and evaluate the more imaginative public library-based schemes for meeting the needs of the disadvantaged'. An experiment in the actual provision of such a service would be a welcome advance in this area.

The future directions of the Councils are difficult to predict. Many would like to see included among their membership some younger and less 'establishment' members of the profession as well as a student of librarianship to add extra dimensions to the debates. The all-important questions they might well be grappling with in the next few years are the twin areas of how to continue to secure a reasonable resource allocation for library services and how to help librarians provide value for money. A further consideration is how best to plan for the period of prosperity, which is predicted for us when North Sea oil finally begins to flow in quantity. In this connection, Jennie Lee's memorable words to the 1968 Public Libraries Conference are well worth consideration:

... there is no reason, although pockets are frozen, why our brains should be frozen. It is those services which think ahead, which have got clear ideas of where they want to go, who are going to be at the top of the queue when the economic situation becomes easier.[43]

References in text

1. Sewell, P. H. Government concern for libraries and information services. *In* Whatley, H. A. ed. *British librarianship and information science 1966–1970.* Library Association, 1972, p. 3.
2. These suggestions were made by Dr A. J. Evans at the County Library Weekend Conference held at Warwick University, April 1973 and reported in *County Newsletter* 60, June 1973. [4]
3. Lomas, Kenneth. Libraries from an MP's point of view. *Libr. Ass. Rec.* 75 (4) April 1973, 71.
4. Great Britain. *Department of Education and Science. OSTI the first five years. The work of the Office of Science and Technical Information, 1965–70.* HMSO, 1971.
5. Sewell, P. H. *Op. cit.,* p. 3.
6. Library Advisory Council (England). *Working Party on Resources. Libraries and their finance.* DES, August, 1975.
7. Great Britain. *Parliament. House of Commons. Report from the Select Committee on Libraries.* ... 1849.
8. Carnegie United Kingdom Trust. *A report on library provision and policy by Professor W. G. S. Adams.* CUKT, 1915.
9. Great Britain. *Board of Education. Report on public libraries in England and Wales.* HMSO, 1927.
10. McColvin, Lionel R. *The public library system of Great Britain.* Library Association, 1942.
11. Great Britain. *Ministry of Education. The structure of the public library service in England and Wales.* HMSO, 1959.

12. Great Britain. *Ministry of Education. Standards of public library service in England and Wales.* HMSO, 1962, and Great Britain. *Ministry of Education. Working Party on Inter-library co-operation in England and Wales.* Report HMSO, 1962.
13. Great Britain. *University Grants Committee. Report of the Committee on Libraries.* HMSO, 1967.
14. Great Britain. *National Libraries Committee* Report. HMSO, 1969.
15. Sewell, P. H. *Op. cit.,* p. 9.
16. Library Advisory Council (England). *Working Party on Resources. Op. cit.,* p. 4.
17. Labour Party. *The arts: a discussion document for the Labour movement.* The Labour Party, 1975. p. 14.
18. *Ibid.,* p. 24.
19. Library Advisory Council (England). *Working Party on Resources. Op. cit.,* p. 3.
20. *Ibid.,* p. 6.
21. DES advisers at Buckinghamshire [news item]. *Liaison.* October 1975, 73.
22. Great Britain. *Ministry of Education. Standards of public library service in England and Wales.* HMSO, 1962.
23. Corbett, E. V. 1965 to 1975: a decade to remember. *Libr. Ass. Rec.* 77 (10) October 1975, 236.
24. Paulin, Lorna. The work of the Library Advisory Councils for England and Wales. *J. Librarianship* 7 (2) April 1975, 133.
25. Shimmon, Ross. Reorganisation—is it working? *Assistant Librarian* 68 (3) March 1975, 41.
26. Great Britain. *Ministry of Education. Standards of public library service in England and Wales.* HMSO, 1962.
27. Library Advisory Council (England) *and* Library Advisory Council (Wales). *A report on the supply and training of librarians.* HMSO, 1968.
28. Schur, Herbert *and* Saunders, W. L. *Education and training for scientific and technological library and information work.* HMSO, 1969.
29. Great Britain. *Department of Education and Science. Census of staff in librarianship and information work in the United Kingdom 1972.* DES, 1975.
30. Great Britain. *Ministry of Education. Working Party on Inter-library Co-operation in England and Wales.* HMSO, 1962.
31. See: Library Advisory Council (England) *and* Library Advisory Council (Wales). *Situation Statement.* DES, 1975 [9].
32. Great Britain. *University Grants Committee. Op. cit.*
33. Wilson, T. D. *Local library co-operation.* Postgraduate School of Librarianship and Information Science, Sheffield 1974.
34. Great Britain. *Department of Education and Science. Local library co-operation in support of higher education* (Public libraries circular letter No. 20). DES, 1975.
35. Chartered Institute for Public Finance and Accountancy *and* Society of County Treasurers. *Public library statistics.* The Institute and the Society, annual.
36. Great Britain. *Department of Education and Science. Public libraries and their use* (Library information series no. 4). HMSO, 1973.
37. For example:
Jones, A. C. Criteria for the evaluation of public library services. *J. Librarianship* 2 (4) 1970, 228–245.
Sewell, P. H. The evaluation of library services in depth. *Unesco Bull. Libr.* 22 (6) 1968, 274–280.
Shimmon, Ross. Assessment of public library services. *Assistant Librarian* 63 (9) 1970, 135–139, 146.
38. Great Britain. *Department of Education and Science. Public library services in mainly rural areas.* DES, 1974.
39. DES advisers at Buckinghamshire [news item]. *Liaison,* October 1975, 73.
40. For example:
Goff, Martyn. The Library Advisory Councils. *Libr. Ass. Rec.* 74 (11) November 1972, 216–217.
Paulin, Lorna. *Op. cit.*

41. Recent publications are listed in the latest *Situation Statement* cited above.

42. Library Advisory Council (England) *and* Library Advisory Council (Wales). *Op. cit.* [3].

43. Lee, Jennie. Inaugural address. *Proceedings, papers and summaries of discussions at the Public Libraries Conference held at Brighton, 1968.* Library Association, 1968, p. 8.

Chapter Seven

The Future of Library Techniques

Rollo G Woods

Introduction: forward to AD 2010

The destruction of our civilisation by nuclear or biological warfare, ecological disaster, or a new Ice Age, would destroy our libraries as well. There are therefore good practical reasons for excluding these prophecies from this chapter. Similarly, to avoid imitating Sci-Fi, it looks no further ahead than AD 2010. Big Brother will then have been watching us for twenty-six years, the meritocracy will have been in charge for fifteen years, and the day of the Triffids will have arrived. It is also the year in which a young librarian, now settling into his first professional post, may expect to retire.

Techniques are means, not ends, and a librarian who becomes too immersed in the minutiae of cataloguing may forget that libraries are for people, and that the librarian's real function is to meet his readers' needs for entertainment, instruction or information, using any techniques that seem appropriate. This chapter is written for those who have achieved a balance between the broader objectives of their work, and the techniques needed to accomplish it. It assumes that new or improved techniques are those which allow librarians to spend more time and money on identifying and satisfying the individual reader's requirements. Of course, techniques for handling new media cannot be entirely separated from a discussion of the media themselves, but in the main this chapter will be limited to the traditional library techniques of selection, acquisition, cataloguing, classification, and circulation, with their more recent extensions into document and information retrieval, and the education of readers using machine-aided systems. There will be no shortage of materials on which to exercise these techniques, though the printed word may appear in some new guises, and will be supplemented, and in some fields replaced, by the newer media. This is dealt with below.

Change is continuous in any living organisation, and a contemporary often sees a revolution where later generations see only a modification of established practices. Because libraries are not only conservationist but also conservative, some librarians have seen a revolution in the various technical innovations of the past ten years. These, however, are rather the harbingers of much more far-reaching changes which will really revolutionise library techniques during the next thirty-five years.

The contents of libraries: the printed word and the newer media
The 'information explosion' has ceased, through familiarity, even to be a librarian's nightmare. The number of significant documents in science and technology issued each year passed the million mark in 1970, and will probably have doubled by 1980.[1] Nor is this growth limited to the sciences. In a recent lecture Shirley Williams said that coping with the sheer quantity of information now available was one of the most intractable problems of modern administration.[2] Moreover, when the graphs level off, it will mark, not a decline, but a stabilisation.

There is, of course, no shortage of plans to control the information explosion, and 1975, when shortage of funds made prospects of doing so even more remote, was the year of NATIS (NAtional Information systems), a Unesco-sponsored project.[3] The EC is also investing large sums in information work.[4] But the figures have a numbing effect. Not only can libraries neither store nor record the material, but the lists and guides are in disarray as well. There is no control over what is published in which journal, who indexes or abstracts it, or what information retrieval tapes record it.[5] Warren Haas commented recently:

It is perhaps this complexity coupled with high costs [of publishing] that is apparently forcing a small number of leading scholars in certain subject fields to establish alternative closed systems for communication of their most advanced work to a very limited number of favored colleagues working with them on research frontiers.[6]

The system of private communication – the 'invisible college' – affects even groups with an interest in open access to information. During the pioneer period of library automation, there was a flourishing college of librarians and computer experts. However, forecasts that the situation would be brought under control because the printed word would soon be entirely replaced by machine-readable records can be discounted on grounds of cost alone. In 1970, Dr W. N. Locke calculated that data in book form could be stored at MIT for 2 cents per megabit/year. Equivalent costs for off-line tape storage were $7.47, and for on-line disc storage $237.[7] A fall in computer storage costs is anticipated, but can hardly cancel this discrepancy. Machines have a part to play in library work – their use is the theme of this chapter – but for the present, they can transmit, index, and record, but not hold the material.

Moreover, book selection remains a librarian's job. Books in print can be listed and sorted by computer, using the large files described below, but intelligent selection from these lists needs a human, not a machine, intelligence. There is, however, a real danger that some kinds of book will no longer be published. Costs are already so high that only assured sales justify publication of the kind of book that may properly be admired as a work of art. A scientific report, typed and lithoprinted in the office, attracts less respect, yet both are means of communicating ideas. 'Hot metal' printing is costly and slow. 'Utility publication' is quick and cheap. In 1974 as many reports were issued in this form as articles in the journals; with xerox copiers in every institution, they are never really out of print. Many of these reports escape the standard bibliographies, and the information may never reappear in periodical articles or books. How many libraries hold a set of Michael Ventris's 'Worknotes', for example? This adds to the problems of book selection, and makes completeness even more difficult to attain. At the least, every research library should try to collect all the reports circulated in the parent institution, so that they do not escape altogether.

The newer media – sound recordings, films, radio and television – will not replace the printed word, but certainly threaten some of its traditional functions. Librarians are involved because all of them now appear primarily in forms which can be stored and lent, as books have always been, and because they are no longer limited to entertainment, but also can be used for instruction, and the recording and presentation of information. The Open University's use of TV is an example of the one. The taping of American TV news programmes by Vanderbilt University, which has also indexed them and can supply copies of any section required, is an example of the second.[8] (The service is now the subject of a copyright case). Nor are these the only materials a library might collect and circulate. Community antenna or cable television (CATV), originally developed to serve isolated communities, is now ready to serve urban communities, and its coaxial cables can not only carry a number of programmes simultaneously, but will be able to transmit in both directions, to and from the viewer.

A 'wired city' could immediately react to local, state or federal legislation enactments. Commercial television could poll the viewers as to their level of satisfaction. Programmed instruction assisted by computers would be available at any terminal connected to the cable system. Classroom instruction would be available to shut-ins with the student being able to respond to the instructor's questions and directives as well as contribute to the classroom discussion. Dial-a-programme could be offered. Specific educational courses, significant meetings, as well as entertainment rebroadcasts, could be called up from the CATV's library.[9]

'Library' is the key word here, and if CATV is introduced to Britain, a new library service, with direct access to readers, may replace the mobile's fortnightly visit.

The new media are now recognised as an alternative form of publication; even *The Times* advertises its range of cassettes in its own *Literary Supplement*. Unlike books and discs, however, tapes can be updated quite easily, and the rules of cataloguing cannot apply. For example, the 'tape magazines', circulated among enthusiasts, who update the tape as it passes, never have a

The Future of Library Techniques

permanent form, merely various states of development. An even more readily updated system is discussed below.

Finally, special machines are required before any of these media can be used, and these, too, will be part of the librarian's responsibility. Since some librarians entered the profession to escape from machines, these must be considered next.

Machines in the library: from the hand-wound film to on-line access
Not all librarians – and this does not mean those who regret the replacement of the quill by the typewriter – wish to become machine minders. Filing cards may be boring and repetitive, but seems more human than feeding similar cards into a gadget. The library manager of the future must ensure that machines do not destroy the personal relationship between the librarian, the book, and the reader. However, for 150 years machines have been called in when manpower could not cope, and some have already been used in libraries. The first, perhaps, that librarians had to use were microform readers. Microforms have appeared in a variety of formats and shapes, each smaller than the last, each announced as a new standard, and each requiring a separate reader. Extreme reductions are now possible with the photochromic micro-image system (PCMI), now used for *Books in English*, and great compression is also possible using holography, which can be used for both microrecording and data storage.[10] The use of microforms will increase, because it already costs more to bind and store a journal than to buy a commercial microcopy. Only the complete failure of the manufacturers to supply a reliable and acceptable reader or reader-printer for any microform prevents a real breakthrough in micropublishing.

Gramophones and other machines for reproducing sound recordings are found in so many homes that they present few problems, and teaching machines, combining sound tape and slides, do not seem to suffer from the design problems that have affected microreaders. Around 25% of schools have videotape teaching aids, and these too will be needed in research libraries and will undoubtedly be found in many homes. The most recent development, teletext, which requires a modification of the

93

ordinary television receiver, is a method of transmitting text by television, using the gaps which occur on the screen between each image. Both BBC (Ceefax) and IBA (Oracle) are already transmitting, and receivers are expected to be on the market in 1977. Ceefax will be virtually a hundred-page newspaper, updated continuously, that is, every half-minute in some cases. The Post Office is now also investigating linking the telephone service to the domestic television screen, and their system, Viewdata, could draw on much larger data banks than Ceefax.

The Post Office could use Viewdata itself for directory enquiries. Students could connect themselves to libraries, or a computer. Housewives could dial the local supermarket to see what was in stock. Estate agents could offer an information bank of all properties for sale in the area. The fact that classified advertisements could be handled in this way would be a nasty shock for the local newspapers.

But one of the far-reaching effects of teletext, should it take off as quickly as the optimists believe, is that it will so reduce the cost of talking to computers and to information banks, that they will quickly become a part of our everyday lives.[11]

All these machines replace the book and the book shelf. The computer, however, is rather a tool which replaces some of the routine functions of the library staff, from recording issues to maintaining a file of abstracts and even, eventually, retrieving the actual information itself.

Computers are not part of most people's everyday lives, however, and even in a library with various automated systems it is rare to find a librarian who is also a professional computer analyst or programmer. Automation does not, in fact, reduce the number of decisions a librarian has to take; it does not imply a single librarian controlling a factory-like resource centre from some remote keyboard. The prime task of the library systems analyst is to determine at what point intelligent intervention – i.e. a librarian qualified to make the correct decision – is needed. A general understanding of computers and data processing is assumed in what follows.

The computers that will be used in libraries will vary in size and purpose, and may include a free-standing mainframe machine,

The Future of Library Techniques

processing data for the library as it does for other clients, a dedicated mini-computer, for on-line updating of frequently consulted files, and the control unit of an information storage and retrieval device. It will probably be part of a complex of computers, linked by telephone lines (and ultimately perhaps by microwave links), and able to transmit data from one to another. The next generation of computers, due about 1985, will have faster processors, will be more reliable, need less maintenance, and be easier to program and operate.[12] The speed of input/output devices is not likely to improve. However, there is at last a prospect of the automatic input of text through the development of Computer Input from Microfilm (CIM). Previous OCR systems foundered on unusual typefaces and paper transport. For CIM, all material must be transferred to microfilm, but almost any typeface, and printscript, can be read. Any character that is not recognised (a broken letter, for example) is shown on a screen, with its context, and the operator can key in a replacement. At present, CIM is expected to be used principally for preserving data. CIM film has a longer storage life than magnetic tape, and can now be converted back to machine-readable form when required. There are, however, obvious possibilities for recording bibliographic data, abstracts, and so on, and only the cost of the machine (£500,000) will delay its installation in libraries.[13] The new computers will be able to control large databases, and the catalogue of a large library is a very big database indeed. Librarians would willingly sacrifice nano-seconds inside the processor for better input/output facilities, and it seems that for the next twenty-five years computers will operate much as the biggest machines do today.

In the pioneering period, up to 1970, any operational system could be considered a triumph. Most of these early systems will be obsolete by 1980, or absorbed into integrated systems. They did, however, reveal certain basic principles that are likely to become standard library techniques. They also made the librarians involved very cautious, willing to advance only step by step, and only too aware that dependence on a man-made machine involves dependence on those non-librarians who maintain, operate, and control it. A maintenance engineer delayed on the road means the disruption of a smooth running system, a careless operator the destruction of a complete catalogue, and of course, notes like 'tape failure' and 'card wreck' still appear all too frequently in the computer logs. Many computer installations are, by library standards, very lax in the care they take of data passed to them for processing. The librarian planning an automated system must arrange at the design stage for adequate manual back-up in the event of a breakdown, and for the duplication of essential files. Close supervision of data preparation is also a library responsibility, especially as the machines involved – currently usually tape typewriters, but within a few years key-to-tape machines, visual display units, etc. – are likely to be housed in the library and operated by the library staff. Quite casual idiosyncracies by one typist in the way accents are typed can stop the whole of a catalogue input program, and cause endless trouble to programmers trying to devise a foolproof validation routine. Librarians who have gone into automation have not only revised the textbooks of librarianship; they have also rewritten and much expanded their own staff manuals.

An automated library benefits from having a staff systems analyst and programmers. Not only can they deal immediately with program failures, but the design, programming, implementation, and enhancement of a new system can all gain from regular contact between them and the librarian directly concerned. Lack of this communication is the commonest cause of an unsuccessful system. However, computer staff have educational qualifications in no way inferior to those of librarians, and it is better to recruit a trained systems analyst than retrain a librarian.[14] Since libraries dare not employ second-raters, computer experts must be recognised as professionals, whose skills are as valuable as those of a qualified librarian. They must have adequate opportunities for promotion, even if this means the systems analyst ranking higher than the chief cataloguer.

Automated library housekeeping routines: circulation, acquisitions and cataloguing
Although in theory a computer is a machine which manipulates symbols, in practice all computers prefer doing mathematical

The Future of Library Techniques

calculations to processing text. Library data processing is primarily a matter of creating a file of data, usually bibliographic records, in machine-readable form, and then keeping that file up to date. The simplest systems, therefore, are those in which the file remains relatively small and constant in size, because at each updating roughly the same number of records is removed as is added, and is based on numbers rather than text.

Circulation systems, currently the commonest operational system, are a typical short file type.[15] At present, almost all involve the collection of data from a punched card or bar-coded label, storing this data, usually until the end of the day, and then processing the day's transactions to update the existing file of books on loan, and to print the necessary recall notices. These systems are basically sound, and are actually economic to operate. Their weakness is that they are always one day out of date, and that for a library to know the actual whereabouts of a book – a requirement in many university libraries – means that the entire file must be output, usually on the line printer, at every updating. If the data collection unit cannot record an adequate amount of bibliographic data, then it must be supplemented by a catalogue file, or recall notices consist only of the book's accession or call number.

Libraries of the future will probably overcome this by installing a mini-computer, adequate to do all the processing needed, with a small printer to produce recall notices, yet with a store large enough to hold on-line records of all books on loan, with at least author/title information as well as accession numbers, all registered borrowers, and lists of defaulting borrowers and reserved books. Desk top data collection units that sense through the cover of the book are also likely. Alternatives to this have been suggested, including a proposal that the system should be linked to the full library catalogue, itself held on-line, so that any reader searching the catalogue by means of a visual display unit will know at once if a book he wants is available. However, such a system, at least at present, recalls the proverbial sledgehammer and nut. So too, at present, are proposals that libraries should issue throw-away copies reproduced on demand from a store held in microform or in a machine-readable store.

It would, of course, save the printing of unwanted copies and provide adequate data for a PLR assessment. Indeed, it has been suggested that bookshops should supply books for their customers in this way, and it is technically feasible.

Acquisitions is another short-file system, obviously related to existing successful commercial purchasing systems, and basically a batch-mode system – even the books arrive by post in batches. Current off-line systems do work this way, but future systems will probably be a mixture of on- and off-line techniques. The problem with an off-line system is partly data-preparation, which amounts to creating a tagged file for each book ordered, and partly correcting and updating this file with new data also prepared off-line and not necessarily error-free.

Very shortly large files will be available, recording all books currently in print not only in Britain, but in most other countries, and updated by weekly tapes from the various national bibliographic centres. Similar records are being considered for other media as well. The library can be linked, at some convenient time in the week, to this file, and can call up in turn each item on the list of books to be ordered, check the data, transferring it to a machine-based order file on the library's computer, and, perhaps, submitting it simultaneously to the computer in whatever agency is chosen to supply the book. When the book arrives, its arrival will be notified to the order file, an accession number added, the data transferred to the catalogue file, and the invoice passed to the finance office files. Off-line data preparation will be needed only for second-hand orders, and for those fringe publications referred to above, which escape the net of the national system – to which the library may add any it finds.

Development of a system of this kind will not be simple, but the Birmingham Library Co-operative Mechanisation Project (BLCMP) already has a potential requirements file (PRF) with nearly 300,000 entries,[16] the BNB and *Books in English* are produced from machine-readable records, and in the USA the Ohio College Library Centre (OCLC) expects in 1976 to have a thousand subscribers linked on-line to its file of data, which

The Future of Library Techniques

contains both entries received from the Library of Congress and those contributed by subscribers. Since the central file records also which libraries stock each title, it is also used widely for book selection and by inter-library loan departments. This co-operative effort has been made possible by two internationally supported systems: the International Standard Book Number (ISBN) and the MARC (MAchine Readable Catalogue) format.[17] The ISBN provides the key to the file, and allows a specific entry to be called up. The MARC format ensures that all entries are in the same machine format, and so can be transferred from one computer file to another. MARC formats are now being developed for other media, including films, music, and teaching aids.

Acquisition systems, then, may be expected to change from short-file, independent systems to large-file, co-operative ones, which require access, though not at all times, to a large computer capable of handling a really large database. The creation of large exchangeable databases naturally affects the work of library cataloguing staff. The MARC system can, of course, be used by a library which needs to create its own data, and many libraries will do this for special collection catalogues and the like. For this a knowledge of the MARC tagging structure will be needed. For most purposes, however, local cataloguers will no longer have to spend time proof-reading the body of the catalogue entry – though checking headings and cross-references will still be necessary – for all entries will be drawn from the central files. The cataloguers' main duty will be to supervise the database and catalogue production.

The problems of holding large amounts of bibliographic data in machine readable form are very complex. They require computers with a quite different configuration from that usually provided, because very large random access backing stores are required. Most smaller second and third generation computers depended on magnetic tape for storage of data. Sorting, for example, 10,000 entries into alphabetical order on magnetic tape can take several hours, whereas to do the same job on a disc takes a relatively short time. The British Library, which for some time has used a mixture of disc and tape for its MARC project, reached in 1975 the point at which more capacity was needed, and this involved the complete re-design of its database structure and its transfer to a new and larger computer. The proposed configuration includes 1.5 million bytes of main store, 6 million bytes of high speed Fixed Head Disc Store and 3200 million bytes of Exchangeable Disc Store.[18] This may seem an incredible capacity, but it must be remembered first, that a computer does not store data as economically as a book shelf, and second, that a library with a stock of 10 million volumes, given that the average length of a machine-readable bibliographic record is 500 characters, will need 5000 million characters of storage for its machine-readable catalogue, even at the greatest imaginable packing density.

OCLC supplies catalogue cards to its subscribers,[19] but this can only be regarded as a stage in the development of automated cataloguing for it makes no use of the computers' ability to file entries alphabetically. However, if the catalogue is produced in a permanent form, printed or microform, then the complete catalogue must be replaced – or a supplement provided – after each updating. This is necessarily an additional expense. Printing costs are high, and may involve some delay. COM output is cheap, but reading equipment must be provided sufficient for all readers likely to consult the catalogue at the same time. In theory, of course, the catalogue should remain in the computer, and be consulted on-line, using visual display units. These units are, however, very expensive at present, though a single unit, linked to a keyboard for file correction, will be needed in every acquisition and cataloguing room.

The MARC format was designed for libraries and therefore reflects the librarian's way of thinking about books. However, it shares some of the limitations of the traditional catalogue as well, for it is also based on cataloguing rules whose main function was to reduce the number of headings used. A computer entry can be searched, if necessary, word by word. A request for a book can be checked by keyword, publisher, date, or any other item tagged in the MARC format. Additional information can also be included. For example, ways of assessing the reading difficulty of the text are now being developed. A computer that could scan a sample of the text, for example, could operate the literacy code

The Future of Library Techniques

used by the College Bibliocentre in Ontario. This allots numbers on a range from 0 to 100.

The ratio shows 0 to be practically unreadable and 100 to be easy. In order to achieve the rating, it is necessary to apply the following formula: Multiply the average sentence length by 1·015. Multiply the number of syllables per 100 words by ·846. Add the results and subtract the total from 206·835.[20]

The development of these large systems has already begun, though it will be many years before any library holds the whole of its catalogue in this form. At present it is more usual to close the existing catalogue, and start a new automated one. There has been some work on catalogue conversion, most notably at the Bodleian Library, Oxford, which is experimenting with on-line file correction. Most libraries, however, have neither resources nor computer facilities for this task.

Automation and information retrieval

Housekeeping systems like those described will probably be used in all kinds of libraries. Why a tired citizen reads a novel, a householder a do-it-yourself manual, or a student a prescribed text, is usually obvious enough, and similar reasons will govern the same people's selections from other media. It is usually possible for a library to meet their requirements. It is the research worker, whose needs are more complex and difficult to understand, who is affected by the information explosion. No one quite knows how researchers (in any field of study) look for or use information.[21] Librarians are merely aware that their needs are not being met, and that no solution has been found so far. The position was recently summarised by R. W. Hamming in this way:

It is fashionable to write about the [information explosion] and to say that computing machines will (somehow, magically) cure the problem if only enough money is appropriated to develop some system or other of information retrieval. I have found it convenient to judge such papers by the ratio of amount of effort they put on saying how important the problem is to how little they say in specific detail on how to do it. The more they stress the importance of the problem, the more it is likely that they have nothing to offer. It is not as if there have not been generations of librarians, from the days of the Library of Alexandria to the present, who have worried and thought about the problem of the storage and retrieval of information ...

One of the major difficulties of research in this area is the utter confusion about how information is actually retrieved by real humans. The models formed are often based on a small, carefully selected field of work and its information retrieval needs, or even on sheer fantasy. A careful examination of actual methods that people use in retrieving information during a 'library search' reveals many differing ways and needs, and it seems unlikely that we will find a single solution to all of the various requirements.[22]

This is a bold statement, for there are already many automated information retrieval systems, some covering wide fields, operating quite successfully, either providing a current information service, or carrying out retrospective searches of their database.[23] Indeed, the us National Technical Information Service has just issued a guide to some 500 databases maintained by various federal agencies, but available to researchers from outside.[24]

However, all systems now operational are extensions of the cataloguing systems described earlier, but without the benefit of an internationally agreed machine format, which makes it difficult to construct an inter-disciplinary database by combining data from several sources. More progress has been made on classification and subject indexing, and both modern faceted classification methods and indexing using a thesaurus of subject terms have advanced so far that professional guidance is normally necessary to construct a valid 'profile' for searching the database. (These classification systems, designed for computer use, are of course too sophisticated for shelf classification, which is really a different field.) Naturally, preparing the data, which may include abstracts as well as classification, is costly. A large computer and a sophisticated program are needed for searching the file, and the cost of the service, when a realistic charge is made, is high. Finally, when the search is complete it produces, not the information, but a list of references, a proportion probably valueless, and many relating to articles and reports not in the enquirer's own library, imposing a further

The Future of Library Techniques

delay before the actual documents are to hand. It is as though the catalogue of a library were available once a month, and the shelves could be inspected a week or so later.

Existing services, then, are up to date, well organised and indexed, and invaluable as a source of basic data to a researcher starting a new project. They are often better than the manually compiled abstracting services with which they are competing or on which they are based. Yet the people for whose benefit they were set up have not welcomed them – and certainly do not wish to pay the charges levied – and this justifies Hamming's remarks.

Users of information have come forward with ideas for better systems. As long ago as July 1945, Vannevar Bush forecast the development of the 'Memex', described as 'a sort of mechanized private file and library':

A memex is a device in which an individual stores his books, records, and communications, and which is mechanised so that it may be consulted with exceeding speed and flexibility. It is an enlarged intimate supplement to his memory.

It consists of a desk, ... primarily the piece of furniture at which he works. On the top are slanting translucent screens, on which material can be projected for convenient reading. There is a keyboard, and sets of buttons and levers. Otherwise it looks like an ordinary desk.

In one end is the stored material. The matter of bulk is well taken care of by improved microfilm. Only a small part of the interior of the memex is devoted to storage, the rest to mechanism. Yet if the user inserted 5000 pages of material a day it would take him hundreds of years to fill the repository, so he can be profligate and enter material freely.

Most of the memex contents are purchased on microfilm ready for insertion. Books of all sorts, pictures, current periodicals, newspapers, are thus obtained and dropped into place. Business correspondence takes the same path. And there is provision for direct entry. ...

There is, of course, provision for consultation of the record by the usual scheme of indexing. If the user wishes to consult a certain book, he taps its code on the keyboard, and the title page of the book promptly appears before him, projected onto one of his viewing positions. ... Moreover, he has supplemental levers. On deflecting one of these levers to the right he runs through the book before him, each page in turn being projected at a speed which just allows a recognising glance at each. If he deflects it further to the right, he steps through the book 10 pages at a time; still further at 100 pages at a time. Deflection to the left gives him the same control backwards.

A special button transfers him immediately to the first page of the index. Any given book of his library can thus be called up and consulted with far greater facility than if it were taken from a shelf. As he has several projection positions, he can leave one item in position while he calls up another. He can add marginal notes and comments....[25]

Since Bush's paper was written before the computer age, its forecasts, some of them now attained, seem remarkably apt. A similar prophecy by J. G. Kemeny, written in 1962, includes one more radical change. In place of, or in addition to, the personal files proposed by Bush, he envisages a national store of information, constantly updated, properly indexed, which the researcher could contact from a terminal in the library, or from his own desk. Like Bush's memex, Kemeny's machine would allow the researcher to follow a 'trail' through the various branches of his subject, and when a paper, or even a page, that was of interest, appeared, to add it to his private file for future reference.[26] All evidence suggests that researchers prefer the control over their own searches given by interactive systems to passive acceptance of a current awareness service, and this is provided in these systems.

Much of the equipment that Bush and Kemeny postulated can now be built. Modern computers are more than adequate as control units, and the Post Office's Teleview and Postfax,[27] though slow, could transmit data from the central store. It would, of course, involve considerable financial investment to put it into operation. To librarians it would bring one enormous change. The learned journal, the scientific report, and most shorter research monographs would simply cease to be published. It would become as much a source of kudos for a young researcher to have his paper accepted by the centre, perhaps with a high grading allotted to it, as to have it published. The minor reports that now never see the light could also be filed, and the invisible college would open its doors to the world.

The Future of Library Techniques

The time scale and detail of these forecasts cannot be guaranteed, but the signs are already here. 'Synopsis journals' limit their contents to indexes and abstracts, supplying the main text on demand in microform. Some 'hot metal' printers are diversifying into demand printing, microforms, and facsimile transmission. There is, of course, an element of danger in this. Professor Ziman pointed out the problems of getting a really new idea into an established journal.[28] If the only large-scale outlet is too rigidly controlled, routine research may be assisted, but really innovative work hampered. There may be *samizdat* publication among the scientists. The copiers for it will still exist.

And after automation, what remains?
The outline given above of a probable path towards a fully automated library has, for convenience, treated each basic system separately. In fact, each system, even though developed and implemented independently, must be designed to be part of an integrated whole. The order in which each library automates its various systems will vary, partly according to its own needs, partly, if regrettably, because progress depends on access to a computer, which may not be available. The actual date for each step on the way will vary from place to place. Some think that the fully automated library, with its entire contents in a cubic yard of storage, will be operating by AD 2000.[29] Others assume that the traditional library will continue much longer. These thirty-five years will be a strenuous time for the library profession, who will have to adapt to new machines, new colleagues, and new opportunities. And when all is done, when there are no accessions, because all literature is available on call from a central store, no cataloguing, no classifying, no shelving or circulation, no readers, for each has a memex in his desk, what will the librarian have left? When the library, as far as it exists, is all screens and keyboards, discs and reels, one library service will almost certainly remain: the training and guidance of readers using the services.

Instruction in using the library in some libraries already includes instruction in the use of a terminal. In some institutions, students must take a course in literature searching which is assessed and marked, and counts towards a degree. The new research facilities will not be easier to use; their very perfection will make them difficult. Someone will have to guide readers through the maze, ensure they do not get a tape of Hamlet in mistake for Coronation Street, and explain why the wrong chemical formula has come up on the screen. That person may not use the current techniques of librarianship, but will still be, fundamentally, a librarian.

References and further reading

To compress the material into the allotted space, some important topics are covered by references rather than discussed in the text.

1. Anderla, G. *Information in 1985: a forecasting study of information needs and resources*. Paris, OECD, 1973. A valuable summary of the present position and likely developments.
2. Mrs Williams' lecture has not been published.
See also
Grayson, L. Urban documentation: its nature and purpose. *J. Librarianship,* 7 (4), October 1975, 229–251.
3. Green, S. NATIS: the theme for the 1970's *Unesco Bull. Libr.* 29(3) May 1975, 117–123.
4. Giles, C. G., Gray, J. C. The European Information Network for Science and Technology: the first stages. *Aslib Proc.* 27 (9) September 1975, 366–375.
See also
The economics of the European Information Network: study on the cost of alternative network configuration and related questions. Prepared for the Commission of the European Communities by Diebold Deutschland GmbH. June 1975.
5. Subramanyam, K. The Scientific Journal: a review of current trends and future prospects. *Unesco Bull. Libr.* 29 (4) July 1975, 192–201.
6. Haas, W. Scholarly communication: new efforts to understand a complex process, in Minutes of the 86th meeting [*of the*] *Association of Research Libraries, May, 8–9, 1975*. Washington, 1975.
7. Locke, W. N. Computer costs for large libraries. *Datamation,* February 1970, 69–74.

8. Wright, C. Inside Washington. *Coll. and Res. Libr. news* March 1975, 73–74.
9. Drolet, L. L. Metropolitan library service via 'the cable' in the United States of America: a thing of the future. *Unesco Bull. Libr.* 29 (2) March 1975, 75–79.
See also
Mead, E. S. *A big ball of wax*. New York, 1954.
10. Gates, J. W. C. The optical basis for holography in information storage and retrieval. *Reprographics q.* 8 (4) Autumn 1975, 141–145.
11. Margerison, T. Switch on and clue up. *D. Telegraph mag.* 525, 26 September, 1975, 25–28.
See also
Darrington, P. Wireless World teletext decoder. I – The background. *Wireless Wld,* November 1975, 498–504.
Hope, A. Beaming magazines into the home. *New Scientist* 1 May 1975, 246–249.
Smith, J. Ceefax and Oracle. *Practical Electronics.* February; April 1975, 134–136; 322–327.
Viewdata: too early to count the costs. *Computing* 2 October 1975, 4.
12. Withington, F. G. Beyond 1984: a technology forecast. *Datamation* January 1975, 54–73.
A useful summary of probable developments in computing to 1985.
13. *Information based on data from the manufacturers*. Information International Grafix Ltd.

14. Minder, T. Library systems analyst – a job description. *Coll. and Res. Lib.* 27 (4) July 1966, 271–276.
15. Aslib ACCWP. *Directory of operational computer applications in United Kingdom Libraries and Information Units;* ed. by C. W. J. Wilson. London, 1973.
16. *VINE*, 10, August 1974.
17. Gorman, M. and Linford, J. E. *Description of the BNB MARC record – a manual of practice.* London, BNB, 1971. See also
Irvine, R. *MARC for Cataloguers: an explanation of its use.* (SoUL/APR4) Southampton, 1972.
18. *Computer Weekly,* 12 June 1975, and documents circulated by British Library.
19. Allison, A. M. and others. The impact of OCIC on cataloguing departments – a study. *Network 2* (1) January 1975, 11–16, 25.
20. Internal document, supplied by the College Bibliocentre.
21. Line, M. B. On the design of information systems for human beings. *Aslib. Proc.* 22 (7) July 1970, 320–335. See also
Rothwell, R. Patterns of information flow during the innovation process. *Aslib. Proc.* 27 (5) May 1975, 217–226.

22. Hamming, R. W. *Computers and society.* New York, 1972. The quotation is from ch. 11: Language and information retrieval.
23. Leggate, P. Computer-based current awareness services. *J. Docum.* 32 (2) June 1975, 93–115.
24. Directory of computerized data files and related software, 1974 – (Washington) NTIS, 1974 – (Annual). Review: *Coll. and Res. Libr.,* July 1975, 310.
25. Bush, V. As we may think. *repr. in* Kocken, M., ed. *The growth of knowledge.* New York, 1967. Orig. pbl. *Atlantic mon.,* 176, no. 1, July 1945, p. 101–108.
26. Kemeny, J. G. A library for 2000 AD *in* Greenberger, M. ed. *Computers and the world of the future.* Cambridge (Mass.), 1962. p. 134–179.
27. Briglin, J. E. The inter-city document service by phone. *P.O. Telecommunications Jnl.* 27 (1) Spring 1975, 2–3.
28. Ziman, J. M. The light of knowledge: new lamps for old. *Aslib Proc.* 22 (5) May 1970, 186–200.
29. Gee, R. D. Library 2k AD. The information explosion, technology's contribution, and the social conscience. *LSE mag.,* 34, December 1967, 10–12.

Chapter Eight

Libraries as Media Centres

Norman Beswick

The recording of information in formats other than that of the printed book has provided fertile ground for the more imaginative futurologists and it is important not to be carried away by undisciplined speculation. Thomas Alva Edison prophesied in 1913 that the film would entirely replace the book as an educational medium within ten years, and it did not happen.[1] Similarly, writers have forecast not merely the transformation of libraries but also their demise, under the onslaught of the so-called 'new' media and computerisation.
C. L. Eatough, writing in 1966, prophesied that even the multi-media library would quickly phase out because of 'expense and inefficiency', leaving us with electronic media made available on screens and through earphones by dial-access.[2]
R. P. Henderson told the Royal Canadian Institute in 1972 that the world's knowledge would soon be recorded entirely electronically rather than on the printed page:

We will see enormous archival computerised knowledge banks replacing books and libraries.[3]

Yet what might happen is not necessarily what will happen; these prophecies may turn out to be as mistaken as Edison's. Much depends, for instance, on the future of raw materials and energy sources, including wood-pulp as well as oil and electricity: not to mention further developments in technology itself, and in social stability, consumer preferences and prevailing social mores.

If we look back at some past ventures into the provision of non-book media in libraries, we shall see that some formats, such

Libraries as Media Centres

as illustrations and photographs, were recognised as appropriate for library organisation very early in the century, and W. C. Berwick Sayers considered their classification in his *Manual* in 1926. Collections of gramophone records were proposed by H. A. Sharp in 1922, and begun by Middlesex County Library in 1935.[4] In the USA, the public library in Kalamazoo (Mich.) began experiments with film distribution in 1929,[5] yet although some academic and special libraries in the UK today have a recognisable film commitment, and some public libraries offer a film service to schools in their area, the bulk of film distribution is still undertaken – and for understandable reasons – by agencies outside the profession, using only the simplest retrieval techniques. One Florence Henry, in 1930, made out a case for the inclusion of piano rolls in school libraries and gave storage advice, but the medium was overtaken by other ways of sound recording.[6] Throughout the 1930s, librarians in teachers' colleges and high schools in the USA collected stereographs, three-dimensional items whose novelty quite disappeared with the development of television. The wave of the future was not there, though no doubt the collections served a useful purpose in their day.

Furthermore, the first standards for school libraries ever devised were published in America in 1918, and known as the Certain Standards after committee chairman C. C. Certain. Among other things they recommended that the school library

> should serve as the center and co-ordinating agency for all materials used in the school for visual instruction, such as stereopticons, portable motion picture machines, stereopticon slides, moving picture films, pictures, maps, globes, bulletin board material, museum loans etc.[7]

Yet apart from pictures and clippings very little of this became standard practice until the late forties and early fifties when changes in teaching methodology combined with the development of more flexible and convenient equipment to make an irresistible movement.

We have to ask, then, not only whether there is some kind of logic that might encourage British librarians to develop along multi-media lines in the future, but also whether this logic is likely to combine with other factors to make the development truly widespread. One can find examples of libraries which contained much more than print-form material throughout many past centuries, but it is only in the last twenty years that the idea of the library as a media centre has really caught the attention and imagination of the library profession, in Great Britain or even the United States, although it is true that American librarians were, on the whole, rather readier for the change. This appears to be paralleled by developments in other parts of the world. When C. P. Ravilious surveyed (for Unesco) developments in bibliographic control of non-book materials in twenty-four countries in four continents, he found a very mixed and unsatisfactory situation but in every case some useful activities, almost all of them very recent.[8] Yet photography has been in existence for well over one hundred and fifty years; motion pictures for over seventy-five; sound recordings for nearly a century. Similarly, with the multi-media school library: a Unesco/International Bureau of Education conference in Geneva in 1974 produced case studies from Britain, USA, Sweden, France and Switzerland, all new starts, and the attendance from USSR, Africa, South America and Asia testified to the wide, varied and recent nature of world interest.[9]

It is arguable that the main reason for the interest today is the rapid development of varieties of audio-visual and other formats in increasingly portable, flexible and trouble-free versions, at comparatively cheap prices. The earliest gramophones were cumbersome, noisy, had to be wound up by hand each time, and used easily-damaged discs; contemporary cassette-players are extremely portable, can safely be loaded and operated by a small child, and can be listened to through ear-phones with nothing but a quiet hum and occasional clicks discernible to others. Slides which once had to be displayed by a large projector, with a noisy fan cooling the lamp, can now be viewed by anyone sitting at an ordinary table or in a comfortable chair, through an inexpensive viewer held in the hand. Films which had once to be wound through tortuous channels and projected in a darkened room can now be purchased in cassette form and viewed on a daylight back-projection screen, or, in the case of film loops, on

Libraries as Media Centres

a simple, user-operated and very compact player. Television programmes can be recorded on a machine no larger than a medium-sized case, costing – for black and white – about a quarter the cost of a new small car, and playing back through a domestic television set.

The simplicity and relative cheapness of the equipment is shown by the spread of their use by individual families. Cameras are nearly as common as wristwatches, and many quite humble families take cine records of their summer holidays and outings with the children. Children in infants schools have made their own little movies as part of class projects. Adolescents tote cassette recorders as ubiquitously as transistor radios, the latter itself an astonishing development when compared with the 'wireless sets' of the 1920s with their big valves and aerial poles at the bottom of the garden. The cinema, radio and television play major roles in our lives, not only in our recreation and entertainment, but in forming our view of the world, giving us information about it and broadening our general education. Nor is the use of the so-called 'new' media entirely passive; it has become easier and easier to take photographs, make movies, and record ourselves, our neighbours and our favourite broadcast programmes, and we do it constantly.

Increasing sophistication in listening, viewing and producing has led us to the realisation that the audio-visual media are more than merely alternatives to what was already possible. The recording of a poet reading his own verse, though not necessarily enjoyable, gives us a different type of information from the bound volume of his own collected poems, even though the items read are apparently the same; we have personal data which the rather impersonal printed page cannot give, and although we may not always want it, it is still a useful addition to our studies. The film of a play or book, though sometimes in practice artistically inferior to the original, is a different experience often reaching a different audience. Musical recordings, which for so long aimed at *reproducing* the concert-hall experience, now combine different takes and make use of a multitude of sound controls and effects, so that what one purchases is an art-form in itself; much that would be acceptable as a single experience is intolerable after multiple repetition. Furthermore, the photograph or film of an event, or its recording in sound, often gives raw data for study which the verbal description by the most scholarly, imaginative or knowledgeable author does not. Film of the two world wars, and of international events between them, is now primary research material for historians on a par with Cabinet documents, preserved correspondence and newspapers of the time.

The world of education has recognised the value of the audio-visual media, most prominently for their ability to make real and vivid the subject matter to be presented. A picture, a sound recording, a piece of film or videotape, can show what it would take thousands of words to describe, and usually describe less accurately or comprehensibly. Language learning has been revolutionised by sound recording, enabling the learner to hear correct pronunciation and compare it with his own. Film and videotape has enlarged the possible range of scientific experiment, geographical exposition and medical detail that can be shown. Backward readers and the handicapped, including those blind or deaf, can be reached by media suited to their special needs. Moreover, the predominance of the mass media of cinema, radio and television requires that schools educate for critical and knowledgeable viewing and listening. In many cases this not only involves analytical discussion in sociology, current affairs and literature classes, but actual creative work in the production of audio-taped interviews, school radio programmes broadcast over the intercom, videotaped playlets and 8mm and 16mm films. Some of the films made by young people in school or as a sparetime hobby are now shown on British television, and in some cases the youngsters are only nine and ten years of age. At professional level, there are now over twenty film-making courses available at polytechnics and universities, despite the current economic recession.

However, what has most significantly influenced and stimulated the involvement of libraries in schools and colleges with the provision of audio-visual and other non-book media is the steadily growing use by teachers of enquiry learning, discovery learning, programmed learning, and what is comprehensively

Libraries as Media Centres

termed 'resource based learning', as educational strategies with pupils and students. This is a development which sets the learner in the active mode, seeking information from a wide range of 'learning resources' and using it in problem-solving exercises, project work, academic research or creative activity. The resources used may be print-format, as with books and periodicals; audio-visual, as with slides and filmstrips and audio-cassettes; three-dimensional, as with educational games and specimens and museum objects; or truly multi-media, as with kits and packs and project boxes. Some of this material is closely sequenced or programmed, so that it can be used only in the way envisaged by its creator, thus guarding against mistaken use in an unsupervised situation; other material may be only loosely sequenced and guided, allowing it to be used in a number of different ways, and presupposing either the teacher's tactful oversight or its use by well-prepared pupils and students. All of it, however, requires organisation for retrieval, and is therefore part of the responsibility of a librarian, or someone acting in a librarianly manner.

Some fashions in education do change, but there is now every reason to believe that these developments will continue, with variations and improvements, and that the recognised usefulness of audio-visual media and self-instructional materials will actually increase. It is not necessary to envisage an immense capital expenditure to set it all up; existing provision is being reorganised and co-ordinated, and improved as circumstances permit, and in many schools and colleges of education there are already impressive collections of material, equipment and production units for staff and students. The Educational Foundation for Visual Aids has identified over 450 organisations producing audio-visual materials for education, some of them quite cheap, and there is a considerable amount of local production of materials within schools and colleges themselves. Some of these latter have been helpfully listed in such catalogues as HELPIS (Higher Education Learning Programmes Information Service) published by the Council for Educational Technology.[10] The school library as a resource centre or media centre has been supported by the Schools Council,[11] the Scottish Educational Film Association,[12] the Inner London Education Authority,[13] the Library Association[14] and the School Library Association,[15] among many others; similarly, for the college library field, the Association of Teachers in Colleges and Departments of Education,[16] the Association of Teachers in Technical Institutions,[17] the Council for Educational Technology,[18] and the Library Association,[19] have produced reports, documents and standards expressing the multi-media view.

Thus education has been a major growth area so far as the development of libraries as media centres is concerned, and so far as it is possible to foresee, this may be expected to continue. In some ways, economic stringencies make more urgent the efficient organisation of what one already has, a task for which the methods of collection and organisation for retrieval which librarians practice are admirably suited. There is, in other words, a librarianship dimension to audio-visual media, because they are essentially information sources. This has, of course, long been recognised by those institutions which specialise in one or more of the audio-visual media, or make extensive use of them in their work. The film collections maintained by the British Film Institute, the Imperial War Museum, and the BBC Film and Videotape Library are each, in their different ways, impressive; their techniques of indexing and (in the case of the BBC Film and TV Library) subject analysis are essentially those of any archival or special-library concern, as is the Slade Film History Register, selectively indexing the holdings of five film archives. Similarly, the British Institute of Recorded Sound and the BBC Record Library, as well as the enormous collection built up by *The Gramophone* magazine, represent the typical librarianship problems of very large libraries of materials gathered for their own sake; and the BBC Sound Archive exemplifies a special library approach with its own information requirements, for instance to be able to retrieve the sounds of particular birds, and particular machines, as well as of individuals and occasions.

Until recently it was common to find collections of audio-visual materials being maintained by, and regarded as the preserve of, specialists in the production or educational use of such materials. There are many signs today that such people now welcome the presence of librarians and no longer feel threatened by the

Libraries as Media Centres

suggestion that we have a major contribution to make in the acquisition, indexing, storage and utilisation of audio-visual materials, and in the giving of suitable bibliographic and reference services in relation to them. The Council for Educational Technology set an early example in the 1960s in collaborating with librarians towards common purposes; and such bodies as the National Educational Closed Circuit Television Association, the Audio-Visual Communications Section of the Association of Teachers in Colleges and Departments of Education, and the Association of Teachers in Technical Institutions, have shown an increasing recognition of the place and value of the service of professional librarians in their work.[20] This does not mean that the librarian as such takes over the functions of producer, or teacher, or educational technology specialist, though there is no reason why a librarian who possesses suitable qualifications should not do so, and no reason why a librarian should not seek and obtain such qualifications if he so chooses; but as with the printed book, there is much that the librarian can say and advise which does not infringe on the prerogatives of others. With regard to a filmstrip, for instance, a librarian can describe the physical nature of the strip, whether it is single or double framed, whether it is in black and white or colour, whether its frames are diagrammatic or photographic and how many there are, whether there is an accompanying booklet, or audio-commentary on record, reel or cassette, whether it is produced in a particular series and by whom, and whether it is associated with a reputable subject specialist; he can draw attention to reviews, and the producer's stated intention, and if he has had a chance to study it himself he can give his own opinion for what that may be worth if anybody asks him. This is entirely in line with his behaviour with any other type of item, including a book, and does not presume to give the same sort of advice or description as might be given by, on the one hand, a university specialist in the subject matter or, on the other hand, a lecturer in educational methodology.

The importance of such expository and guidance work, as well as of professionally executed indexing and descriptive cataloguing, lies in the fact that many audio-visual formats are inherently unsuited to browsing. One cannot, at present, flip through a film or an audiotape as one flips through a book or journal, sampling its contents; and even when the equipment becomes more adaptable to such a practice – as is now happening – the wear and tear on the item itself may make it undesirable. Moreover, the packaging of most audio-visual items at present tends to give insufficient or unreliable data about the contents. Libraries offering audio-visual provision must therefore expect to provide more descriptive data in their catalogue entries, so that the enquirer has a fuller understanding of what the item is, what its provenance was, what equipment he will need to make use of it and enough details of its contents to be sure that it is worth his taking the trouble. This has been recognised by those concerned with the devising of cataloguing codes for non-book media: not only in Part III of the *Anglo-American Cataloguing Rules 1967*,[21] now universally agreed to be in need of revision, but in the *Non-book materials cataloguing rules* issued by the Library Association and the then National Council for Education Technology in 1973,[22] as well as in Anthony Croghan's code published the previous year.[23] International discussions for the revising of Part III of *AACR* are forthcoming, and the recommendations of C. P. Ravilious' Unesco study cited earlier in this chapter included the proposal that an IFLA Working Group be established under Unesco sponsorship to recommend an International Standard Bibliographic Description for Non-Book Materials. This has now taken place.

An important necessity for librarians developing media centres however, is not only a standard code for cataloguing data but also a national and international system of bibliographic – or rather, 'materiographic' – control, supplying to libraries and other users standard information about items published in a form similar to that already provided for the printed book in such services as *British National Bibliography*. It is a further indication of the increasing importance of non-book media as information sources that the whole question of the development of a national cataloguing and information service for audio-visual materials was urgently considered by a study sponsored jointly by the British Library and the Council for Educational Technology, reporting in May 1975.[24] The investigators examined the difficulties of bibliographic control of non-book

Libraries as Media Centres

media and the attendant problems for public, educational and special libraries, and saw the need for a national data store which could be used to generate a current catalogue, a catalogue of available materials, a MARC tape service, a printed card service, or lists by format, subject, audience, producer or any other retrieval facet. A pilot experimental programme was accepted in principle and is now being developed on behalf of the two concerned institutions.

The involvement of the British Library with non-book media is empowered by the Act which set it up, requiring it to provide a comprehensive collection of 'books, manuscripts, periodicals, films and other recorded matter, whether printed or otherwise'. Its concern with bibliographic control stems from its legal role as covering 'reference, study and bibliographical and other information services'.[25] It is likely that, in view of the enormous range of materials and activities within its purview, as well as prevailing economic conditions, its progress as a fully multi-media national collection will be slow, and that it will be content to develop liaison between those existing institutions having substantial audio-visual responsibilities.

Public libraries, meanwhile, are required by the Public Libraries and Museums Act 1964 to

have regard to the desirability of securing ... that facilities are available for the borrowing of, or reference to, books and other printed matter, and pictures, gramophone records, films and other materials, sufficient in number, range and quality to meet the general requirements both of adults and children.

In North America, and in some Scandinavian countries, examples can be found of public libraries offering a very considerable range of materials and service, although in no country is such service regarded as an already achieved standard. In Britain, public libraries have tended to make their provision in three types of service: in sound recordings, in the local collection, and in service to educational institutions.

Sound recording provision began with gramophone records, and as most of these were of music they tended to become the responsibility of the music librarian. One suspects that this situation will not last, as plays, historic speeches, comedy, poetry, language teaching, debates and sound effects proliferate on disc, reel and cassette: quite apart from other developments to follow. The local collection has long been the store of illustrations, maps, posters, theatre programmes, press cuttings and aerial photographs, as well as books and periodicals; there is every likelihood that the future will see audio-tape, 8mm and 16mm films, and video-recordings, not only collected for the local collection but sometimes created for it, either by staff of the public library itself or by some co-operating body such as a Local History Society. We shall therefore be able, and relatively cheaply, to gather together the sights and sounds of our locality as well as printed accounts of it: local accents, interviews with local notabilities, recollections of elderly people and motion pictures of festivities, customs and major events.

Services to educational institutions are already being developed in a multi-media direction, notably at present by Wiltshire, Somerset and Leicestershire. There can be no doubt that as education increases its use of audio-visual and other resources, it makes excellent economic sense for the public library to become involved, and to offer for these materials the sort of service county libraries have already offered for books. A common feature of modern publishing has been the book with a record in the back cover, and many of the productions of curriculum development agencies such as the Nuffield Foundation and the Schools Council projects have been genuine multi-media kits, including printed material, filmstrips and slides, audio-cassettes and three-dimensional models. Other publications, such as the Sussex Tapes and the units of the Open University, have made considerable use of non-print formats and will be sought equally by educational institutions and students. It will therefore be difficult to separate out the traditional print-form items which libraries have hitherto regarded as 'their' prerogative.

The Regional Resource Centre experimental project, which began at Exeter University Institute of Education in 1970 and is still proceeding, sought to maximise support to schools in the provision and manufacture of learning resources, and has been developing a network of teachers' centres, colleges and other bodies in association with schools on the one hand and the Institute and its library on the other.[26] This is happily in line with the Council for Educational Technology's advice that

in each local authority area the various services concerned with the identification, provision and utilisation of resources should be properly aligned and co-ordinated, perhaps through a specific administrative responsibility.[27]

Richard Fothergill in exploring this matter saw useful areas of co-operation between the library service, museums, teachers' centres, archives departments and local authority audio-visual services where in existence, and believed that the public library might have a useful co-ordinating role in the provision of catalogues and a van delivery service for all the different bodies concerned, without impinging on the autonomy or special responsibilities of any.[28] Such developments, already being considered in some areas and explored more fully in Wiltshire,[29] are inherently logical, so long as the problems of some local authority structures are reconciled – I am thinking particularly of areas where the public library is classed under leisure and recreation rather than with education.

Meanwhile within schools, colleges, polytechnics and universities, we are seeing a steady if uneven development of book libraries into organisations with multi-media aspirations. It is likely that it is this field which will see the most rapid innovations, as educational pressure comes to terms with economic constraints. The provision of facilities for viewing and listening, as well as reading, is increasingly becoming standard in new libraries and being developed in old, and with the market already gearing itself to meet these new demands the greatest economic problem is likely to be, not the cost of equipment, but of servicing and staff. The Inner London Education Authority has pioneered the development of a new type of ancillary worker, the Media Resources Officer, whose job is to stimulate and advise on the production of educational materials, give guidance on the use of audio-visual equipment, and organise resource centres in collaboration with librarians;[30] such a person has already played an important role in educational advance and it is likely that this will increase as schools and colleges persist with resource-based learning. However, the MRO is not a technician, though he can offer first-line maintenance and diagnosis where necessary. Equipment is becoming increasingly foolproof, but there is still disturbing evidence of audio-visual apparatus and materials lying uneconomically idle in educational institutions because of lack of immediate servicing and repair. It is, of course, not entirely impossible for suitable librarians to add such skill to their portfolio, but this is not likely to provoke co-operative responses from technicians' unions.

The rapid development of new models and media formats is unlikely to slow down, and has already been the cause of exasperation and embarrassment to institutions and librarians whose decisions have become unexpectedly out of date. 8mm film appeared in two incompatible versions; several incompatible types of video-recording exist; and quadraphonic sound recording is currently being promoted in a number of different systems which do not necessarily conform with their rivals'. Libraries will move with due caution, therefore, and it may be hoped that as the number of multi-media libraries grows, librarians will be able to play a role in restraining the wilder enterprises of commercial companies and encouraging intercompatibility of software. Three recent developments are worth closer attention, indicating the possibilities for the library and perhaps the ways in which further advance will come in the immediate future.

The first, least spectacular but arguably most immediately helpful example is the development of machines shaped rather like small television sets and allowing sequences of slides to be played and viewed to the accompaniment of a linked cassette audio-recording. With such equipment, individuals or small groups can make use of slide-tape sequences without fuss or difficulty in ordinary light; most machines enable the cassettes to be given an inaudible pulse so that the slide change can proceed automatically. Commercial firms and university departments, for instance, already use such machines in exhibitions and on open days for publicity purposes, and libraries can easily make

Libraries as Media Centres

use of them for library induction, as well as for ordinary study. The slide-tape sequence is a popular, inexpensive and effective method of communication, well suited to in-house production as well as to commercial distribution, and likely to show rapid proliferation.

The second development has been forecast for some years and has not yet quite arrived in popular form, although its potential is considerable: it is video-recording. Not only is it possible for institutions and individuals to record television programmes – broadcast and closed-circuit – but at least two major companies have been actively exploring the commercial possibilities of selling video packages for replay through the domestic TV set. Videotape is comparatively expensive for such purposes, and subject to unacceptably rapid deterioration after successive playings; experiments with high-resolution film as an alternative have been proceeding for nearly ten years, though not with completely satisfactory results, and another company has announced the imminence of video-disc, where the recording is made and replayed by means of a laser beam. Both formats offer the possibility of retrieving individual frames in the recording, as well as the whole programme, and would thus be useful for specific data storage. There seems little doubt that in one form or another – and perhaps, unfortunately, both – we shall soon be able to purchase television programmes, both educational and recreational, and no longer be dependent on broadcast schedules.[31] Some public libraries are already looking ahead to providing a stock of video records just as at present they stock sound recordings, with striking changes to our domestic habits as well as to library practice. In North America, and occasionally in the UK, college and other libraries already have collections of conventional videotape.

The third possibility, at present in active research, is of widespread use of holographic techniques providing a genuinely three-dimensional image. Already 3-D holograms have been produced, giving an apparently conventional photographic picture which when rotated presents views round the side and back as if one were rotating the actual object or moving around it oneself. The front view of a house, for instance, can be rotated so that the sides and even the back terrace come into view. The process is another instance of the versatility of the laser beam, the results of whose scanning can be laid down in this remarkable and disconcerting fashion. Industrial uses are already in development, and we can only speculate on the possibilities it may offer for information storage. Certainly the 3-D hologram will be much more than the stereograph of the thirties, whose use was mostly for educational novelty.[32]

Many other experiments are possible: one could discuss the likelihood that more material will be published directly into one or other of the micro or ultra formats without an intervening print stage; one could speculate on further uses of facsimile transmission. In the United States large sums of money have been poured into random dial access: the user dials the number of an audio- or video-tape, a computer makes a rapid copy of the master in thirty seconds, and is playing the copy to the user in his carrel within a minute; another person can ask for the same item one minute later, and hear another copy of it – within a further sixty seconds.[33] The expense of such installations is still considerable, and British libraries will need a great deal of persuasion before they accept their provision as an important priority, if indeed it is important at all. Experiments in computer-assisted learning, however, where the insights of the 'programmed learning' or 'systems approach learning' movement are developed with the use of the computer for presentation and monitoring, are still proceeding across the Atlantic, with results said to make economic sense with large enough student numbers,[34] and it may well be that we shall find sufficient uses for the computer for its 'dial access' possibilities to be more financially tempting.[35]

But all such forecasts, as we saw at the beginning, are perilous. Dial-access, for instance, pre-dates the cassette and lost some of its immediate impetus when this easily produced, easily copied and easily operated form of packaging became cheaply available. One can only predict that in general the use of a wide range of audio-visual and other formats will become standard and surely increase. Many students come to library schools today with considerable experience with the simpler audio-visual media,

Libraries as Media Centres

although they do not recognise the fact and it is not always built upon in their subsequent courses. All students will need to develop a multi-media attitude, to information sources as well as recreational provision, and to be prepared for a future of change. These attitudes will be greatly helped if library schools themselves do much of their teaching in the newer ways, and include considerable stocks of audio-visual and self-instructional items in their libraries. Moreover, the pace of change and development will make it increasingly necessary for librarians in post to seek refresher courses from time to time in the potentialities of the new devices. It is unsafe to assume that the assumptions of the last decade have not recently been overtaken and overturned.

Some forecasts have included their glimpses of horror, of students penned in like battery hens connected to monitoring dials. A National Conference of Professors of Educational Administration in the USA took comfort when assured that

It is highly improbable that by 1985 chemical gases will be released through the school ventilating systems to keep pupils and teachers, with or without their knowledge, alert during formal school sessions.[36]

Let us hope so. There need be no threat in the non-book media; they can indeed, as many of them have impressively shown us, make important contributions to the understanding of arts and to the quality of life. But of one thing we may be sure: they will not go away, nor should we wish them to do. As Dr Enright advised the Library Advisory Council (England):

Far from proving a threat or an irritant, the arrival of new media promises to be an opportunity for developing still further the concept of active librarianship in the service of the user.[37]

It is good to be able to report that the Council agreed, setting up a Working Party to study the whole field. Its final report, which has been submitted and set before the Secretary of State, followed Dr Enright's lead in stressing the positive as well as the urgent advantages to libraries of most kinds in considering themselves as centres for the collection and active use of all information media in whatever format. It is to be hoped that the existence of the currently flourishing Audio-Visual Group of the Library Association, in co-operation with its Aslib counterpart, and jointly responsible for the admirable quarterly *Audiovisual Librarian*, will help to keep the Council and the profession at large in tune with the developments of the times.

References in text

1. *New York Dramatic Mirror* 9 July, 1913: quoted in Saettler, P. *A history of instructional technology*. McGraw-Hill, 1968, p. 98.
2. Eatough, C. L. What tomorrow's library will look like. *Nation's Schools*, 77 (3) March 1966, 107–109.
3. World knowledge banks foreseen by Honeywell executive. *Automated Education Letter* 7 (12) December 1972, 6–7.
4. Landau, T. *Encyclopaedia of librarianship*. 2nd revised ed. London, Bowes & Bowes, 1961, p. 154.
5. Saettler, *op. cit.*, 113.
6. Henry, F. A. Fugitive material in the school library. *Wilson Bull.*, 5 (1) September 1930, 519–524.
7. National Education Association. Committee on Library Organization. *Standard library organization and equipment for secondary schools of different sizes*... C. C. Certain, Chairman. Chicago, ALA, 1920.
8. Ravilious, C. P. *A survey of existing systems and current proposals for the cataloguing and description of non-book materials collected by libraries, with preliminary suggestions for their international co-ordination*. Paris, Unesco, March 1975. (Typescript).
9. Unesco. International Bureau of Education. *Meeting... on the development of school libraries into multimedia centres in secondary-level education, Geneva 10–13 June 1974*. Microfiche copies of some of the papers presented to this gathering may be obtained from the IBE.
10. *Higher Education Learning Programmes Information Service: a catalogue of materials available for exchange*. I–, March 1971–. Councils and Education Press for Council for Educational Technology.
11. *School resource centres: Schools Council Working Paper 43*. Evans/Methuen Educational, 1972.
12. See, for instance, *A resources centre... is a state of mind,* Scottish Educ. Film Ass., 1973.
13. See, for instance, Briault, E. *The allocation and management of resources in schools*. Council for Educ. Technology, 1974. (Occasional Paper no. 6).
14. Library Association. *School library resource centres: recommended standards for policy and provision*. 1970. *A supplement on nonbook materials*. 1972.
15. Waite, C. and Colebourn, R. eds. *Not by books alone: a symposium on library resources in schools*. School Library Ass., 1975.
16. *The organisation of educational technology in colleges of education and other institutions of higher and further education: a policy statement*. Association of Teachers in Colleges and Departments of Education Audio Visual Communication Section, July 1973.
17. *Educational technology – a policy statement*. Association of Teachers in Technical Institutions, June 1974.
18. Fothergill, R. *Resource centres in colleges of education: NCET Working Paper 10*. National Council for Educational Technology, 1973.

19. Library resource centres in schools, colleges and institutions of higher education: a general policy statement. *Libr. Ass. Rec.* 75 (3) March 1973, 52.
20. A useful example of this was the Seminar on the availability, management and application of learning resources in teacher education, held at Windermere, 19-21 February 1975, at the invitation of the Council for Educational Technology.
21. *Anglo-American cataloguing rules: British text.* Library Association, 1967, pp. 198-265.
22. Library Association Media Cataloguing Rules Committee. *Nonbook materials cataloguing rules: integrated code of practice and draft revision of the Anglo-American Cataloguing Rules British Text part III.* National Council for Educational Technology and Library Association, 1973. (Working Paper 11).
23. Croghan, A. *A code of rules, for with an exposition of, integrated cataloguing of non-book media.* Coburgh, 1972.
24. British Library and Council for Educational Technology. Joint feasibility study into the development of a national cataloguing and information service for audio-visual materials. 1975.
25. *The British Library Act.* HMSO, 1972.
26. Walton, J. and Ruck, J. eds. *Resources and resources centres.* Ward Lock Educational, 1975.
27. *Educational technology and the expansion of education.* London, National Council for Educational Technology, 1973.
28. Fothergill, *op, cit.*, pp. 120-128.
29. Hallworth, F. Public libraries and resource centres. *Libr. Ass. Rec.* 74 (3) March 1972, 39-41.
30. Briault, *op. cit.*, pp. 33-36.
31. Burke, J. G. Coming through your front door: pre-recorded videocassettes. *Am. Lib.* 1, December 1970, 1069, 1073. Meanwhile, videodisc is being pioneered by Philips Electrical.
32. Barson, J. and Mendelson, G. B. Holography: a new dimension for media. *Audiovisual Instruction* 14 (9) October 1969, 40-42.
Spencer, J. R. Applying holography for the storage of information. *Video & Film* September 1975, 17-18.
33. Ofiesh, G. D. *Dial access information retrieval systems: guidelines handbook for educators.* US Dept of Health, Educ. & Welfare, Office of Education, 1968.
34. See, for instance: Peltu, M. Computers aren't just for the mathematicians. *Times Educ. Suppl.* 5 April 1974, 42-43.
35. National Conference of Professors of Education Administration. 1985 Committee. *Educational futurism 1985: challenges for schools and their administrators.* Berkeley, Calif., McCutchen, 1971, p. 49.
36. *Ibid.*, p. 55.
37. Library Advisory Council (England). *Report of the New Media In Libraries Working Party.* 1975. (Typescript).

Chapter Nine

The Library in the Cultural Framework

Brian Arnold and Bob Usherwood

Prognostication does not cause blindness but an article that uses it as its basis by definition cannot rely on references to worthy, learned, official and semi-official documents of the past. Thus, the reader will not find a long list of citations to professional literature at the end of this piece, for we have deliberately set our faces against producing a résumé of previous utterances. This chapter is the result of several brain storming sessions in which we have considered and reconsidered our professional philosophies and aspirations, and attempted to project them to the Brave New Library World of the year 2000. As is the case today, the library world of the future, if it is to be relevant will have to relate to the *real* world; to the aims, hopes, aspirations, needs, and culture of a future people. This, in turn, will depend on the socio-economic order that governs Britain at the turn of the century.

The word 'culture' offended Goebbels, and for different reasons it offends the writers with its 'nice' middle-class and élitist overtones. However, we intend to consider the word in its broadest sense so as to include as wide a range of human activity as possible. Reminding himself constantly of how much is embraced by the term, T. S. Eliot, in *Notes towards the definition of culture*, said:

It includes all the characteristic activities and interests of a people: Derby Day, Henley Regatta, Cowes, the twelfth of August, a cup final, the dog races, the pin table, the dart board, Wensleydale cheese, boiled cabbage cut into sections, beetroot in vinegar, nineteenth-century Gothic churches and the music of Elgar. The reader can make his own list.

The Library in the Cultural Framework

This seems to us to be a good working definition; at least our list runs parallel to Eliot's as we pick our way between the traditional culture vultures and the well meaning but slightly patronising purveyors of 'good art to the masses'.

Crystal-ball gazing is a dangerous activity even today when young and old alike often seem to return to earlier aeons in their avowed allegiance to astrological and magical Gods – the solace of the ouija board is a comfort to some. The omens on this occasion could be propitious, and indeed by the time this appears in print we might be in the midst of an artistic and cultural renaissance. But so far in the abject, sullen and soporific seventies we have seen or heard little to excite the senses, or set the pulse racing; culture, be it popular, mass, high or low, appears to be in a dry and arid valley.

The sixties were much more productive and exciting years; possibly they seemed 'swinging' to the writers, who were younger then and perhaps particularly receptive. Youngsters in the seventies still have fun, albeit of the 'cool' variety, and it is possible that in using the sixties as a basis for our prognostications we shall be accused of nostalgia for a fast fading youth. However, we think it of value to take down those lost years from the shelf, fast gathering dust like some half-forgotten basement collection in the British Library, and take a look at how librarians and library authorities responded to those days. They may guide us a little in assessing the library world's future cultural response.

The era of bomb culture, pop culture, the alternative society, flower power and the hippie saw a determined assault on the élitist framework for living. It saw, for example, solid and exciting developments in the formal as well as fringe theatre. The West End drawing-room 'puppets' were replaced by the heirs of the Porters' one-roomed flat; the English Stage Company and others scoured out the soufflé dish and offered us instead, pie and chips (with everything) and spotted dick with custard for 'afters'. In music, in writing, and in most forms of the creative arts, the response was the same. A culture with a working-class hero on the stage as well as in popular song; one which allowed positive identification and involvement by the ordinary people, perhaps for the first time in some areas of creative activity.

Of course, the tradition of music, dancing and entertainment for the masses had been with us on and off for centuries. The darlings of the Edwardian East End or Tyneside music-hall were largely swept away by the First World War along with the winkles and champagne. Sir Henry Wood, Sir Hamilton Harty and others had pioneered concerts for the working man and student early on in the century; Sir Malcolm Sargent popularised the Proms but the London Symphony Orchestra was yet to be revolutionised into shirt sleeve order by André Previn.

The one area where the class barrier was really defeated in the sixties was in opera and ballet. Sadler's Wells, Scottish Opera, Welsh National Opera, London Festival Ballet and others, alternatives to that hitherto hallowed haven for the monied and privileged, the Royal Opera House Covent Garden, engaged the attention of new and wider audiences from other strata of society. The first polo-necked sweater was seen at the 'Garden' as was caustically noted by a critic in one of the 'post Sundays'. Provincial tours by these companies became commonplace, and we could at long last claim that steel workers in Britain could partake in a cultural experience to which their counterparts in Eastern Europe had long been accustomed.

The abandonment of censorship in the theatre, the arrival of TW3, the Establishment satirists and a liberalising, civilising Labour government came almost at the same time as the first drag artist pulled on his knickers for a show in the local pub. The mini skirt and hipsters were followed by the abandonment of 'his' and 'hers' for 'theirs'. The long hair, beads and drugs on the 'Dilly' infuriated some, but looking back, it seemed natural in a decade that lay in ambush for, and finally embraced, a new democratic culture. Did the library world notice all this? Did it react, did it care, or did it, like some fading Queen, smile serenely through it all?

The Library in the Cultural Framework

We must conclude that the profession took a regal stance, as if expecting some future royal accolade. The Library Association, local and central government and the garden gnome attitude of many librarians, young and old, ensured that the response of the library world was too little, and possibly too late. A few cared enough to try out new ideas, and their names are familiar enough. However, the profession's good middle-class background, and concern with the bestseller, traditional reference libraries, 'nice' books for 'nice' kids, all washed down with a good dose of syrup of education, was a long way from reflecting developments in the cultural mores of the sixties.

Nor did there appear to be a firm conviction of the role libraries could play in the whole of society. The alien, the unwashed, the unkempt or downright disadvantaged, all portrayed in the drama on the stage, on the television, and in many of the novels on our shelves were not welcome clients in the majority of our libraries. Slowly the profession began talking about its wider responsibilities, but the seventies have provided a cultural stop rather than a cultural shock, and we now seem to be in a holding position.

One aspect of life in the sixties that we have not mentioned so far was the growing number of immigrants from the West Indies, Asia and elsewhere who began to live and work in our towns and cities, bringing with them new and exciting cultures, providing libraries with a challenge to which few of them responded.

A speaker at the Library Association one-day conference on 'Library Service in a Multi-Racial Community' held in November 1975, spoke of British libraries offering a very conservative and racist service. He stressed the need for greater sympathy with, and empathy for, sub-cultural values, and for the elimination of bias. He claimed that some 'black' sub-cultural groups had rejected the library service, and that it must be restructured to their needs if they were to be persuaded to use libraries once more.

The audience stirred uncomfortably in their seats at these

statements. However, the harsh reality remains that few librarians or library authorities are really prepared for the challenges and opportunities which are provided by a multi-racial and multi-cultural society. Unless there is a more imaginative response by those working in the library profession by the turn of the century, the traditional library service with its white racial structures coated by a veneer of 'do-goodery' will be totally irrelevant to Black Britons.

Black writers and black culture in general have shown what can be added to life, let alone the cultural life of any community. The lesson here is clear – the library, like any other cultural institution, must reflect the culture of the various groups in society rather than impose its own values.

The impetus towards black awareness has resulted in a greater interest in materials for all cultures. This has had positive results in some library authorities and no doubt their number will grow. If it is to survive in any meaningful way, we predict that the library world in the future will have to be less middle-class, more multi-racial, not to mention multi-media.

It is not a new thought – we owe it to Raymond Williams – but it is a relevant one that culture is responsive to new political and social developments. There are, of course, countless examples but the following from near or during our own time may contain pointers to the sort of political and social problems that could confront libraries during the next thirty years.

The so-called decadent art in Germany exemplified by George Grosz, who caustically depicted the spendthrift vulgarities of Weimar Germany's top people, or the celebrated film, *Cabinet of Dr Caligari*, conceived and written as a pacifist demonstration against militarism, or again, Paul Hindemith's impassioned plea on behalf of the artist working in a repressive society in his opera *Mathis der Maler*, all show culture struggling against and finally being stifled by bitter oppression. As we have already said, Goebbels despised the word 'culture', and this must still be a warning to us for the future.

The Library in the Cultural Framework

During the sixties one particular cultural response to social and political change was 'The New Chilean Song'. Begun in 1967, this movement assumed its place in the struggle for freedom which Chilean workers had been sustaining since the beginning of the century. The impetus bestowed by the Allende government developed Chilean folklore into a fully effective contemporary expression, which flowered particularly in the music of Violetta Parra and also in the songs of Victor Jara, the Chilean singer and composer. New Chile, new man, new song – the songs made people feel that Chile's history belonged to them, and that they were part of the revolution they were living through. But this power was suppressed with swift and terrible violence by the enemies of the movement – book burning did not end with the Nazis.

Even in our own time, and our own land, judges, policemen, and self-appointed guardians of public morality have endeavoured to prevent free trading in the market place of ideas. Under the false banners of freedom and public decency the 'Thought-Police' have already been in action. What political and social developments can we expect during the next twenty to thirty years? Will they produce a climate that will stimulate or suffocate those who are concerned with the communication of information and ideas? Interviewed in *Peace News* in 1969, the playwright Edward Bond forecast a time when the creative writer would fail to find a responsive audience. He asked 'Could my plays be understood by the new people who will be imprisoned all their lives in concrete towers? Who will never see an animal outside a cage or off a lead? Whose education will be a sort of remedial therapy to make them quiet, docile, wage-earning slaves? And who will be vicious towards anyone unusual, unobedient, or simply called an enemy of the government?'.

Further questions about possible developments inevitably arise in our minds. Will the promised increase in leisure time have arrived, or will it continue to be, as we believe it is now, a media myth, as men and women moonlight to keep pace with the inflation produced by a capitalist economy? Will the new and fashionable emporiums, the all-purpose Leisure Centres become half-heated refuges for a vast army of the unemployed, gaining weekly entrance on a Social Security 'Leisure Entitlement' ticket? Will cut-backs in public expenditure continue to blow like gusts of stepmother's breath down our cultural necks?

As a result of our economic ills many now fear a future repressive society – either of the extreme right or left; a society where ideas, let alone publications, are censored. Far from being cultural agents, libraries could find themselves agents of the State and the State line of policy. Ideology through culture has been tried before, and not just through the totalitarian regimes of Eastern Europe. At least one old Bette Davis movie graphically portrays the plight of a librarian who is thought to be contravening the party-line – that of Senator Joe McCarthy!

Hopefully, the society that will develop will not be of either extreme, but some kind of social democracy. On current evidence gleaned from many 'socialist' countries, the cultural function of the library is afforded a greater degree of social importance in those countries where such political structures exist. Poland, Czechoslovakia and the Soviet Union, all now relatively well-known to librarians in the West, are notable examples. In these countries there seems to be a greater awareness of cultural tradition and heritage. The response by the people to this awareness is quite astounding to us, living as we do in a country where we can seriously contemplate letting the Royal Shakespeare Theatre Company, or the few remaining repertory companies, go to the wall for the sake of a few million pounds.

The printed word, the spoken word, the whole cultural ethos, has been of importance to the liberation of peoples through the generations. We suggest that catering for the workers, and not just for their technological needs, but for their whole social, cultural and political development could and should be a great area for exploration and exploitation by libraries during the next quarter century. We have hardly begun to emulate experience elsewhere in this respect – we are hopelessly out of tune and in any case probably singing the wrong song.

The Library in the Cultural Framework

Workers' libraries began in Sweden as long ago as 1903. They grew out of the Swedish Workers' movement which began to develop during the 1880s and was a struggle to ensure equality and civil rights, and equality of opportunity to take part in the intellectual and material culture the workers saw around them.

In 1968, a Literary Commission was appointed in Sweden to investigate publication of literature and the distribution of books. They began a series of experiments in libraries and persuaded the librarians to place books in revolving racks in factory lunch-rooms – workers could take a book without any form of restriction or control. In 1971, the City Library of Malmö received a grant of 75,000 Swedish crowns to continue and expand their activities with factory collections, and branch libraries throughout the City became responsible for the collections located in their areas. There was back-up from the main library with personnel from the whole system involved in the activities.

In Poland, where a factory's employees exceed 500 the management is required by the Ministry of Culture to provide a library. At the huge Cegielski engineering works in Poznań, in addition to a large central library, small collections of books are held in dining and recreation rooms and on shopfloors. Both technical and recreation books are provided, and collections are frequently circulated and exchanged. The librarians are responsible to a Users' Committee, consisting of employees and management, the main criteria for selection to serve on the committee being sufficient interest in the library's work and the opportunity to devote free time. Not only the employee, but any member of his family including his children may use the main library, and the employee has access to the collections elsewhere around the factory at any hour of the day or night. The library also holds regular meetings with writers and critics talking about their work, the events numbering about fifty a year, and advertised in the factory's newspaper.

Truly, 'Books at the Job' could become a very important aspect of library activity. It is happening in Sweden and Poland but who is doing it here? The County of Cleveland libraries have begun a factory loans scheme, and other libraries in the

North-East have considered following this example. We believe that this type of service should be given in some form or other, probably by existing library authorities, but that industry should be persuaded to contribute money and facilities for such libraries. Factories need not only be places of labour but centres of informed leisure and culture as well. The time is now ripe for the Library Association to enlist the support of government and the trade unions to bring this about.

A further interesting point to note from the Eastern European situation is that the term 'culture' does not carry the élitist overtones which tend to be attached to it in the West. We recognize that there are some restrictions on what people in these countries are allowed to see, hear or read, but within these limitations we believe this argument holds good. 'Culture' is still not totally accepted by the masses in Britain; the term, and the activity, is at the very least treated with suspicion, and at the worst, with total derision. This is not to say that every Russian loves the ballet – people in Eastern Europe enjoy and have greater access to Western pop culture than is generally believed. Pop culture is not the complete answer to the British problem however; the solution is not to let them eat bread when cake does not appeal. The cultural taste-buds of people in Eastern Europe have not been blunted to the same extent as ours by the mass produced mediocracy of the media moguls. The need here is to sell, sell, sell, and this attitude is predominant; the price of bread continues to rise as the media moguls create a false hunger in the consumer.

Culture is a response to personal and social relationships as well as to political and social developments, and we must wonder what will be the level of acceptability of popular taste in the year 2000. During the revolutionary – for some, revolting – sixties, Kenneth Tynan shocked the television viewing public when he filled in the **** on a late night TV show. The recent box-office success of the film *Lenny* demonstrates that it is now possible to say in a mass market, albeit an up-market movie, words that a decade ago would have brought a prosecution if uttered in an expensive night-club. Words indeed that had the performer, Lenny Bruce, threatened with deportation.

The Library in the Cultural Framework

Today, no one turns a pubic hair when Anna Raeburn gives advice to lower middle-class mums in *Woman* on how to achieve an orgasm, alongside serial stories portraying traditional 'romantic' love, while at fashionable dinner parties cannabis is served along with the port and After-Eights. It is now respectable commercial cannon-fodder to talk about and illustrate advanced sexual techniques within the marital bed-sheets, and even outside them. Other sex behaviour patterns are cautiously tolerated by an increasing number of people, 'Gay-Lib' badges are worn at meetings at the Library Association, and a self-professed 'Gay' librarian has stood for election to LA Council. Sex manuals proliferate on some of our library shelves, and the passions which Enid Blyton and Biggles still arouse in some librarians curiously enough do not extend to the supply and display of volumes of 'sex made simple'. 'Lassie' has truly 'come home' in some respects.

Today's culture reflects a greater concern about racism and sexism. The role of women and the role of the family are being revalued and reassessed. At the same time, despite the activities of the Jesus freaks and similar groups, religion is playing a decreasing part in life styles and patterns, and we would suspect that this progression towards a secular society will continue. This takes on greater significance if we consider the former cultural role of the Church as patron of the arts. We must adopt a responsive attitude to all these continuing changes in personal and social relationships, and not merely adopt a belated and passive stance, safely hidden behind our own bookstacks.

In addition, we can envisage over the next three decades a continuation of urban change that has presented so many challenges to those of our colleagues working in inner city areas. We have seen or read about highly encouraging attempts by many different people to relate the library service to multi-racial groups, one-parent families, battered wives, homelessness and social deprivation of all kinds. It is doubtful if librarians of the forties and early fifties ever thought that they would face this kind of challenge in their everyday work. It is a tribute to a few far-seeing librarians that this challenge is being met by some libraries.

All this is a natural development of our work with children, the elderly, the sick and the housebound, but some library authorities in deprived areas have not even begun to react to *these* problems at all adequately, let alone to tackle all the other areas of concern staring them in the face. We are as yet only scratching the surface; nothing is static, particularly in these days of economic uncertainty, and the stress present in contemporary inner city areas may tomorrow exist in today's quiet suburban streets. Services to the disadvantaged cannot be considered 'frills' as some librarians would have them described. Libraries and their services must be for all times, good and especially bad, when they are squeezed between the dual forces of increased expectations and decreased resources.

The scale of technological change is perhaps more predictable than that of urban change. Pundits have been forecasting the death of the book for years but by the year 2000 there can be little doubt that libraries will exist in a society that values not only literacy but media literacy. Today, many children are better able to cope with the intricacies of a cassette recorder than those of the index to an encyclopaedia. This, we predict, will be even more true in the years that lie ahead. Indeed, it is somewhat ironic that the literacy movement has gained influence at a time when some would argue that print culture is becoming less important. We would not deny the importance of current and future literacy programmes, or decry the fundamental role that libraries can play in the literacy campaign. However, we suspect that in the future the shape of such programmes may be rather different.

In the area of general technological change it is difficult to escape the socio-political implications. There is a relationship between the control of the means of production and the control of the dissemination of information and ideas. If production is to be concentrated in fewer hands, it might well follow that the dissemination of information will also be in the hands of fewer people – an information élite. The process can already be seen at work in the newspaper industry and if the trend continues it will be even more important that libraries of the future reflect the full

The Library in the Cultural Framework

range of available opinion. By the turn of the century they could be one of the last bastions of true democracy.

How then will the library world respond to the future cultural framework? The experience of the sixties suggests that librarians, with a few notable exceptions, have not been innovators or gospel carriers in the cultural field. Rather they have thought it proper to reflect culture at a safe distance: how apt the phrase 'extension activities' appears in this context. Too often there has been a time-lag between a cultural feature emerging and a positive reaction from the library world. Traditionally libraries have been book-bound and behind the fringe; witness the response, or lack of it, by library authorities to the alternative press. By and large, examples of the counterculture were not stocked until they were safely and respectably bound in hard covers. Writing in the *Los Angeles Free Press* in 1971, Sandford Berman said:

If you're a bank manager, real estate broker, or stock market player you'll emphatically dig at least one large, obviously well-funded public library in the Los Angeles area. It's got everything to satisfy the financier and the major league rip off artist... But if you are young, hip radical, impecunious, Black or into one of the many liberation scenes maybe you won't dig it so much... The library offers its readers only safe orthodox, Establishment type literature.

Is there any evidence to suggest that the type and kind of response to the cultural framework will change thirty years on? Certainly the profession now has its own brand of radical chic but we wonder in practical terms how effective this will be in the long run. Certainly there are external forces which are making librarians view their cultural role in far wider terms than before. In local government, corporate management has brought into being the super Directorates of Leisure, Recreation, Amenities and other euphemisms for 'nice things', of which the library is only a part, but an integral part none the less. One wonders whether in the long term libraries would not be better placed in a Directorate of Communications to include libraries, the arts, public relations and information and advice services – this would perhaps rationalise some of the strange alliances that have occurred in some areas. Surely even outreach must stop at the crematorium?

However, the alliance with sports, entertainments, recreation and so forth has presented library services with opportunities to enhance their cultural activities. We know many of our colleagues feel there is a danger that libraries will be regarded as just another recreation/leisure/amenity service and suffer in consequence. There is always the danger the ultra-conservative viewpoint held by some librarians that 'a library is a place for books' may lead to these fears becoming self-fulfilling prophecies. The attitude of individual librarians and that of the professional bodies will do much to determine the future role of libraries in the cultural framework. Bibliographical backwoodsmen notwithstanding, those that are aligned with an arts orientation will need to be convinced that the cultural framework must also include science and technology, the local Wimpy bar, and the weekly visit to the launderette.

Our conclusions must rest on what we hope to see rather than the unsure base of prophecy. We believe that the library service of the future will need to relate and respond to the cultural framework. To do so it will have to respond to the complex situation presented by a multi-cultural society. In addition, if we believe that the library is to face increased competition from a mass produced, artificial and generally mediocre 'culture', the role of the library must be to make 'culture' available in the market-place, and we mean that quite literally. We would hope library services would not be restricted by the four walls of a building, but that the cultural response of the profession would be to place information, ideas and creative work in the path of Everyman.

As we have indicated above, the library has to exist in a socio-economic system, indeed in a cultural system. If in the year 2000, Britain is a free society, and by that we mean freer than the false freedom we have today, then the library profession must make full use of such freedom. If, as is not beyond the realms of possibility, our society has been taken over by the forces of oppression, we would wish to see the library world in the

The Library in the Cultural Framework

vanguard of any opposition movement. Underground libraries were not unknown in Nazi-occupied Europe, and we would hope to see them if 'it happened here'. The past has seen negative attitudes on the part of the profession result in a diminution of library power. Another thirty years of such attitudes and this essay, this Festchrift, indeed the library service itself could well be regarded as being of historical interest only in the 'Year of the Sex Olympics'.

Chapter Ten

Libraries and Their Users

Barry Totterdell

Whose libraries?
The history of librarianship could be said to be the story of a search for identity. Librarians, even if only subconsciously aware that the profession is essentially one of the means rather than the end, have striven for status by either exaggerating the complexity of one or the significance of the other. Like most generalisations, of course, this is neither fair nor even completely true. It would be very wrong to underestimate or belittle, for example, the vital pioneering work and generosity of time, effort and money, which was necessary first to establish the principle that the general public should be allowed libraries at all, and then to ensure that everyone, in town or country, should have access to some sort of library service. However, an examination of the professional literature up to the 1960s will show a preponderance of writings on individual libraries and collections, on literature and bibliography and on the various technical aspects of library administration. Only rarely in these articles, or in other public statements by eminent librarians, have the needs of the library user been considered. No doubt, if asked, these librarians would say, as some still do, that a distinction has to be made between the individual's wants or desires and his real needs, and the librarian's task is to decide on the nature, and if necessary the order of priority, of satisfying these needs. Stanley Jast, 'one of the great creative forces in 20th century librarianship',[1] considered that letting 'those who pay the piper call the tune' was the negation of government. 'People rarely want things according to their needs', he said, 'but according to their desires'.[2] Such paternalism, although long taken for

Libraries and Their Users

granted by the profession, was certainly not done so by the public. One of the many of Mr Jast's readers, who wrote to the local paper of the time deploring the censorship exercised in book selection and the deliberate discouraging of fiction borrowing, appealed to 'those in authority to descend from their library pedestals and try to understand the people's needs'.[3]

The paternalistic attitude has even less relevance to today's climate of participative democracy. As long ago as 1942, Lionel McColvin[4] considered that the first tenet of the philosophy of librarianship was that

The library service exists to serve – to give without question, favour or limitations. It is an instrument for the promotion of all or any of the activities of its readers. Therefore it must be catholic and all-embracing. Whenever, as may often be the case because of financial and other limitations, it must choose between types of provision, this must always be in accord with the value of the services to the individuals requiring them – not because of our own idea or opinion of what the demands should be.

Even before then, Ranganathan was propounding his *Five laws of library science*[5] and while modern librarians may smile at his apparent simplicity and naïvety, the importance and relevance of these laws are as vital today as ever. 'Every reader his book', says Ranganathan, and this his Second Law knows no exception. 'It can have no rest until it has arranged... for the supply to every one, normal or abnormal, his or her book.'

The term 'reader-centred library' was coined by A. W. McClellan,[6] and he suggested that such a library would 'take into account the complex range of motivations for reading, and the associated differences in pressures of interest which they evoke'. McClellan was one of the first librarians to translate such ideas into action by proposing a physical layout which promotes 'service in depth' thus encouraging a

natural and unimpeded movement of the reader from the conditions appropriate to the 'diversionary' interests through to those most appropriate to the more 'purposive' and thus the more intensely specific.

There is a danger at this point of assuming that the utterances of a vocal minority within the profession are necessarily representative of the theory and the practice of librarianship as carried out by the (comparatively) 'silent majority'. Herbert Gans[7] has made much the same point, when he distinguishes between 'user-oriented' and 'supplier-oriented' library service, the latter based on the assumption that the library is an institution which ought to achieve the educational and cultural goals of the librarian and his profession, and the former arguing that the library ought to cater for the needs and demands of its users. The solution to this dichotomy, he says,

is a pragmatic one taken by other institutions in the same dilemma. On the whole, user-oriented objectives guide the everyday operations, while supplier-oriented objectives are reserved for journal articles, convention shop talk, and other in-group communication.

If it is agreed that a 'user-oriented' service is to be preferred, it is surely better that rather than a surreptitious, even guilty approach based either on vocal demand or intuitive hunches about users, the principle should be employed with enthusiasm and with the greatest possible degree of information on the users and their needs.

Why libraries?
'But surely', it could be objected, 'the purpose of any library is well established as that of satisfying the needs of those that it serves?' Not so. Just as the library of an organisation is intended to serve the ends of that organisation, and of individual users only in so far as their stated demands coincide with those ends, so the purpose of the public library has often been seen in terms of society's needs, rather than those of individuals.

John Allred[8] traces the development of the public library idea, and with this the variations in the views both of its supporters and opponents as to its purpose from 'the preservation of order' to the supposed increases in productivity which would accrue from an educated working class. In the mid-twentieth century the concept evolved of the library as a 'bulwark of democracy'. Michael Harris[9] points to a similar development in the United

States, where a nineteenth-century élitist attitude which attempted – and failed – to 'elevate the masses', gave way to the view of the library as an 'institution which could play a vital role in promoting and preserving democracy by assisting the successful working of self-government'. Only recently has the concept of 'outreach' to the disadvantaged emerged, together with a view of libraries as a factor towards reducing inequalities in society.

In recent years, individual librarians, library organisations and library authorities have attempted, with wishful thinking and much talk of 'development of whole personalities', 'promotion of democratic society', or 'enrichment of life' to frame sets of public library objectives. In the meantime the user, oblivious of these well-meaning attempts at self-justification, continues through the library to seek satisfaction of a wide range of needs, limited only by his own expectations of success or his knowledge, based on previous experience, of which of his needs the librarian appears to consider valid.

It is significant that a study of the 'goals and objectives movement' in the United States revealed that in almost all libraries which had engaged in the setting of goals and objectives, community involvement was minimal, and even more significant that a suggested explanation was that 'librarians may fear that the community's idea of what the library's role should be may not coincide with theirs'.[10]

User studies

There has been some awareness that libraries do not and cannot exist in a vacuum, however, and over the past thirty years a growing number of studies have been made of users and of non-users. Some, like the community surveys carried out for the Public Library Inquiry in the United States[11] or those by Groombridge[12] and Luckham[13] – neither of whom are librarians! – have attempted to identify the library's public and to observe the chief characteristics of both users and non-users.

A natural development from this is to look more closely at the non-users and their needs. It is notoriously difficult to get at the underlying reasons for non-use and the extent of the library's responsibility for this. The straightforward questionnaire has proved too blunt a weapon for this delicate task, and the Hillingdon Project[14] has shown that in-depth studies are able to reveal more of the complex motive and anxieties which can affect even such a (to a librarian) simple and unfraught act as visiting a library.

Other studies have concentrated on the library's clients, not only who they are in terms of age, sex, social class or, in the case of a special library, their department or group, but where they come from, how often, by what means, with whom, and have studied their behaviour within the library – the use made of services, type of material or number of copies borrowed. This is the most common type of user study and a very large number investigating some or all of these factors have been carried out in public, academic and special libraries. The most comprehensive conducted in this country was that undertaken by Taylor and Johnson for the Department of Education and Science,[15] for which nearly 50,000 visitors to public libraries in South Cheshire, North Staffordshire and the Lincoln area were questioned.

The next step – a most important one – is to examine the library's success, or otherwise, in meeting users' demands. This may be, and in the past has only been, done by the use of checklists of authors, subjects or titles, but it is difficult by this method to ensure that the supposed use is representative of the actual users' demands. Direct questioning of users was carried out in a 'frustration survey' conducted at Lancaster University Library in 1968[16]. Changes made as a result of these surveys enabled measurable improvements to be made in the effectiveness of the University Library. Cambridge University Library Management Research Unit has conducted surveys along the same lines.[17] In public libraries, it has been shown[18] that, in spite of a higher level of non-specific use, a simple questionnaire administered direct to users can achieve a high response rate, and can be a valuable guide to users' demands and to the library's achievement in meeting those demands over the whole range of material provided. It is important, however, that the results of 'user satisfaction' surveys are considered in conjunction with the volume of use. One could argue that the lower the quality of library service, the fewer clients that service will have, and therefore the better the selection on the shelves, and so those who do use it are more likely to have their demands satisfied! Incidentally, these surveys have shown that the whole way in which the stock of a public library is usually arranged is not such as to best meet the actual demands of those who are using the service.

Linked with this proliferation of use studies has been the realisation of the importance of 'relating standards of book availability to the needs and behaviour of library users by examining the effects of activities that are critical in this relationship',[19] and this study of 'book availability' in one form or another is central to measurement of library performance.

Time for reappraisal
Any consideration of future proposals for libraries and their users in this country must be viewed in the light of the serious economic conditions prevailing at the time of writing. All libraries are going to be under severe financial pressure, are unlikely to be able to expand and, indeed, may well be called upon to justify expenditure on all or some of their services. During 1973 the Public Libraries Research Group carried out a 'Delphi exercise'[20] in which the prognostications of thirty-one experts in the field were collected, and their level of agreement compared on the 400 statements collected about future developments in public libraries. The statements show a continued emphasis on materials and methods rather than use and users, but there was general agreement that library collections will become more closely related to the needs of users, and the majority view was that 'public libraries will become more concerned with identifying and attempting to meet the needs of non-readers . . . and will adopt novel means of serving them'. While the general tenor of the predictions is one of cautious optimism, many of the statements on which there is a fair measure of agreement are frankly expansionist, and one wonders whether, in the light of a deteriorating economic

climate, the same experts would not now make very different predictions.

It is just at this point in time that a reappraisal of basic concepts is required. The need to obtain the maximum possible benefit from diminishing resources makes it more imperative to ensure that the real, not the imagined or more readily acceptable, needs of users are taken into account. No longer can librarians be justified in making the invidious distinction between needs and wants – or 'desires'. This time-honoured practice has too often been the excuse to relegate embarrassing demands from the first to the second category where they can conveniently be ignored. There is a feeling, justifiably held, that public libraries are at crisis point, and that unless a new sense of direction is found, they are in danger of foundering. There is no contradiction between this suggestion and the scepticism, already expressed, about recent attempts to redefine public library objectives. What is required is a readiness to adapt in response to changing circumstances and need, rather than yet more groups of librarians seeking some sort of eternal truth that will once and for all demonstrate the library's goals to be synonymous with some theoretical societal goals. With this readiness to adapt to the needs of users must go an increasing awareness and knowledge of those users. As Lowell Martin says:

A service agency that does not know who it is serving or how well it is serving is likely to be more satisfied with what it has done than concerned with what it could do. The weaknesses and mistakes of the library do not come clearly to light, and in time become built in, accepted, and even defended. This is a condition that library administrators have had to live with, and not many have been able to break free and see their institutions fresh and clear. Under these circumstances the need for basic adjustment and redirection can readily be obscured or missed entirely. When the public library comes to know itself, will it wish it was something else? And how can that something else be envisioned, except in relation to present and potential use and users?[21]

User studies – the future
So where do we go from here? There will continue to be a need to collect whatever information is required to identify the user

population. For special and academic libraries, where the clientele usually share certain characteristics, or can be relatively easily grouped, this should not be difficult. For public libraries, it may be that with money less available for large scale community surveys, the next few years should be devoted to assimilating the information which has already been collected. While it is true that we cannot know too much about our users, it is also true that sufficient is already known to identify reasonably readily the predominant social and educational level and age group structure of the existing clientele.

The real problem over the next few years is going to be to extend the user population with possibly ever-decreasing resources and it is for this task that knowledge is needed on the reasons for non-use. This is also the area where accurate information has been much more difficult to collect and it is suggested that the most rewarding avenue to be explored is that of 'in-depth' studies of non-users. This does not mean, however, that the librarian does not have quite a number of clues as to where the emphasis should be placed if more non-users are to be attracted to the library. The Hillingdon Project has shown that while many people do not, and probably will never, see the library service as relevant to their needs – and here there is quite a considerable gap between the librarian's concept of the library as an information source and the public's view of that aspect of the library's role – it is nevertheless true that there is a considerable body of potential users, and in many cases past users, who could be attracted to the library and have been, or are being, deterred for various reasons that can be attributed to failure on the part of the library. Failure to create the welcoming atmosphere necessary to overcome the fears and suspicions of libraries which exist in many people's minds, failure to relate bookstock adequately to demand, failure to take account of real use patterns in arranging stock, and failure to publicise services widely enough – can all have an effect on the level of library use, and not all of these are the effect of lack of resources.

The time has now come to establish experimental libraries, perhaps in areas that are already well served by conventional public library services, in which an attempt is made to do away with any preconceived ideas of what a library should be like, but deliberately setting out to attract non-users and then to monitor success in doing so. This would go hand-in-hand with an imaginative development of outreach. It seems likely that unless the library is to identify more closely with the community, then the community itself will set up some sort of 'alternative' library service. There is no reason, of course, why the local authority service should not encourage others to do what it has found difficult to undertake itself, as with the Highfield Community Library[22] in Belfast.

The establishment at the University of Sheffield of a Centre for Research on User Studies is a significant step, and an indication of the increasing importance attached by the profession to the continuing need to collect information on users of all types of libraries, and a recognition of the wasteful duplication of effort that has so far gone into separate and unco-ordinated research methodologies. A priority must be to bridge the gap between the academic and the practical, and there is a very real need for some sort of package to be produced so that the working librarian can carry out his user survey without needing to examine the methodology of previous surveys or to go through the lengthy, involved and often unreliable procedure of developing a questionnaire each time. Certainly in the field of user satisfaction surveys, enough work has now been done to enable any library system to conduct such a survey without any great problems. In fact, this is one area of user study where very relevant and basic information can be obtained at a minimum cost.

Throughout this period of economic stringency the emphasis must be on the practical benefits of user research, and as has been already suggested, it is during such a period that the librarian needs at his disposal the maximum possible amount of information on which to base any decisions, not only as in the past, on the establishment of new libraries and services, but to be sure that any reduction or cutback in services is also made in such a way that it will cause the least hardship to the least number of people.

The Future of Library Studies

Relevant to this whole business of user studies and user surveys is the question of output measurement, and here it is worth mentioning that significant information on the performance of a library service can be obtained from data that is readily collected as part of the normal administrative routine of the library. Over the past few years there have been a number of attempts among individual library authorities and by organisations such as the Chartered Institute of Public Finance and Accountancy (CIPFA) and the Public Libraries Research Group to develop and refine output measurements for libraries. This is an area where a considerable amount of work still needs to be done, for there have to be satisfactory measures of output before we can begin to gauge the effectiveness of library services.

Despite the likelihood that shortage of funds is likely to continue for some years to come, there is one immediate improvement to library services that involves little expenditure in financial terms but a considerable expenditure in terms of imagination. Librarians and their staff must make the imaginative effort continually to see the service through the eyes of the individual user, and if they are, as one hopes, anxious to attract more users, then to see it through the eyes of the community. This may appear to be stating the obvious, but any articulate library user can usually be persuaded with little difficulty to recount horrifying tales of treatment by library staff. How much more easy it is to deter the nervous, uncertain or disoriented client! It is all too common for the service to the public to be seen by librarians and assistants as some sort of battle of wits in which both sides are trying to score. Close attention must be paid in recruiting staff, through in-service training and in the library schools, to this vital and fundamental question of reader-relations. The library service could be forgiven many of its shortcomings attributable to lack of resources if only one could be sure that every library was an informal, pleasant and enjoyable place to use.

Prospects
This chapter has so far considered the past, present, and the desirable developments for the future, but has not as yet indulged in much prognostication. This is in many ways the

worst possible time for forecasting the future. At the present time it seems that any attempt at futurology is doomed as one is writing from a constantly shifting base. Several trends seem clear, however. There is the move towards greater user orientation, and this can be expected to gather momentum, provided the economic situation does not tempt librarians to regard it as some sort of frill, and that they see it as increasingly more necessary. There are other changes forced upon the librarian by influences outside, or almost outside, his direct control. The increasing uncertainty in the book trade, for example, may very well bring about a complete polarisation in bookstock provision between the ever-increasing need to conserve material no longer available because of the lack of economic viability in publishing, and the other extreme, the move away from conventional hardcover publishing towards the setting up of paperback libraries on a large scale. Not only do paperbacks, if handled in a much simpler and more flexible way than hardcover books, as far as accessioning, cataloguing and processing are concerned, make economic sense. It is possible by the use of paperbacks to break down many of the barriers to use, often in the past caused by the librarian's own need for order and permanence. The same economic stringencies are going to make much less likely the establishment of prestigious and impressive library buildings which, although by their very impressiveness and permanence may give the librarian responsible a feeling of pride and achievement, in fact are more likely to deter potential users than attract them. Economic necessity may require a new type of library building – less permanent, more makeshift, but in the process possibly more flexible, colourful, attractive and inviting.

One thing seems certain, that unless the library can adapt, unless librarians can take the imaginative step necessary to look at their services afresh from the point of view of the user, unless strenuous efforts are made to discover and meet the real needs of those users and potential users, then library services, having to compete with other services and institutions for a slice of a cake which almost daily grows smaller, will become of less and less significance.

The Future of Library Studies

References in text

1. Fry, W. G. *and* Munford, W. A. *Louis Stanley Jast: a biographical sketch.* Library Association, 1966, p. viii.
2. Jast, L. S. *Whom do ye serve? An address given . . . at the Jubilee celebrations of the Gilstrap Public Library, Newark-on-Trent.* 1933.
3. *Croydon Advertiser,* 10 June 1911.
4. McColvin, L. R. *The public library system of Great Britain.* Library Association, 1942, pp. 4–5.
5. Ranganathan, S. R. *The five laws of library science.* 2nd ed. repr. Asia Publishing House, 1963.
6. McClellan, A. W. *The reader, the library and the book: selected papers 1949–1970.* Clive Bingley, 1973.
7. Gans, H. J. Supplier-oriented and user-oriented planning for the public library *in* Gans, H. J. *People and plans.* Basic Books, 1968.
8. Allred, J. R. The purpose of the public library: the historical view. *Libr. History,* 2 (5) Spring 1972, 185–204.
9. Harris, M. The purpose of the American public library: a revisionist interpretation of history. *Libr. J.,* 98 (16) 15 September 1973, 2509–2514.
10. Bone, L. E. The public library goals and objectives movement: death gasp or renaissance? *Libr. J.,* 100 (13) July 1975, 1283–1286.
11. Campbell, A. *and* Metzner, C. A. *Public use of the library and of other sources of information.* Rev. ed. Institute of Social Research, Michigan University, 1952.
12. Groombridge, B. *The Londoner and his library.* Research Institute for Consumer Affairs, 1964.
13. Luckham, B. *The library in society.* Library Association, 1971.
14. Totterdell, B. *and* Bird, J. *The effective library.* Library Association, 1976.
15. Taylor, J. N. *and* Johnson, I. M. *Public libraries and their use.* HMSO, 1973.
16. Buckland, M. R. *Book availability and the library user.* Pergamon Press, 1975. 41–45.
17. Urquhart, J. A. *and* Schofield, J. L. Measuring readers' failure at the shelf. *J. Docum.,* 27 (4) December 1971, 273–286.
18. Totterdell, B. *and* Bird, J. *op. cit.*
19. Buckland, M. R. *op. cit.,* p. 136
20. Kennington, D. *and* Pratt, G. *Public libraries and long range planning.* Public Libraries Research Group, 1976.
21. Martin, L. A. *Adults and the Pratt Library: a question of the quality of life.* Enoch Pratt Free Library, 1974, p. 13.
22. Martin, W. J. The Highfield Community Library, Belfast. *New Libr. Wld,* 75 (893) November 1974. 240–242.

Chapter Eleven

The Book Trade and Libraries

Brian H Baumfield talking to Clive Bingley

BHB   At the present time the financial crisis and inflation is colouring so much of the affairs of libraries and the book trade, it is difficult to see beyond the veil. Perhaps we should look at the short term economic factors first.

CB   First, perhaps, as they are affecting libraries, before we consider the book trade.

BHB   I think, today, libraries are experiencing possibly the most difficult period that they have encountered over the last quarter-century. It's only a reflection of the national picture – or perhaps even the international scene – but I have never known a time when the essential parts of the library service – and I am thinking principally in terms of books and staff – have been under such massive attack. Although this comes mainly from the local authorities, it has not been without some encouragement from central government. There seems to be less and less regard for the service element to the community, and whilst social services and education continue to reap substantial harvests, libraries have become unfashionable in terms of priorities, despite their heavy use and popularity with the public. As far as the future goes, in the short term I can see little change from the present situation, and I imagine we shall be working with, certainly, no increase in book funds – which means much reduced purchasing power, as the cost of books continues to rise – and the prospect of fewer staff, which will mean cuts in opening hours, and a general drop in the level of service which we are giving at present.

The Book Trade and Libraries

CB   Yes, that looks to be the scenario. The book trade tends to feel that in times of hardship it is the libraries' book fund which is axed first of all, and chopped to the bone, and that perhaps staff establishment costs do not bear their fair proportion of cuts. It's a stigma which, let's say, the private sector of industry attaches to the public sector at large – that the jobs are always secure, they're just cutting expenditure on materials and products; and by cutting book funds, for example, without reducing staff levels, libraries are in fact throwing on to the publishing industry a greater level of redundancy than would be necessary if the libraries also took their share of staff cuts.

BHB   I think this is true of the past – I don't think it's any longer wholly true of the present situation, and I'm sure it's not going to be so in the next few years. Local authorities are looking very hard at staff salary bills, and in many authorities at the present time there are cuts ranging from 3% or 4% up to 20%, and, as I said before, I think this means that libraries will close – or at least reduce their opening hours. For the first time in my professional career, the word 'redundancy' has cropped up, and perhaps it is the first time it has related to local authority staff since the General Strike.

CB   The short term economic problems for the book trade are no less severe, and the cuts in expenditure by the libraries are going to have a considerable effect on the future for a wide range of publications. If you superimpose on the cost levels which are now involved in producing books the fact that libraries are going to buy fewer of them, so that the print runs are going to have to come down, then you have to cut out of the publishers' lists quite a substantial category of short-edition general trade titles, in the subject areas of fiction, biography, travel and so on; the 'list-fillers', if you like.

BHB   I think, too, that it is going to affect marginal material even more, particularly since local government reorganisation. Where you might previously have had twenty authorities each buying, say, a copy of an expensive art book, equivalent new systems will only buy one or two. This is particularly sad when libraries are increasingly being orientated towards providing for the leisure needs of the community. There are other factors, such as PLR, which are going to have an equivalent effect, but I am quite sure that there will be a growing number of books for which publishers will not continue to see a profit, if that profit in the past has been largely dependent on local authority purchasing.

CB   That's absolutely right, and in this context we have seen, not perhaps the death, but the very severe decline of the pulp-fiction reprint industry, which was booming away two or three years ago, and now has virtually ceased. I don't think that for specialised publishers the problem is likely to be quite so severe, because in most cases, such as my own for example, the libraries were not, by and large, buying more than one copy, or perhaps two copies of a title anyway, and, as a generalisation, the cut-backs will therefore tend to be of eight Graham Greenes down to five Graham Greenes, rather than one Bingley title down to none.

BHB   Yes, this makes sense. Fiction publishing, I think, is in a parlous state, whether it is a question of new titles or reprints. The boom in reprinting out-of-print titles is largely over, apart from well-known authors. In any event, the bottom of the barrel has been scraped pretty hard, but unless new fiction begins to be published at a reasonable price, by which I mean a good deal less than the present levels ranging up to £4 and £5, I cannot see conventional fiction publishing remaining viable; so that unless titles are available in paperback, and unless libraries go over to paperback stocking on a fairly large scale, we shall find that much of the range of material which people have traditionally expected to obtain from the libraries just won't be there any more.

CB   I quite agree with that. Part of the difficulty is that nobody's ever been able to establish what is the 'barrier' price for a novel which the book-buying public won't go above. Possibly that's because fiction has not, other than in the paperback imprints, been marketed in the mass quantities which would enable publishers to test the water by price variation. In the 1930s, for example, when a novel cost 7/6*d*, an average edition was no more than 750 or 1000 copies. Publishers could get away with it in those days, because all the various costs of the publishing process were comparatively very much lower than they are today.

But the difficulty with fiction is that you can only reduce the price of books significantly by cutting out part of the conventional cost-attribution process; so that, for example, you can cut a substantial amount off the published price of a book publication if you do not market it through bookshops, but can sell it direct to your customers. You can't save all the bookseller's usual discount, because you have to spend money on the alternative methods of marketing. But fiction, of course, can't do without the bookshop, because a novel is almost always a random-purchase item – people don't know whether they want to buy it until they have had a look at it – and there's no way in which it is possible, as I see it, to build up any kind of satisfactory, reliable, mailing list which would enable a publisher to market novels, or indeed general trade books of any kind, direct to his customers instead of via the bookshops.

BHB   I think there's a great danger that the bookshop as we know it today may well disappear from many parts of the country. I know we have slightly different views on this, but the question of direct supply is very much in the minds of some local authorities. To date, to my knowledge, there has been no Central Purchasing Officer who has not gone to the chief librarian for guidance, or failed to accept his recommendations as to the way in which books shall be bought; but it doesn't follow that if times get even harder financially this will still obtain and, if it didn't, we have the hoary old question of what would happen to the Net Book Agreement? I really cannot see this lasting in its present form for many more years, although its perpetuation has many advantages for the librarian.

CB   Well, I suppose my own thesis – which has, at different times, been regarded as pro-bookshop, anti-bookshop, and right across the spectrum of affiliation to or away from the bookshop – is that basically the conventional retail bookshop is not equipped to market the entire output of the publishing industry. Different resources are required for marketing, say, paperback fiction from student textbooks, to take two obvious examples. In the context of ability to market particular types of books, I think that the Net Book Agreement is of only secondary relevance.

What I would like to see is either much greater specialisation by bookshops within certain subject areas, or else a decline in the number of bookshops, so that the fewer become bigger and better bookshops, serving a wider clientèle by going out to meet it, prepared to deal by mail, prepared to grant credit accounts and this kind of thing, which is not widely done. Bookshops have got to realise that new marketing methods are required as their numbers decline, in order to hold the affiliation of that desperately small sector of the population which does regularly buy books.

BHB   Yes, I have seen little evidence of a growth of stockholding bookshops, which is the sort of thing which you envisage.

CB   There has been little growth because of the capital investment needed to fill up the shelves, and if a bookshop is established to be a stockholding bookshop, that is to fill x metres of shelf space with a representative range of British publications, without having first discovered who its clientèle is going to be, it's a recipe for probable economic disaster.

BHB   It's a marketing problem, isn't it? How is your bookshop, as distinct from your library supplier, going to widen his net, and still make something more than the 5% or 6% net profit which seems to be the optimum figure that a retail bookseller could make by the end of the year? Which is not enough for working.

CB   No, indeed.

BHB   I think the specialist bookseller will certainly continue to exist, because as long as the things he is selling are wanted, his trade is much more certain than that of a small general shop.

The Book Trade and Libraries

CB   That's undoubtedly the case. A lot of people make a good living out of nominally 'bookselling', who in fact have a mailing list of their customers to whom they send information about new books within their own special interest areas, receive back orders by post with cheques, send the corresponding order straight to the publisher with an instruction that the book be sent direct to the original customer, and the invoice back to the bookseller. The bookseller in this case need never handle a book throughout the course of his whole career.

BHB   Yes, well that's good business, isn't it? I think we have seen evidence of this in the marketing methods of some of the big shops.

CB   It's very good business, but of course what it doesn't do is sell general books – it sells specialist books, and it's the sensible way to do it, because this kind of specialist bookseller can operate on much lower overheads than the large stockholder.

BHB   I think this can work as far as the sale of books to the public is concerned – I'm not so sure that it can work sufficiently well to keep libraries supplied, because of the enormous number of titles in their through-put, and this is where the library supplier comes in, where he has come in and prospered, and is still prospering, despite present difficulties.

CB   And doing a useful job. Of course, a number of the larger library suppliers do act as stockholders in order to provide a speedier, more convenient service for the library customers whom they service, and sometimes they find themselves over-stocked, so that they are not acting, as it were, as forwarding agents, but as a kind of 'bookshop' which is not open to the general public. The pure library-supply function is really no more than a clerical one, which saves the library work making out orders and cheques for different publishers. It therefore ought to be a perfectly assessable service in terms of value. A library could say, if we did our own ordering direct, instead of one order a week we'd have to write out x hundred, and then y hundred cheques, which would cost us so much; we should probably expect to negotiate an average direct-supply discount of 20%, so if the extra clerical cost is equal to 15% it is worth doing; but if the extra cost would be 30%, then it is not worth doing. The library supplier's function could be assumed by libraries if it was cost-effective to do so.

BHB   We could say, however, that we see the library supplier continuing more or less in his present role, with probably a considerable increase in his stockholding function, which will obtain as long as profitability obtains. We see the diminution and the reduction in the number of small High Street booksellers, and I am not sure quite how much we shall see in terms of direct supply – the clerical work involved in a large library system would be huge, and one would have to do a fairly detailed analysis of the costing of one as opposed to the other; so far as I know, no local authority has attempted such an operation.

CB   I would add that I think there is developing amongst publishers some recognition now of the fact that the function of a library supplier is much more to assist and save the time of the library customer than to advance the marketing objectives of the publishing house, and this is something which some publishers feel should be reflected in the nature of the terms granted to library suppliers. I'm not talking necessarily of reduced discounts, but if publishers have to give large discounts to library suppliers whose function is designed purely to ease the workload on the libraries, then the library supplier should offer the *quid pro quo* of sensible stocks and a minimum of single-copy orders. They are saying, 'you exist for the benefit of the library customer rather than to 'push' our books, and therefore your costs must be met out of the library's resources as much as possible, rather than be thrown wholly onto us, the publishers'.

BHB   One or two book suppliers have foreseen this and have set up regional centres in different parts of the country, and this bears out one implication of what we said earlier – that people will have to go further if they want to see a good range of books.

CB   Which is reasonable! In my firm, we have stopped supplying at-publication sale-or-return library inspection copies, because we were finding that inevitably some of them

The Book Trade and Libraries

came back; and where you are sending out single copies, which tend to be uneconomic anyway, if you get one back out of five, the cost of cancelling that one sale probably removes the notional profit on the sale of the other four. Our reply to library suppliers who asked us to continue this was that this is done for the convenience of the libraries, who don't pay any extra for having a book conveyed to them for their yea or nay, which may then be sent back to the publisher unsold. We think that the libraries should carry these costs. If they want to buy the book then they can certainly buy it at full price, and that's it. But if they want us to send it along to, say, Huddersfield, and ourselves foot the cost of their saying no after all, then our answer as publishers must be 'sorry, we're not interested'.

BHB I agree with this entirely – in fact, I've always been an apostle for real costs being charged, whether it's a question of library servicing or on-approval systems. Library suppliers, in my view, have made a rod for their own backs in providing a vast offertory of servicing, ranging through plastic jackets, strengthening, catalogue cards, book cards and stationery, and charging a nominal amount which is actually a hidden discount. Librarians cannot really be blamed for taking full advantage of this.
On another tack, a lot of publishers, not so much in the public library market, but on the schools side, fall over themselves to send inspection copies to professors and lecturers, and there are hundreds of copies of new textbooks which go out gratis, which contradicts your argument somewhat.

CB I'm not sure I agree that there are hundreds. Different publishers have different methods, but the usual practice is to allocate a fixed number of copies as 'desk copies' for professors who might recommend them to students for class use; these books are the same as 'review copies', and they are not usually taken into the unit costing which fixes the price of the book. Another way, which we have adopted from American practice, is this: when we get a request for a desk copy from a professor or teacher, we send it to him with an invoice, and we say on the invoice, 'If you return this book to us within thirty days we will cancel the invoice; if, within thirty days, we receive from your college bookshop an order for ten copies or more of this title, you may retain the book and we will cancel the invoice; if neither of these things happen, we shall hold you liable for the invoice'. This works fairly well.

BHB   Well it has an incentive bonus!
Of course, one of the things which is hovering like the sword of Damocles over the whole thing is the upward surge of book prices. We all – publishers, booksellers, and librarians – hope that it will soon become possible to stabilise them, but we can't stabilise them when manufacturing costs keep going up.

CB   There are two principal factors affecting book prices – one is the level of manufacturing cost, the other is the reduction in print runs. Of the two, probably the more significant for book price levels is the reduction in print runs, because a book's price is fixed according to the unit cost of manufacturing each single copy of that book in an edition, and there are certain static costs, like composition, which don't rise according to the number of copies you print; so the more copies you print, the cheaper your unit manufacturing cost, and the lower your retail price. The only way of avoiding a rise in the price of books due to a reduction in the general levels of print run is, of course, to sell more books – there's not much more than that one can say about it!

BHB   Undoubtedly, in certain areas, more books are selling. Far more members of the general public are buying paperbacks than they have done for years, despite the fact that the price of paperbacks has escalated almost in proportion to the others.

CB   I think that's right, even though there has been a very sudden jump in average paperback price levels in 1975, which may have created selective customer resistance. That, I think, will probably stabilise itself as people get adjusted to the different values of money.

BHB   This is one of the things which makes it so difficult to forecast a trend, because as long as prices keep on changing, keep

The Book Trade and Libraries

on going up, the pattern of demand from libraries will change too.

CB   Clearly that is the case. As regards manufacturing costs, though, – and speaking in Autumn 1975 – I think we have topped-out the 1974/75 inflationary spiral. One is certainly finding among printers, binders and paper-merchants a readiness now to stabilise their prices for a foreseeable period in the future. It's been a horrifying spiral, there's no doubt, and publishers' overheads have done exactly the same thing as manufacturing costs. The wage slice of the cake throughout the whole country has gone up quite dramatically, but people seem to have realised that if too much is being paid in wages, the net result is unemployment, because you then have to achieve from fewer people the same amount of output as more staff were producing before.

BHB   Yes, it's a reflection of the national pattern. I think we shall be on the prongs of Morton's Fork, insofar as we can't prevent world prices increasing; we just hope they will slow up. It's a fact that customer-resistance, certainly in local authorities, is with us now, and we have agreed that book funds are not going to go up in the same sort of proportion that they have gone up over the last decade. Therefore, there could well come a point where it's no longer economic to publish certain types of book. In this sense the book could therefore be in a decline.

CB   That is right, because it's also the case that probably the most squeezed sector of the public in 1974/75 has been the middle and upper management people earning between £5,000 and £8,000, who have seen personal taxation increased substantially, while at the same time price-inflation has eroded the value of their remuneration; and the kinds of things which get cut out when incomes are severely squeezed, as they have been for these people, are non-essentials like theatre, gramophone records, books, newspapers, and so on.

BHB   How far is this going to affect the general picture over the next ten or twenty years? Are we going to see the book disappear as we know it today?

CB   This is a broad question, of course, and one can forecast, but nobody really knows. I judge that we will see the conventional format change radically; the orthodox hardcover edition must be in decline, because although the additional cost of putting boards rather than paper wrappers round a book is not dramatic, none the less it's significant, and with the differentials which exist between hardcover and paperback prices, the former are meeting customer-resistance.

BHB   It's not for me to teach publishers their business, but I'm quite sure that this is so. I have maintained for a long time that the differential in some publications is far too great, and where a paperback book is priced, say, at £1·50, when the hardcover edition – which is no different except for its binding – is priced at £6, however popular the title, the librarians will not buy the hardback book; although I'm sure that the vast majority of librarians would still prefer to buy hardcover books if they could.

CB   You are talking, of course, of dual editions rather than the issue of a novel by one publisher, who then sells the paperback rights to a paperback publisher, who re-issues it – such as a book on, say, economics, in hard cover at £6 with a student's edition at £1·50.
I have some sympathy with the publishers here, the rationale is this: the market for this book is a maximum of 5000 copies; if we produce 5000 copies in hardcover, it will have to be priced at £3·50, which may lose us some potential student purchase. So we produce a paperback edition at, say, £1·75, but since the savings between the cased boards and the paper wrappers are not sufficient to permit a reduction on that account from the initial £3·50 price down to £1·75, we must 'load' the price of the hard cover to make up the revenue differential. The hardcover subsidises the paperback.

BHB   Yes, I accept that, but all I'm saying is that in some instances the publishers have wrongly estimated the cut-off point.

CB   Well, that may be true. I'm not the least surprised to hear publishers get their maths wrong. All one can say is that in individual cases of apparent over-pricing the answer is for the

The Book Trade and Libraries

customer, and in particular the local authorities, to write and query it.

BHB   Yes, I think we can deal with this in individual cases; it's really general trends that we're concerned with, and this is perhaps a small part of it. If we get right down to the basics, we should be very much concerned with whether reading itself is diminishing. How far is the influence of the visual media taking over from the printed word, and will it mean that the people who regularly used to read even the popular Sunday newspapers now no longer do so?

CB   This is a hobby-horse of mine, but it's an entirely speculative one. I think reading is in decline, at least relatively; that is to say, the reading habit is not expanding in proportion to the growth in the receptivity of the population to communication generally.

BHB   And in the general increase – which we are led to believe is growing – of leisure activities.

CB   Yes, and of literacy and cultural development. I believe that the slice of the communication cake held by the book and the printed word is diminishing. I don't suggest the book will die within the foreseeable future, which can be as many years as you think it sensible to say, but it will increasingly become the province of a smaller section of the community. Now, it's also true to say that when I have spoken on this theme at library conferences, the discussions from the floor afterwards have always refuted the proposition; they say 'we see no evidence of this, the reading habit is as strong as ever, our issues are fine, lots of youngsters are coming into the libraries', and so on. It is really a 'gut feeling' with me that our product has not, over the last thirty years, been marketed as an essential part of ordinary everyday existence, and because of that, the price levels now being demanded for books, newspapers, magazines, are encountering strong customer-resistance; and that seems to me a sure recipe for a decline in reading – particularly when you consider what alternatives are available for leisure activities.

BHB   Are you suggesting that books in future may be restricted, to use an old-fashioned word, to the intellectual élite?

CB   They may be restricted to a *use* which is élite, let's say – not to a certain proportion of the population which is intellectually endowed. But they will be very much categorised in their forms of use, so that students will read them for study purposes, for example, or intellectuals will read them for particular purposes related to the content of the book, and so on. What I think we're likely to find is a decline in the automatic turning to a book on whatever subject as a valid means of filling leisure hours: I've got half-an-hour, or three hours, in which to do nothing, let's go to the shelves and take down a book. I don't think that habit will disappear, but I think it's declining and will continue to decline.

BHB   This is a fair assumption and it applies too, for another reason, not only in the field of leisure reading, but also in the field of information reading. We have seen such an enormous revolution in methods of information retrieval – the use of micro methods, the use of computers, have become so sophisticated over the last few years, and I see no evidence that this is changing; in the field of documentation and the recovery of facts, which are, after all, very much part of purposive reading, this too could contribute materially, not to the death of the book, because I don't think the book is going to die, but to its reduced use in the conventional form that we know it.

CB   Yes, the stratification of its use if you like. I may add that the development of SDI, Selective Dissemination of Information, – in industrial and scientific libraries in particular – is contributing to this, because instead of the scientists scanning a journal as a whole, they receive the explicit advice from their information department to read pages 27 to 34 – not to browse through the journal.

BHB   It's part of the ever-increasing complexity of everyday life as we know it. If one looks back, even in my lifetime – the palmy days in publishing, bookselling, and in librarianship relied on a far simpler and much more direct approach than we have today, and I don't think that the modern product, whether it's practical or intellectual, is necessarily any better than that which we had 30 years ago.

CB   No. But the implications of any kind of decline in reading for the publishing industry as a whole, including newspaper and magazine publishers, are very considerable. You recently asked me whether publishing is likely to become a cottage industry. The quick answer to that is that book publishing always has been a cottage industry, because even the biggest British firms' sales are but a fraction of those of big firms in other industrial spheres. I think that not only is publishing likely to become increasingly a fragmented industry, with some large groups dissolving back into the fragments from which they were originally formed ten or twenty years ago, but even for the smaller units it's going to be less a cottage industry than a sort of garden-shed industry. One's talking of a number of years from now, but the industry is bound to fragment as publishers concentrate more on specialisations which don't need expensive capital gearings, large-scale overhead resources of staff, buildings, computers, and the rest.

BHB   Yes, this of course is a direct contradiction of the post-war publishing tendency, where we saw so many of the small, independent publishers disappear into large cartels. There is also a school of thought which believes that local government reorganisation as we saw it first in London, and more recently in the rest of the country, is not viable, and we may even see a return to smaller units of government.

CB   Certainly in the book trade you can already see a move towards a disengagement and re-fragmentation. A number of companies have fragmented or hived off parts of their operations recently, and I find this sensible because I believe that the nature of publishing as an industry is not such as to be able to support large administrative structures.

BHB   I think this applies again over the whole field of industry. In some areas, such as the heavy manufacturing industries of the country, firms have to be large to be really efficient, but in many spheres we find a new fragmentation and decentralisation, because only in that way can the concern or the person exist, and make a reasonable living.

CB   I don't know what proportion of the total of British books is published by firms which employ perhaps no more than fifteen or twenty people, but I bet it's a pretty high one. It is not axiomatically true, for example, that because you've got x thousand sales invoices going through your firm every month or week or year, therefore you must have a computer to prepare them.

BHB   Some may call it heresy, but it's been a hobby horse of mine that computers have often been used because they're there, because they're a new fashion, and the human error factor is just as liable to occur when information is being fed into a computer, as with the old-fashioned ways of working. This is not to say that computers are not the best way of dealing with certain large-scale problems. As a customer, since publishers generally adopted computerisation, it seems to take much longer to obtain books, and it is often impossible to get accurate and speedy reporting. Let us leave this one, and move on to the subject of PLR.

CB   Well, my views are fairly well known through the medium of *New Library World* – or perhaps nobody reads *New Library World!* What do you think about PLR?

BHB   I think that like the poor it will always be with us, and I think, despite the many delays hitherto, that a measure will be introduced in due course. Apart from a small core, I think librarians on the whole don't have blazing passions about this. As I see it, the main bone of contention is the fear that the book fund may be further eroded by the introduction of PLR.

CB   Yes, but on this account the defence by librarians over the years has been so resolute that this one is now largely by-passed, isn't it? I think some kind of PLR is going to come in, but all the signs are that it will take the form of a straight central government subsidy, however much they may disguise it. What the libraries may be left with is a work-onus of attributing loans to titles, or operating whatever other method they select. But apart from that, the signs are that the battle which libraries *wished* to fight over PLR has actually been won.

BHB   I would like to think that that was true. We are concerned with cost, which is where we came in on this discussion. Cost, not only with regard to the book fund although it is primarily so in this special area – but cost as far as staff time is concerned. Library staffs are being cut; it's becoming more and more difficult to maintain our existing services. We're worried that an additional workload will be put on to existing staff, in whatever form it comes. I think, as I said at the beginning, the consensus is that if this comes as a straight state grant, librarians will not oppose it greatly. I have, from the early days when I had an exchange of letters with A. P. Herbert on the subject long before it became a national issue, maintained this particular position, and the book fund is still something of a sacred cow; but it's a sacred cow not only on which the general public depend, but on which the publishers, the library suppliers, and the booksellers also depend for their general well-being.

CB   Yes, that's a very acceptable standpoint. My own opposition to PLR has, I suppose, been intellectual, and 'selfless' in the sense that I am both a publisher and an author. It's no longer suggested that publishers should actually benefit from any PLR, which is another illogicality in the basis of the scheme, but I have always felt that the concept is intellectually untenable. PLR is an attempt to give greater remuneration to writers under a trumped-up pretence that they have some kind of enduring 'right' in particular situations in which their books are handled, and it's absolute nonsense logically and intellectually.

BHB   Would you not say that the principles have been argued over and over again, and that now we are more concerned with practicalities rather than principles?

CB   I agree with that, and I see no reason why PLR, if and when it does become law, should not provide that where any work is required of the libraries in providing information upon which the loan-payments are to be based, that work must be remunerated out of the same central fund. The libraries should be reimbursed for their costs in helping to work the scheme.

BHB   That's extremely fair, and I hope that will be incorporated into it. Time alone will tell. In conclusion, then, what would you offer as a quick forecast of 'the prospects for British librarianship'?

CB   The distant prospects are good – in terms of the profession's role as the organiser and distributor of information; as purveyor of leisure entertainment for the literate, however, the prospects are much more circumscribed than hitherto. But then, the same could be said for publishers!

BHB   That, I am sure, will continue to be our role, and I think we are agreed that prospects over the next decade look rather gloomy for everyone whose business is with books. On the other hand, do you remember what Sinclair Lewis said in *Dodsworth:*

'The trouble with this country is,' observed Herndon, 'that there are too many people going about saying "The trouble with this country is . . ."'

Chapter Twelve

International Directions

J S Parker

At the time of its foundation at the Conference of Librarians held in London in October 1877, the Library Association could already claim, with some justification, to have opened the way to new directions in international librarianship. The Conference itself was an exercise in international librarianship, and was, indeed, the first real international library conference, with a substantial proportion of the 216 delegates attending from overseas, including sixteen from the United States.

Fifty years later, the Association's fiftieth anniversary conference in Edinburgh provided further and more concrete evidence of the Association's concern for international co-operation in the library field, with the establishment of the International Library and Bibliographical Committee, the forerunner of the International Federation of Library Associations. The other main topic at this conference was the Kenyon Report – the *Report of the Departmental Committee on Libraries* which surveyed the British library scene and put forward recommendations for the development of a national library service. The Kenyon Report had only limited impact on the development of library services in Britain, but had considerable influence on library development overseas, being taken as an example of the British lead in the field of national library services by librarians in Canada, South Africa, Australia, New Zealand, the West Indies and elsewhere in subsequent years. The development in Britain of the county library movement was also a comparatively recent innovation at the time of the Edinburgh Conference, and this, too, was widely regarded as an illustration of British leadership in seeking new solutions to characteristic problems of the time – in this case, the problems of ensuring book supply to rural areas and of attaining a uniform level of library provision over the whole country.

The 1927 Conference was a focus for the discussion of these issues and for the dissemination of information about these developments; and many distinguished visitors from overseas who took part carried away with them new ideas and new approaches to old problems, which were to have widespread influence on library development in other parts of the world. It seems appropriate to begin our consideration of future directions in international librarianship in the period following the Library Association's one hundredth anniversary by asking whether contemporary developments in British librarianship are likely to have the same widespread influence throughout the world as did these earlier developments some fifty years ago.

The world of international librarianship has changed in the last fifty years, not least because of the efforts of that International Federation of Library Associations which had its roots in the Library Association Conference of 1927. The wider opportunities for international discussion of professional problems which have come about through the activities of IFLA and other international bodies have led gradually to the growth of a consensus of opinion on the key issues confronting the library profession throughout the world. The international influence of professional developments in any one country, therefore, seems likely in the future to be directly related to the relevance of these developments to world-wide key issues.

Key issues in the field of librarianship, however, cannot be viewed in isolation from key issues in world society as a whole, and it therefore seems necessary to commence with a consideration of some of these broader issues, and of their possible implications for librarianship, before looking in any detail at the problems of librarianship itself. The very development of a widespread international consensus of opinion on professional problems, and the limited potential influence of even the most advanced developments which do not relate to

International Directions

this consensus, are themselves a reflection of what is perhaps the most significant trend in contemporary world society, namely, the approaching end of world dominance in many fields – librarianship among them – by the industrialised nations of the 'developed' world, and its replacement, hopefully not by world domination by some fresh power grouping, but by a more natural balance of interest and influence involving all the nations of the world.

In a paper[1] published in October 1974, the writer emphasised the importance of the relationship between library development and the development of society as a whole, and suggested that the possibility of a shift in economic and political power away from the industrialised nations of the West might bring with it significant changes in the development of library and allied services. In the twelve months which have elapsed between the publication of that paper and the writing of the present one, this shift of power has accelerated rapidly; and it seems more than likely that some of the tentative forecasts of future development outlined in the present paper may have become established fact by the time it is published. Even the rapid developments which are now taking place, however, seem likely to mark only the beginning of a much longer term movement towards the establishment of the 'new world economic order' propounded by the United Nations General Assembly at its Sixth Special Session, and it is this long term movement which seems likely to have the most important consequences for the future development of library services.

A new world economic order will not come about overnight, nor will it be achieved without opposition. A redistribution of the world's wealth on a more equitable basis inevitably means that some of those who now have most may be called upon to give up some of what they now have or, at the very least, to forgo some of the further improvements in their wealth and standard of living which they had been anticipating for the future; and these considerations are as likely to apply in the field of library services as in any other. Irrespective of the amount of lip service paid to the idea of 'development' as a means of increasing the wealth of poor nations, the wealthy cannot be expected to give up a part of their wealth without a struggle; and perhaps the central problem confronting the world in coming years will be, not so much the economic problems of creating a 'new world order', but the political problems of achieving this with the minimum of international ill-feeling and the maximum of international goodwill.

Perhaps the first steps in this direction have already been taken. The Seventh Special Session of the United Nations General Assembly, held in September 1975, adopted a resolution on relations between rich and poor countries which, despite the expression of reservations by the United States and other developed nations, is seen as a big step forward in commitment by the rich to the poor. Greater emphasis is to be placed in future both on agricultural development and on the industrialisation of the developing countries, with UNIDO, the United Nations Industrial Development Organisation, becoming a specialised agency of the United Nations and in that capacity organising major discussions on the industrialisation of the developing countries, with emphasis on the redeployment of industrial capacity from the rich countries. In support of these objectives, the United Nations itself is to organise a world conference on technology in 1979 and set up a technology data collection system.[2]

Despite the many practical and political difficulties which will doubtless continue to arise in the future, it does appear that the first steps, at least, have been taken towards the redistribution of industrial capacity – and thus of wealth-producing potential – coupled with a recognition of the need also to redistribute technological knowledge. In the opinion of one current affairs commentator,[3] it is now evident that the West will transfer tracts of its traditional industries to the poorer countries and the newly oil rich, concentrating its own educated manpower on creating a service economy instead. The implications of these projected future developments for library and information services are manifold, both in terms of the role of such services in supporting the transfer of technology to poor countries, and in terms of the redistribution of library and information resources themselves.

International Directions

The relocation of traditional industries in the developing countries will require, not only the transfer of appropriate technological knowledge and information and the establishment and development of suitable information handling systems, but also the improvement of more general school, public and academic library services as a contribution to the creation of the educated manpower which will be needed to run the newly-transferred industries. These objectives are not new; but they are being given a new urgency by the growing pressures for change which are now coming to a head. Almost by definition, the solutions to the problems created by this new situation will be international in scope and character, involving the further development and improvement of existing and proposed systems for the international transfer of information, and concerted efforts to raise the level of library and information systems in all countries to levels appropriate to their needs.

It seems likely that the resources for research and development required by this expansion of international information transfer systems will continue to be found, as at present, chiefly in the increasingly service-oriented economies of the West. The establishment and development of library and information systems and services may thus in part replace the production of goods in these reoriented economies; and it seems possible that the differences in research and development capacity in such fields, as between the new service economies and the new industrial economies, will perpetuate the existence of a gap between them – more qualitative than quantitative by this time, one hopes, but still a gap. In the field of library and information services, the awareness and effects of this gap may perhaps be mitigated by the improvement and development of library and information services in the newly-industrialised countries themselves – that is, by improving their capacity to utilise the products of the international information transfer systems developed in the West. In terms of current international library and information programmes, this means that the extension to all countries of the NATIS concept of integrated national information systems is essential if the full potential of the UNISIST programme for a world information system is to be realised. We shall return to a further consideration of NATIS,

UNISIST and the closely associated programme for universal bibliographical control, UBC, at a later stage. For the moment, however, we must give at least cursory attention to another aspect of the situation, that of the redistribution of library and information resources.

Central to the whole concept of NATIS is the idea of information as a national resource – a resource, therefore, which must inevitably be affected by plans for a large-scale redistribution of the world's resources of all kinds such as those outlined above. The problems likely to attend such a redistribution in our present field of concern may, to some extent, have been obscured by the very use of the term 'information' in this context, with its suggestion of discrete items of data, easily communicated, reproduced, stored and retrieved by electronic and other means, to virtually any part of the globe. The use of the more traditional term, 'knowledge', in this context, may perhaps remind us that a vast proportion of the world's existing store of 'information' is housed in more traditional documentary formats which are far less readily transported to distant parts of the globe – even when they are readily accessible – except in the form of copies which may not always be acceptable substitutes for the originals.

The great libraries of the industrialised nations of today contain rich and extensive collections of books, manuscripts, archives and other documents, many of them rare and irreplaceable, which are of inestimable value as sources of 'information', but far less easily transferable than items of data stored electronically in the memory banks of a computer. Many of the riches of these libraries are true products of the cultures of which the libraries are part. They have their rightful places in these libraries, and perhaps the libraries of other nations with different cultures can never have access to them except through the imperfect media of facsimiles or copies of one kind or another. But the libraries of the West also contain many of the documentary riches of other cultures; and if the above argument holds good for the products of Western culture, it must also hold good for the products of others. In other words, there is, in the libraries of the industrialised nations – and, indeed, in their

International Directions

art galleries and museums also – a great deal of rare and even unique material, the product of other cultures and other times, which is essential to a true appreciation of those cultures and their histories, and which may well be thought to have its rightful place in the libraries which serve those cultures, now or in the future. It would be unfortunate, from the point of view of international scholarship and understanding, if this quite reasonable viewpoint were allowed to harden into a kind of bibliothecal chauvinism, but there seems little doubt that, as the transfer of resources from rich to poor gathers momentum, the great libraries of the West are likely to come under increasing pressure to transfer some, at least, of their more important holdings of foreign material back to their countries of origin.

Such demands are likely to remain sporadic and unco-ordinated whilst the levels of educational and library development in the poorer countries remain low; but, as indicated above, the future industrialisation of today's developing countries will call for rapid and substantial improvements in both educational and library services. We have already suggested that the development of the latter in line with the NATIS concept of an integrated national information system for each country is essential if poor countries are to benefit fully from the potential for information transfer of the expanding range of international information systems being developed under the UNISIST umbrella such as DEVSIS, AGRIS, SPINES, and so forth. A somewhat worrying feature of the NATIS concept as at present formulated – if such a miscellaneous collection of objectives, strategies and methods can truly be called a 'concept' – is that the idea of a totally integrated national information system, comprising all kinds of library, documentation and information services and planned integratively with national development in other fields, is so very far in advance of reality in developing countries, most of whom have yet to achieve adequacy even in the establishment of the national public library systems which they were being exhorted to develop at Unesco regional meetings twenty or more years ago. Nonetheless, even though the NATIS concept is still far from realisation in most countries of the world – and not only in developing countries – it remains true that it is only through the planned and integrated development of all types of library, documentation and information services in a country that full use can be made, not only of the country's own information resources, but also, through international information transfer systems, of the resources of other countries and ultimately of the world at large.

The proposed international framework for the development of these international information transfer systems is the UNISIST programme, and whilst both UNISIST and NATIS received the approval of the Unesco General Conference at its Eighteenth Session in 1974, it is the former which is considered to be one of the major programmes of Unesco, and to which responsibility has been allocated for 'all conceptual and operational activities relating to scientific and technical information and documentation services, whether financed by the Regular budget or through UNDP funds'.[4] This step was proposed by the UNISIST Steering Committee at the close of its first session in November 1973,[5] and adopted by the Director-General in the preparation of Unesco's Draft Programme and Budget for 1975–1976, where he stated that, in deciding to transfer responsibility for scientific and technical documentation from the Department of Documentation, Libraries and Archives to UNISIST, rather than bring UNISIST under the wing of the Department, he had been 'prompted by essentially practical, and not intellectual, reasons ... in view of the dynamism displayed by the scientific circles which have devised and are supporting it, it is desirable above all to preserve the coherence of UNISIST and give it every chance of success'.[6]

At an earlier point in his introduction to the Draft Programme and Budget, the Director-General had also made it clear that the inclusion in UNISIST of information relating to the social sciences and humanities was also to be encouraged.[7] Whilst the transfer of these various responsibilities to the existing UNISIST sector of the Unesco Secretariat is intended as a 'transitional phase which should not last too long',[8] and the ultimate aim is to gather together into one complex all the documentation, information and library activities of Unesco, it seems more than likely that the philosophy and practices of the present UNISIST programme will be predominant in any such reorganisation. If this

International Directions

development is seen by librarians as some kind of 'take-over' of their rightful spheres of professional responsibility by the information scientists, perhaps the library profession has only itself to blame, for not having displayed the same dynamism in devising and promoting a world library network, as the scientific community has clearly done in relation to the UNISIST programme.

If UNISIST is to form the international operational dimension of any future regrouping of international programmes in the library and information field, and NATIS represents the national organisational dimension through which the objectives of UNISIST are, in part, attained, then UBC will inevitably – and rightly – come into the same complex as the essential complement to these other elements. The relationship between UBC and UNISIST has been clearly defined by Chaplin, who declares that 'If UNISIST, the organisation of specialised bibliographical information on an international basis, is fully to achieve its aim, it must rest on the foundation of UBC, the recording of general bibliographical information on a national basis';[9] and he points out that the world centre for the collection of data for the International Serials Data System, ISDS, which is a key element in the UNISIST programme, has been established in a national library – the Bibliothèque Nationale in Paris – thus emphasising the vital importance, for the success of the UNISIST and UBC programmes, of an adequate institutional basis.

Within Unesco itself, UBC is still clearly seen as having closer links with NATIS than with UNISIST. A recent report on the Eighteenth Session of the Unesco General Conference records that the approved programme for documentation, libraries and archives provides for 'a new project for the improvement of bibliographical control which could ultimately be expanded into universal bibliographical control',[10] and a joint Unesco/IFLA conference is to be held in 1977 to further the aims of UBC within the NATIS concept. It is clearly only a matter of time before these three programmes, UNISIST, NATIS and UBC, are fully integrated, together with other library and information operations, within the Unesco Secretariat; and this must inevitably lead to a more integrated approach to these three aspects of the same central problem in the wider world outside. The problems of overlapping responsibilities for libraries, documentation and information services within the Unesco programme, important though they are to the future development of such services throughout the world, constitute only one aspect of the many and much more serious problems confronting Unesco at the present time, which may have equally important effects in the library and information field.

At the Seventeenth Session of the Unesco General Conference in 1972, the Director-General submitted for consideration by the Conference a Medium-Term Outline Plan for 1973–78. This plan was not accepted as such by the Conference, which asked the Director-General instead to prepare, for presentation at the Eighteenth Session, a document analysing major world problems in Unesco's field of competence and including a table of objectives arranged in order of priority which would serve as the basis for a new Draft Six-Year Outline Plan to be submitted for consideration by the Nineteenth Session of the General Conference in 1976. The document[11] submitted to the Eighteenth Session identified twelve key problems in four main problem areas, and proposed solutions to these problems in a list of fifty-nine objectives. Whilst the four main problem areas – respect for human rights and the establishment of conditions for peace, development of man and society, balance and harmony of man and nature and communication between people and exchange of information – were retained intact, the Conference reduced the number of problems to be considered to ten, and the number of objectives to thirty-seven; and on this basis, the Director-General was asked to prepare a medium-term plan covering the period 1977–1982. If this plan is adopted by the Nineteenth Session of the General Conference, five years will have elapsed since the submission of the original plan for 1973–78; five years of increasing difficulty for the Organisation on many fronts, not least that of attempting to initiate and promote, in the library and information field as in others, long-term programmes of action without an agreed long- or medium-term policy and plan to provide a firm framework.

Among other problems have been the clashes of opinion arising from the adoption of predetermined political stances, which have been an increasingly noticeable feature of the General Conference proceedings in recent years. At the close of the Eighteenth Session in 1974, these conflicts had reached such proportions that the new Director-General, Mr Amadou Mahtar M'Bow, was constrained to declare that 'I cannot pretend that I have not felt some anxiety about the future of the Organisation because of the serious dissensions which have emerged within the General Conference in the last few days, some of which could easily have been overcome'; and he made a plea for delegates to rise above their unavoidable differences of opinion in the cause of international co-operation and the future development of mankind.[12]

Political disagreements are not the only cause for anxiety about the future of Unesco. Its present and future financial position is serious, due in no small part to the fact that many Member States are substantially in arrears with their subscriptions; and the structure and functioning of the General Conference itself is now stretching the Organisation's facilities – and the health of its staff – to breaking point, with no less than 279 meetings, 789 documents and 482 draft resolutions in 1974. The rates of implementation of Unesco operational projects have declined substantially in the last three years, and there is an urgent need for the development, not only of means of assuring more effective operational action, but also of improving programming methods and the evaluation of programme activities.

Faced with problems of this magnitude, and despite the determination of the new Director-General and his staff to tackle them energetically, it cannot be said that the future of Unesco is completely assured. Without the whole-hearted support of Member States, and of non-governmental organisations such as IFLA, FID and ICA, there must remain the ever-present danger that, at any time in the next few years, Unesco could cease to exist. The implications of such an event for the future of world library development – and of many other fields of activity – would be catastrophic. Whatever the faults and failings of the Organisation, there can be little doubt that its achievements, since its establishment in 1946, have been substantial, in the library and information field as in others; and it is hard to envisage how the future development of such programmes as UNISIST, NATIS and UBC could proceed satisfactorily without the backing of Unesco – or another body of the same kind.

Even if the extreme of the total collapse of Unesco is avoided, the effectiveness of its activities in the future could be seriously diminished if the problems referred to above are not soon solved. This would inevitably affect, not only the Organisation's own operations in the library and information field, but also those of bodies such as IFLA, which rely so heavily on Unesco support for their own programme activites.

IFLA itself is in the throes of an organisational review at the present time, and a Draft Medium-Term Programme for 1975–80, compiled by the Programme Development Group and presented to the 41st General Council meeting in Oslo in 1975, not only contained detailed proposals for the restructuring of the Federation itself, but also included no less than seventy-eight programme activities covering a wide variety of professional topics. Presenting the Programme for consideration by the Council meeting on 11 August, 1975, the President emphasised that, whilst the Programme Development Group had incorporated some of its own ideas in the programme, it had 'first and foremost . . . respected the plans as formulated by the groups themselves in reports, resolutions, statements, letters, etc'.[13] Important though such respect for the views of the various sections and committees may be, it has in this instance clearly been responsible for a programme of such scope and diversity as to recall to mind the description of the proposals put before the First Session of the Unesco General Conference in 1946 as 'a parade of hobby horses'.

Among the proposals included in the programme are a mixture of forward-looking activities relating to UBC and UNISIST, the study of national planning methods for library services and the creation within IFLA of a forum for the study of planning and management, and activities which, for all their importance, call

International Directions

forth echoes from the past, such as 'the role of public libraries in adult education' – the subject of one of Unesco's earliest international seminars in 1950 – and 'the administration of large libraries with departments for different functions or materials'. The problems of compiling a meaningful and coherent programme for an organisation such as IFLA are very considerable, and not to be underestimated; nevertheless, it seems unfortunate that the opportunity was not taken to emulate the Director-General of Unesco and begin by attempting to identify a small number of key areas of concern, and within these then to establish a limited number of objectives designed to produce solutions to the problems in an integrated and effective manner. The very presentation of the Medium-Term Programme in terms of type of library and library function is itself on the verge of becoming out of date, and certainly inappropriate for the presentation of a development programme, if the NATIS concept of integrated systems and user-oriented services with minimal emphasis on institutional barriers has any validity at all. There is also evident a rather worrying degree of naïvety in the planning field in the presentation of a five-year development programme two-thirds of the way through the year in which it is meant to take effect.

The problems of IFLA, like those of Unesco, are to some extent problems of size; and it is interesting to note that both the new Director-General of Unesco and the President of IFLA referred, in the documents mentioned above, to the near-universality of their respective organisations' membership. This is clearly an essential prerequisite if these organisations are to act as suitable forums for the discussion of the many problems which will attend the transfer of wealth and technology to developing countries in the future, but it does create very serious practical problems of organisation and management, and if IFLA's problems have not yet quite reached the same crisis level as those of Unesco, the volume of documentation and the number of scheduled – and unscheduled – meetings at IFLA General Council meetings must give grounds for similar concern.

These considerations are particularly relevant in view of the possibility, at some time in the perhaps not too distant future, of some form of amalgamation taking place between IFLA, FID and ICA, and possibly other international library and information organisations. The three non-governmental organisations mentioned have for some time been acting in concert in their relationships with Unesco, and a joint policy core group was set up at the 40th IFLA General Council meeting in 1974 to liaise with Unesco on matters related to the long-term programme for NATIS.[14] This development is but one reflection of the increasing awareness among professionals in all three associated fields that they share a common interest and a common core of professional knowledge and responsibility, and it can be only a matter of time before the three bodies establish a closer relationship, perhaps leading eventually to their total integration. Such a move would bring many benefits in its train, not least in enabling the 'information professions' to speak with one voice on the international scene; but it would also bring increased problems of size, excessive bureaucratisation and the stifling of individual initiative, and firm steps would have to be taken to guard against these dangers as far as possible.

It is unlikely that any international organisation of this kind, operating on the basis of delegated representatives of various member organisations, would ever be able to rid itself wholly of these problems, and there may well be a place, in the not too distant future, for an international association of individual librarians which would provide for personal membership of those interested in international librarianship itself – a topic which has received little attention from the major existing international bodies in the library field, and which might best be studied within the framework of such a separate organisation. International librarianship is, after all, a form of international co-operation, and, as such, is deserving of intensive and continued study in an effort to understand its processes and problems more fully.

A Delphi survey on the future of comparative librarianship carried out by S. Simsova for the International and Comparative Librarianship Group (ICLG) of the Library Association in 1974[15] demonstrated a considerable degree of support for the idea of establishing a 'Comparative Librarianship Society' on an international basis. If, as the present writer suggested in an earlier paper,[16] comparative librarianship is essentially a research method which can be effectively applied in the international field, it may be more logical to establish an 'International Librarianship Society' which had a clear commitment to the study of the international aspects of comparative librarianship. At present, the ICLG is the only professional group concerned with the promotion and study of international and comparative librarianship as such, and, like other groups of the Library Association, its role hitherto has been primarily to provide a forum for discussion. Under the recently approved proposals[17] for the restructuring of the Library Association, the ICLG, along with other groups and sections, will be able to exert direct influence on Association policy within its field of competence. Recognising the important implications of this new development, the Group's committee, at a meeting in October, 1975, established a small working party to draft preliminary proposals with regard to the Association's future policy in the international field, which it hopes will receive serious consideration by the newly restructured management of the Association.

The preparation and consideration of these initial proposals should be only the beginning of a continuing process of interaction between the Library Association's policymakers and those of its members with an interest in international librarianship and a concern for the Association's role in the international field. For this interaction to be effective, it will be essential to ensure that the membership at large – not just of the ICLG – is kept informed of major trends and developments in the international field, and their possible implications for British librarianship.

The future of librarianship is going to be international. Developments such as UNISIST, UBC and NATIS will affect the daily working lives of library and information workers at all levels, and it will be vitally necessary to keep all of them fully informed on such matters through the adequate dissemination of information through sources which will be read by all librarians, not merely through those internationally-oriented journals which are read mainly by those already interested in the field.

Contemporary British librarianship will have much to offer by way of example to foreign visitors to the Library Association Centenary Conference in 1977, and has played an important part in many of the significant international developments in recent years. British librarians and information scientists have contributed much to the development of UNISIST and its more specialised offshoots, and to UBC; and if Britain has still a long way to go towards the full implementation of the NATIS concept, the first steps have been taken with the establishment of the British Library, and in one sense, at least, Britain may be leading the way towards the eventual integration of these programmes by extending the terms of reference and membership of the British National Committee for UNISIST to cover both the UNISIST and the NATIS programmes.[18] These and other recent developments on the British scene will doubtless be the subjects of considerable interest and discussion by overseas visitors to the Centenary Conference; and it is important that British librarians, too, should be kept fully informed about them. As far as the Library Association is concerned, a better-informed membership will be better equipped to contribute, through the newly-opened channels mentioned above, to the formulation of sound international policies for the Association; and perhaps a well-conceived, long-term policy statement, setting forth the Association's views on its future role with regard to UNISIST, UBC, NATIS and the whole question of the transfer of technology and resources in the library and information field to the developing countries, could have the same widespread influence and long-term impact on the participants in its Centenary Conference as did the discussion of the Kenyon Report and the foundation of the International Library and Bibliographical Committee fifty years ago.

References in text

1. Parker, J. Stephen. International librarianship – a reconnaissance. *J. Librarianship,* 6 (4) October 1974, 219–232.
2. *Sunday Times,* 14 September 1975.
3. *Economist,* 20 September 1975.
4. The eighteenth session of the General Conference. *Unesco Chronicle,* 20 (12) December 1974, 411–421, p. 413.

International Directions

5. Unesco. General Conference. 18th session, Paris, 1974. *Report on the activities of the UNISIST Steering Committee.* Paris, Unesco, 12 July 1974. 18 C/78.
6. Unesco. General Conference. 18th session, Paris, 1974. *Draft programme and budget for 1975–1976.* Paris, Unesco, 1974. 18 C/5, p. XXVII.
7. *ibid.*, p. XXIII.
8. *ibid.*, p. XXVII.
9. Chaplin, A. H. Basic bibliographic control; plans for a world system. *Aslib Proc.*, 27 (2) February 1975, 48–56, p. 55.
10. The eighteenth session of the General Conference, *op. cit.*, p. 415.
11. Unesco. General Conference. 18th session. Paris, 1974. *Analysis of problems and table of objectives to be used as a basis for medium-term planning (1977–1982).* Paris, Unesco, 1974. 18 C/4.
12. Unesco in the last quarter of the 20th century. *Unesco Chronicle,* 20 (12) December 1974, 422–442, p. 423.
13. International Federation of Library Associations. Programme Development Group. *Draft medium-term programme, 1975–1980; working document for the 41st General Council meeting to be held at Oslo, 11–16 August 1975.* The Hague, IFLA, 1975.
14. Liaison IFLA/FID/ICA. *IFLA J.,* 1 (3) 1975, 239.
15. Simsova, Sylva, *and others. Comparative librarianship; the next ten years: an exercise in the Delphi technique. In* Library Association. International and Comparative Librarianship Group. Conference, Scotland, 1974. *Proceedings.* London, ICLG, 1974. pp. 75–87.
16. Parker, J. Stephen, *op. cit.*
17. Restructuring the Association; the Working Party on Association Services. *Libr. Ass. Rec.,* 77 (10) October 1975, Supplement.
18. British National Committee for UNISIST and NATIS. *British Library Research and Development Newsletter,* 4, July 1975, 8.

Chapter Thirteen

Hospital Libraries and Service to the Handicapped

The multidisciplinary professional library in the hospital/Jenny Wade

It is not easy to look into the future at all, and to decide exactly how far to look brings even more problems. The usual distance chosen by those who attempt to survey our professional future seems to be ten years, which would take me well past the notable date of 1984. However, this particular year has ceased to be so significant and fearful a landmark as it appeared in 1949. The future arrives so quickly that it would seem necessary to look further, and perhaps a more suitable date around which I may construct an imaginary future is 2001, less than thirty years distant, and with slightly more hopeful literary associations than those so inseparably linked with Big Brother.

It seems likely that, despite the assurances of present day planners, our current crop of new hospitals will be as outdated in thirty years as pre-war hospitals are today. Thanks to a growing awareness of the importance of information services for health professionals during the past decade, most new hospital buildings include a library of some description. Many are inadequate, some may be well enough equipped to deal with current demand, but almost all have been conceived as traditional bibliographic information centres. Indeed, it is difficult to persuade the medical and allied professions to accept a library service which is any less traditional in approach than themselves. New techniques may be grafted on to the old stem, but there is little real acceptance of the need to uproot the whole plant and develop a totally new approach to information storage and dissemination in order to cope with the requirements of the future. It is, however, hardly possible that hospital libraries in the year 2001 will still operate with methods as close to the traditional techniques of librarianship as they do today.

A great temptation in writing about prospects for the future is to construct an imaginary picture of the twenty-first century library and its services. Such a picture should certainly contain an impressive array of technical equipment, since the present growth in the importance of technology in librarianship and information science can only accelerate. It will also, and comfortingly, contain people, since an interaction between people who are sick and people who are skilled in some aspect of caring for the sick is the very essence of the hospital and health services.

In my picture of the future of library services for health professionals I shall concentrate on two areas: people, and the use of machines and technology. I make no apology for omitting the book which, while still physically unsurpassed as a vehicle for information storage, will without doubt have a less important role in the future literature of the health sciences, simply because of production time lags. The emphasis is now on speed of communication in medicine and science, and even the periodical in its present form is not an ideal medium for high speed dissemination of information. The future would seem to belong to communication methods less constricted by physical format and more adapted to fast and cheap production and distribution.

There is no shortage of current literature describing the necessity for comprehensive library services in hospitals. 'Medical' libraries are slowly becoming 'health science' libraries. The unfortunate and misleading term 'integrated library' which was used to describe the new type of service to all health professionals is now being replaced by the cumbersome but more accurate term 'multidisciplinary professional library'.

The number of distinct professions and occupations to be found in the modern hospital and health service approaches a hundred, and most of these need a continuous flow of information in order to update their knowledge for day-to-day requirements and for support in fresh training courses. In addition to a knowledge of the literature of medicine, in itself an extensive and demanding subject, the hospital librarian must become familiar with material in the diverse fields of nursing, public health, all of the paramedical professional subjects such as radiography and occupational therapy, as well as administration and management, sociology, social welfare, some engineering, and probably computing for good measure. Some hospital librarians may also be responsible for providing a service to patients, and will thus require ten days in every working week.

It is to be hoped that the future will produce a rearrangement of the system of provision of libraries in hospitals so that the two branches of the service, work with patients and work with health professionals, will be staffed separately by specialist librarians. It is not possible to discern more than a slight trend towards this at present, but at least its desirability is recognised. The current practice of appointing hospital librarians with dual responsibility certainly creates administrative difficulties for them, but it has another major disadvantage. Through lack of time and excessive commitments the librarian is unable to develop a full professional relationship with the potential users of the library.

A hospital librarian needs detailed knowledge of the information needs of each of the library's clients, of their work and the stresses and constraints which it imposes, and of the activities and problems of the hospital 'society' in general. Work with patients demands a similar knowledge of the hospital and of patients, their physical and psychological problems and the therapeutic potential of the library to them. However, a librarian encumbered by dual responsibilities is likely to be able to develop neither relationship adequately.

It is now a commonplace that in health sciences the growth of published literature is such that no individual can read all relevant material. The future of hospital library services must include a significant contribution to the solution, or at least easing, of this problem for its clients. If it cannot do this then there is no justification for its existence, and it is precisely here

Hospital Libraries

that a knowledge of the client's professional activities is important for the librarian. Through the provision of a personalised information service, filling the specific requirements of individuals or groups within the hospital, a library can make a positive contribution to patient care. This requires an active information dissemination programme, and immediately raises problems of provision, access to, and storage of material. Further there is the question of the desirability of extending the involvement of the health sciences librarian in direct contact with the patient as a member of the clinical team, responsible for information provision on individual cases.

The next thirty years must bring a more rational distribution of health information resources. There is a wealth of medical and associated literature in the libraries of Britain, and updating these collections is becoming more expensive with each passing year. If small hospital libraries are to have easy access to such material as the full Excerpta Medica abstracting service, they must be part of a larger information network. Such networks, containing one or two large centres and a number of smaller libraries, permit more effective planning of acquisitions policies, and facilitate the purchase of expensive material, as well as the provision of more extensive information dissemination service. These merits are well known, and do not require elaboration here. Fortunately, there is now a trend towards the establishment of such networks, and although progress has been relatively slow, the year 2001 should see such systems well established throughout Britain rather than limited to a few favoured areas as at present.

Regionally organised library networks will also help to ease the difficult problem of storage of old and less used material. However, it seems unlikely that many libraries, even library networks, will still continue the attempt to preserve files of periodicals in hard copy. The change to storage of back runs in microform is at present accelerating, and this must continue if libraries specialising in any of the scientific subjects are to maintain comprehensive collections.

A major difficulty which must be overcome if microform storage is to become a reality in health science libraries is the re-education of readers in the use of this type of material. While librarians have long recognised the need for, and value of, microform as a method of storing older material, the reader is still reluctant to use it. An important reason for its present unpopularity, in addition to purely traditional dislike of non-book material, is the lack of a small, cheap but efficient microform reader. Development of such a reader should not be too great a technological achievement to expect in an age of miniaturisation of equipment. Until the microform develops some of the attributes which make the book so convenient, such as portability and easy access, it will not be possible to make it the important part of hospital library stock which it so clearly should become.

Even a full acceptance of the microform will only provide half a solution to the problem of access to the whole of periodical literature in the health sciences. A simple reduction in the physical size of a serials collection in this way obviously does not reduce either the total number of articles contained within it, or the number of new periodicals published month by month. It is necessary to obtain access to this flood of information, which is unlikely to abate in the future, even though it may not rise at the startling rate which has been predicted. In order to do this effectively there seems to be only one answer for the future: the increased use of computer technology. At the time of writing, the development of the use of on-line systems for access to medical literature is in its infancy in Britain. The use of MEDLARS (MEDical Literature Analysis and Retrieval System) is well established, but its on-line facility, MEDLINE, is a recent arrival, and the number of terminals available is limited. The use of other similar services, such as CANCERLINE, is also restricted. Without doubt, by the time that this volume is published a larger number of hospital libraries will be equipped with MEDLINE terminals. Far more librarians will have been trained in the techniques of on-line information retrieval, and some library users will be able to carry out their own literature searches using this method. By the end of the century the present MEDLINE will certainly have been replaced several times by improved systems, but there can be no question that this type of automated information retrieval will form a vital part of the health science library of the future.

Developments of this kind may still wear something of a science fiction air for the harassed librarian in the average district general hospital. Perhaps it would be as well to return for the moment from technology to people. An important requirement for the future of the hospital library is a change of the attitudes of all those involved in the provision and use of this type of service. I have already mentioned the need for the librarian to develop fully his or her professional relationship with the various professions which are users, or potential users, of the hospital library. This implies the increased acceptance of the librarian as a member of the health team, and raises the interesting question of whether the health sciences librarian has a place in the hospital wards, working more directly with the clinician in order to provide information at first hand, rather than at second hand in the library, as at present. Two recent reports from the United States[1] describe projects, funded by the National Library of Medicine, which aim to study the effectiveness of 'clinical librarians in patient care – teaching settings'. The 'clinical' librarians taking part in these projects are library based, but attend clinical ward teaching rounds regularly with the team of clinicians and other health professionals. During these rounds they aim to gain a more exact picture of the information needs of those in the health care team. In addition they have developed an entirely new system of information dissemination in the form of sets of bibliographies and key articles, relevant to the condition of a specific patient, which are attached to that patient's record chart for consultation during ward rounds.

This more intimate involvement of the librarian with patient care raises a number of ethical questions, and may perhaps prove unacceptable in Britain. However, it is an exciting development in an area of librarianship which is already dynamic, and it may point towards a new trend in librarian – clinician – patient relationships. British librarians will possibly feel that there is little likelihood of their acceptance in such a team, when full acceptance of professions more obviously involved in care and treatment of the patient is still developing very slowly.

A major problem in introducing the concept of the multidisciplinary professional library in the hospital has been traditionalism in the medical profession. The difficulty in some centres of even altering the name of the 'medical' library to 'health sciences' library or something similar is symptomatic of the whole situation. Many nurses and paramedical professionals still hesitate to cross the threshold of a room which has traditionally been doctor's territory, and each newly appointed librarian discovers that it is necessary to supply considerable proof of professional competence before any acceptance by medical users of the library can be obtained. The challenge, needless to say, is rewarding and stimulating, but an important requirement for the future must be re-education of members of the various health professions to accept each other, and the librarian, as equal members of a team whose primary concern is the welfare of the patient. The maintenance of outdated professional privileges has no part to play in this process.

If this desirable state of affairs is to be reached, considerable attention must be given to the training and education of those librarians who seek acceptance as professional colleagues by those whose training has been long and whose responsibilities are considerable. The emergence of a graduate library profession can do no harm in this respect, and if more life sciences graduates can be attracted into hospital librarianship, so much the better. At the same time, however, the practical aspects of our profession must not be forgotten in academic ivory towers. In addition, once appointed, the hospital librarian must be given, and accept, more responsibility as a departmental head in the hospital structure.

Although I have stressed the importance of the place of the hospital librarian in patient care teams for the future, patient care is not the only activity in hospitals. The librarian must expect to provide support for research activities, and the amount of research in district general hospitals is likely to increase in the next decades. A third major activity, for which an effective library service is vitally important, is training and continuing education. A telling sentence in the Merrison Report[2] emphasises the need for the newly qualified doctor to 'recognise the limitations of his own knowledge and abilities and ... be prepared for a career in medicine that is based upon continuing education'. This applies equally to all health professions, and while the value of a well organised library service to support the training and education of hospital staff is recognised, there is considerable scope for development of the library's role in this area. The nurse in training and after basic qualification, the postgraduate clinician, paramedical personnel and administrators are all involved in study for higher degrees, diplomas and a multiplicity of courses. The time may yet come when district general hospitals provide clinical experience courses as part of an Open University degree in medicine. All need study material and study facilities from the library, which should be able to anticipate the demand rather than simply attempting to cope with it as it occurs. In an article which encouragingly describes the hospital library as 'an awakening giant', Charles Stewart, an American hospital administrator, emphasises the future importance of hospital libraries as learning centres.

Changes in kinds of illnesses and patients, development of out-patient preventive care programs, an increased emphasis on teaching programs all will have an impact on the hospital library. The hospital library is developing into both an information center and a learning center. Hospital personnel, both professional and non-professional in all departments, are becoming more and more education oriented and they are looking to the library for guidance and support.[3]

Such support must now and in the future include the provision of not only books and periodicals, but also many kinds of audiovisual materials for use in group teaching and for self-instruction. The value of this form of material is well established, and it is becoming increasingly popular with users of hospital libraries. In particular the tape–slide programme has attained an important position in many areas of education and training. However, the major growth point for the future in this field would seem to be the use of videotape systems. It is easy to appreciate the extra value given to a programme when it is actually made in, and for the requirements of, the individual hospital where it is to be used for training. The videotape system and closed circuit television have so much obvious value in the hospital situation that their use is certain to spread, particularly when economic constraints lessen.

However, developments of this kind are only achieved at the expense of simplicity, and while an expert is not required to use a slide viewer, a trained technician is necessary in order to operate videotape and closed circuit television systems. It may be that when the use of audiovisual aids in hospitals generally reaches this stage of sophistication the librarian will not be justified in seeking to retain involvement. Still, it would be regrettable if the future saw a complete divorce between the activities of the librarian and the media technician, since however complex the equipment used, the basic educational material is no more than an extension of the book. Perhaps the answer is inclusion of courses on educational media technology in the librarian's training.

Involvement of the librarian with education will not be able to stop at the hospital gates. Since the 1974 reorganisation of the National Health Service there has been an increasing interaction between health and social service staff working in the community and those in the hospital itself. Community health staff now look to the hospital library for day-to-day information and support in education. They cannot find, and should not be expected to look for, a specialised health science library service in the local branch of their public library, which is not equipped for this, either in stock or appropriately trained staff. It seems likely that distinctions between community and hospital based health service staff will continue to disappear as emphasis on preventive medicine grows and health care becomes less hospital based. There will at some time be a case for opening information units in local health centres, perhaps another opportunity for on-line links or some kind of videophone complete with printer for reproduction of documents held in a central file. But these really are flights of fancy for the year 2001.

Long before that, there must be a serious consideration of the need to supply the sick and their families with more information on health matters. As the effects of current health education programmes in the community become more obvious, the general public will be increasingly articulate, and will require more information from those who provide health care than these professions at present feel that the 'layman' has a right to request. The hospital librarian should now be considering the potential role of library services in this situation. There is scope for action now, and opportunities should be grasped and exploited as they present themselves.

Health science librarianship is frequently described as a dynamic field, but this is no more than a necessary response to the dynamic nature of the health sciences themselves, to changing patterns of health care, and the requirements of the library clientele. This in turn, as Estelle Brodman has described,[4] reflects the dynamism of contemporary society. Hospital libraries must continue to possess this characteristic in the future, despite economic difficulties and possible public and professional disenchantment with the whole concept of the National Health Service. If this can be done then prospects for the next few decades in this field of librarianship will be both exciting and challenging.

Library services for hospital patients, prisoners and housebound readers / Brian Cooper

Although library services for health professionals and those they serve are considered separately, a total hospital library service is more than a service to professional staff plus a service to patients. The whole is greater than the sum of its parts. Access to and knowledge of patients quite often comes through service to professionals and sympathetic understanding of the library needs of patients is often awakened by the librarian, who encourages and helps health care professionals with their own reading. The staff member who is introduced by the hospital librarian to picture books suitable for his own children is half way towards understanding the possibilities of books for the mentally handicapped patients he cares for and he is certainly going to be sympathetic towards the librarian's plans for a library service to the mentally handicapped.

The integrated library has confused the issue for through it we have brought recreational reading to the patient and information to the professional staff. Appreciating the value of recreational reading and that of information are not at all the same thing and I should like to see the incipient trend for nurses, doctors, psychologists and warders and patients and prisoners to receive a common library service of recreational reading continue. It is the non-reading nurse or doctor who refuses to allow or admit book trolleys on the wards, for books are of a very low priority to them. Hospitals are very different in location, size and function, but it is clear that in most hospitals if library services can be combined in a single area there are economies of staffing and transport to be achieved. Clearly, the library with a single professional librarian giving a service to staff and and patients is a first stage of library development, and as the service develops additional staff are needed and there has to be a division of function. Many new large general hospitals have divided professional and patient services and made them physically separate. This is alright for hospitals with great wealth who can afford separate professional library and patient library staff structures, but it is highly unsatisfactory for the vast majority of hospitals and runs contrary to the concept of total library use in which one hopes that professional men and women read novels, poetry, plays and biographies. Hopefully the last quarter of the twentieth century will see full appreciation and support given to this holistic approach to hospital library services.

Librarians concerned with hospital patients, prisoners, the mentally handicapped and the housebound have brought a new dimension of caring and concern to their professional work. They see suffering humanity and they want to do something about it and the job becomes more than books. Librarians on housebound visiting become the friends of their readers and provide support and information about the outside world, reveal the mysteries of form filling, listen to the stories of the mantlepiece photographs, and provide thoughtfully chosen reading. These qualitative caring services are very time consuming, but they represent one of the highest achievements of our profession in a period when increasingly the able have fallen victims to computers, magnetic timetables and

Hospital Libraries

management needs. Bookmen have declined and this breed of caring librarian, bookman by necessity and inclination, and humanitarian by inclination, represents a hope for the future.

There are unchanging qualities about hospital librarians; they now have both a tradition and a future and the present author is an adamant sentimentalist, proud of the great hospital library tradition and 'hooked' on the looks of delight on the faces of his readers when he brings the 'right' book at the 'right' time. One hopes that from this tradition of the hospital and institution librarian there will emerge in the present generation outstanding men and women who will lift the library profession as a whole to a higher level of caring and bookmanship. They will spearhead a new humble 'reader-centred' librarianship and in this lies the true hope of our profession; they represent civilisation in a systems-dominated world. A note of pessimism: there will be no change of heart, the band will remain small, the managers and organisers will pay lip service and see no readers, the lecturers will withdraw further behind more theses and will increasingly lose touch as their professional experience – often very slender – recedes into the distant past; but hospital librarian, as you read this, do not despair; the band has always been small but it has survived through its belief in people, loyalty and friendship and because it has revelled in books and service and these are satisfaction enough.

The world will not get better; if there is economic decline the needs of suffering humanity will be greatly increased and we must needs become a true caring profession. Current obsessions with hours of duty and parity between professions have produced the meanest breed of people we have yet seen on this island. We who traffic in the records of man's thoughts, travels and dreams must not stoop to those levels. We must show our profession an example of service and care; we will visit the sick, the lonely, the insane and the incarcerated and be proud and confident of the balm we bear. Our pride must be in service to our readers.

A hospital to most people is a general hospital, but there are others, mostly neglected by librarians or given a basic book box service such as the great stone-and-brick mental subnormality hospitals. They may have populations of up to two thousand, many of whom will be old and illiterate, for whom the hospital is home. Society put them away and now promises to integrate them into the community in other people's streets. The long-suffering staff who care for them are condemned by society on the slightest suggestion of malpractice, and little thought is given to the stresses under which they work and occasionally break. In settings like these libraries are beginning to play a meaningful role and this will grow. They contribute to the quality of life, the maintenance of human dignity and help to combat the institutionalization both of staff and patients. Libraries should emerge as the great catalysts of this type of hospital. Staff rediscover themselves and regenerate their relationships with their wives and children through books; through their own appreciation of the library they become aware of its value for those they care for. The borrowing and returning of books, caring for them, looking at their pictures, turning their pages, these are highly satisfying social skills and activities which have on the whole been denied to the mentally handicapped patient. Hopefully the King's Fund paper, *A Library service for the mentally handicapped*[5], will become the blueprint for such libraries and we shall see resource centres with stimulating toys, music, and books making their appearance in subnormality hospitals. These libraries will require librarians who can work confidently with other professionals and feed them with books, information and news of innovations.

In all types of hospital and institution, libraries should increasingly emphasize their capacity to provide peace, quiet and a measure of privacy to combat the stress of communal living. Hospital libraries will reconsider their functions and peace and a quiet pace must be able to rule at least in one area. Bustling activity may satisfy the librarian, but it may be anathema to the elderly library user. A quiet read or browse can still lift, calm and heal and delicious privacy rearrange our scattered thoughts.

For many years, we in England have talked of bibliotherapy whilst our North American colleagues have put it into practice. To many the name sounds pretentious and we are put off, but

Hospital Libraries

Eleanor Brown's *Bibliotherapy and its widening applications*,[6] which may prove to be a landmark in the history of bibliotherapy, helps us to distinguish clearly between the 'art of bibliotherapy' and the 'science of bibliotherapy'. The art of bibliotherapy involves a reader with a mental or physical problem: a sympathetic and unusually perceptive individual with a broad knowledge of human psychology and books. The science of bibliotherapy involves a member of the medical profession drawing on the librarian's knowledge and skill to prescribe reading material for a specifically diagnosed complaint. As more and more psychiatric hospitals appoint librarians, bibliotherapy both as a science and an art should increasingly be practised in Great Britain in the latter quarter of the twentieth century. It would be sad if the implementation of so useful and beneficial a practice should be delayed because of disputes about definitions. Margaret Monroe in a 1968 address at the University of Wisconsin Library School said,

Is there a correct definition? Obviously none is agreed upon. Let me suggest that the essence of help through books is more important than the term 'bibliotherapy'. We must not let our uneasiness and insecurity about our proper function mislead us into irrelevant bickering on terminology. Let us spend our energies exploring what books can do for people and how we as librarians can help.[7]

Possibly in prison libraries will be seen the greatest progress as librarians become more skilful in personal relations with other professionals. Progress has been held back by the inability of librarians to win the confidence of prison staff. Perhaps the way ahead may be to begin to supply good services to the staff themselves. The first full-time professionals who are appointed to prisons will have a very grave responsibility, for the success or failure of their efforts will set the pattern for a long time to come. Custodial staffs in most kinds of institutions feel threatened by incoming professionals and are very reluctant to co-operate until the 'comer-in' has shown that he or she is sympathetically disposed towards their difficulties. If librarians come forward who can win the confidence of the custodial staff, then we shall see a higher level of library service in prisons. The part that libraries can play in tense and stressful institutions, such as prisons, cannot be overestimated. Their contributions towards the quality of life could be enormous. The librarians who take on these early full-time prison posts should be given all the support possible by their fellow librarians as the prestige of the whole profession would benefit from a successful development in the prison library field.

With so much emphasis on maintaining community contact by the aged and the infirm and with the very high cost of housebound visiting, some real move towards bringing people to libraries by buses or other means of transport should develop. Nurses of geriatric patients constantly emphasise the value of 'getting out' and no doubt we shall see this practice developed on a modest scale. It may even become common practice as our population ages. The mentally handicapped and physically handicapped too would benefit from library excursions.

As the needs of various handicapped, housebound and imprisoned groups grow from current library practice, all these services will be outstripped by the demand they stimulate and, depending on economic conditions, staffing adjustments made. Librarians will have to work hand in hand with volunteers and organise their services in order to bring to the public the talents of volunteers. The careful selection of volunteers will become regular practice.

The capacity of various reading aids and books to improve the quality of life is hardly known to the general public. The public must be made aware of them and demand them from public finance. Too often public libraries and social services work to keep their most vocal users quiet. The disabled need champions and the general public will, hopefully, champion them when they are fully aware of the provisions of the Chronically Sick and Disabled Persons Act, 1970.[8]

Throughout history the tiny flame of altruism has kept alight and distinguished man from his animal companions and the caring section of our profession must fan this flame if the highest ideals of our profession are to survive the great leap forward into a systems-dominated world.

References in text

1. Algermissen, Virginia. Biomedical librarians in a patient care setting at the University of Missouri – Kansas City School of Medicine. *Bull. Med. Libr. Ass.*, 62 (4) 1974, 354–358.
and
National Library of Medicine. Clinical librarians accompany physicians on ward rounds. *Nat. Libr. Med. News,* 29 (11) 1974, 3.
2. *Report of the Committee of Inquiry into the Regulation of the Medical Profession.* Chairman: Dr A. W. Merrison. London, HMSO, 1975, 25. (Cmnd 6018).
3. Stewart, C. C. Your hospital library – an awakening giant. *Hosp. Top.,* 53 (3) 1975, 6, 46–48.
4. Brodman, Estelle. Users of health science libraries. *Libr. Trends,* 23 (1) 1974, 63–72.
5. King's Fund Centre. *A library service for the mentally handicapped.* King's Fund Centre, 1973.
6. Brown, E. F. *Bibliotherapy and its widening applications.* Metuchen, New Jersey, Scarecrow Press, 1975, p. 10.
7. Monroe, M. E. Reader services and bibliotherapy. In: *Reading guidance and bibliotherapy in public, hospital and institution libraries.* Edited by Margaret E. Monroe. Madison: University of Wisconsin, Library School, 1971, 42.
8. Chronically Sick and Disabled Persons Act 1970.

Chapter Fourteen

Future Library Co-operation and the British Library

Jean M Plaister

Library co-operation in its widest sense means the sharing of resources and the adherence to agreed standards which make such co-operation possible. It is interesting to reflect that the founders of the Library Association spent much time and thought in working out systems and standards for the administration and organisation of libraries and for the education of librarians, which provided a basis for movement of staff between libraries and the exploitation of resources by co-operation. One has only to think of the Anglo-American Cataloguing Rules 1908, the work on bibliography and charging methods in this country, as well as the development of classification schemes by Dewey and Cutter in the United States to appreciate the systems which became standards for libraries and librarians.

Once these standards had been developed and accepted, it would appear that for the next fifty years librarians were concerned with building up library systems, and that although the mechanics of library co-operation were developed, very little was done to investigate the fundamentals of library systems and management. It was, if you like, the era of the individual library and of the individual librarian. Services were being established to meet the needs of users; and librarians were devising schemes of classification for their own special collections and requirements. The wheel has now turned full circle and librarians and others have during the past decade been analysing and questioning the standards and systems which we use in our libraries.

Co-operation and the British Library

As early as 1942, Lionel McColvin in his Report on *The public library system of Great Britain*[1] was taking a hard look at public library provision in Britain, and this was a prelude to other studies and reports such as the reports of the Working Parties appointed by the Ministry of Education on *The standard of public library service in England and Wales* (1962),[2] and *Inter-Library co-operation in England and Wales* (1962),[3] the Dainton Committee Report on the National Libraries[4] and the National Libraries ADP Report by Maurice Line.[5]

It is interesting to speculate that the concept of the British Library, and the services it will provide, might not have been acceptable to many libraries forty years ago when the climate of thought favoured self-help and individualism.

It may well be that this self-examination and analysis of the library services of this country has prepared the ground for far-reaching developments in library co-operation and provided the framework in which the automation of library systems by the use of computers can play a part.

In attempting to prognosticate future developments and prospects in library co-operation it is necessary to make a number of assumptions:

i   That librarians accept that library co-operation is practical and apparently economic and will show benefits in the use of library and personnel resources extending beyond the purely cost effective;
ii That, given that there is no single body which has authority for a national library policy which would apply to all libraries, the principal co-ordinating bodies – the Department of Education and Science and the British Library – can count on voluntary co-operation and adherence to standards which would make co-operation effective;
iii That collaborative systems for library automation, and co-operation at all levels of development and use of computing systems in libraries are acceptable to librarians, and practical and economic in operation;

iv That the objectives of the British Library as set out in the White Paper (Cmnd 4572)[6] – **a** preserving and making available for reference at least one copy of every book and periodical of domestic origin and of as many overseas publications as possible (the aim will be to provide as comprehensive a reference service of last resort as possible – if a reader cannot get what he wants near at hand he will know he can find it in the British Library), **b** providing an efficient central lending and photocopying service in support of the other libraries and information systems of the country, and **c** providing central cataloguing and other bibliographic services related not only to the needs of the central libraries but to those of libraries and information centres throughout the country and in close co-operation with central libraries overseas – are implemented in accordance with the expressed intentions of the British Library Board.

In addition to making these assumptions it is also necessary to consider current trends and proposed developments in library co-operation. A whole new field of co-operation may be opened up if the proposals in the report on *Local library co-operation* by T. D. Wilson and W. A. J. Masterson of the University of Sheffield Postgraduate School of Librarianship[7] are implemented. This project financed by the Department of Education and Science investigated the library needs of those involved in higher education in a locality and the resources and services provided for these needs, and assessed the potential for and the means of implementing library co-operation and co-ordination in a locality. The transport system for inter-library loans in operation in the Yorkshire Region and the current investigations into a national transport system for inter-library loans may have a significant effect on the pattern of inter-library lending. The development of consortia such as the Birmingham Libraries Co-operative Mechanisation Project (BLCMP)[8] which provides cataloguing services based on MARC and is looking ahead to a joint acquisition system, and SWALCAP which covers the Universities of Bristol and Exeter and the University of Cardiff[9] and is involved in the installation of dedicated hardware to provide its members with automated circulation systems, are

Co-operation and the British Library

providing new avenues for co-operation.

We have in fact already progressed far beyond the original concept of inter-library lending as the sole component of library co-operation. Library co-operation now encompasses many library functions and exists at local, regional – in the sense of a group of geographically related libraries working together at a regional level – and national levels. There would appear to be a need to define the library functions and to identify those areas of responsibility which are best carried out at each level – local, regional and national.

There are so many strands involved in library co-operation, that it is difficult to talk about it without reference to a general system model. The diagram in Fig. 14.1, based on current practice and possible future developments, sets out a model which appears to be practical and also likely to permit or encourage co-operation. The model contains certain concepts about the structure of the British Library which do not necessarily coincide with present expressed intentions of the British Library Board, but which appear to be worthy of consideration. In order to simplify it, two major aspects of library functions have been identified:

i   Bibliographic Resource System – answering the question what is in theory available
ii Material Management System – how in practice it can be made accessible

The concept of a Bibliographic Resource System will depend on the implementation by the British Library of its objective to provide central cataloguing and other bibliographic services related not only to the needs of the central libraries, but to those of libraries and information centres throughout the country and in close co-operation with central libraries overseas. It implies that the British Library will develop as a matter of urgency its plans to establish a data base in machine-readable form which will be available on-line to individual libraries and regional centres. It also implies that librarians will be willing to accept within their systems bibliographic records prepared according to a nationally and internationally accepted standard.

Bibliographic Resource System
This is a fundamentally radial system centred on the National Bibliography, and concerned with the conceptual identification of books and other library material; it includes large scale information retrieval systems.

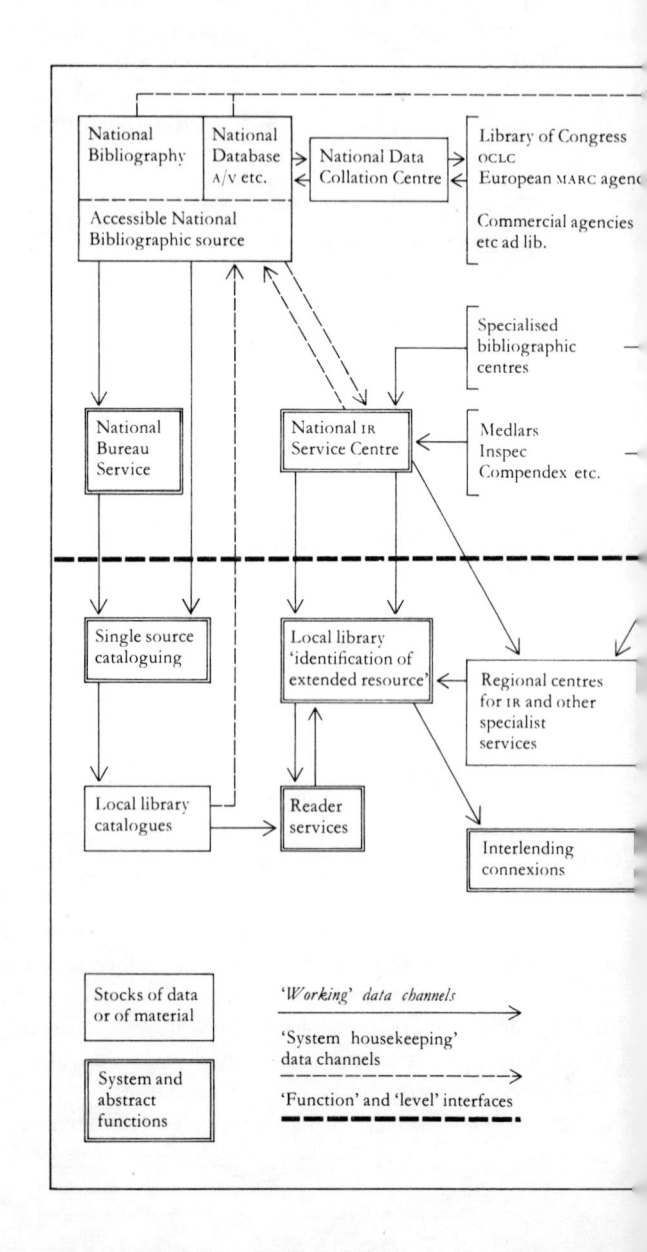

National Bibliography	National Database A/V etc.

National Data Collation Centre

Library of Congress
OCLC
European MARC agenc[y]
Commercial agencies etc ad lib.

Accessible National Bibliographic source

Specialised bibliographic centres

National Bureau Service

National IR Service Centre

Medlars
Inspec
Compendex etc.

Single source cataloguing

Local library 'identification of extended resource'

Regional centres for IR and other specialist services

Local library catalogues

Reader services

Interlending connexions

Stocks of data or of material

System and abstract functions

'*Working*' *data channels* ⟶

'System housekeeping' data channels ----⟶

'Function' and 'level' interfaces ▬▬▬

Material Management System

This is a network with multiple connexions at working level, supported by radial links to a national record of resources in abstract form. The material resource management of BLLD is regarded as a special type of 'library region' characterised not by geographical location, but by its function of holding special resources of serials, and of 'support stock' of monographs. Its function as a communication centre is separate.

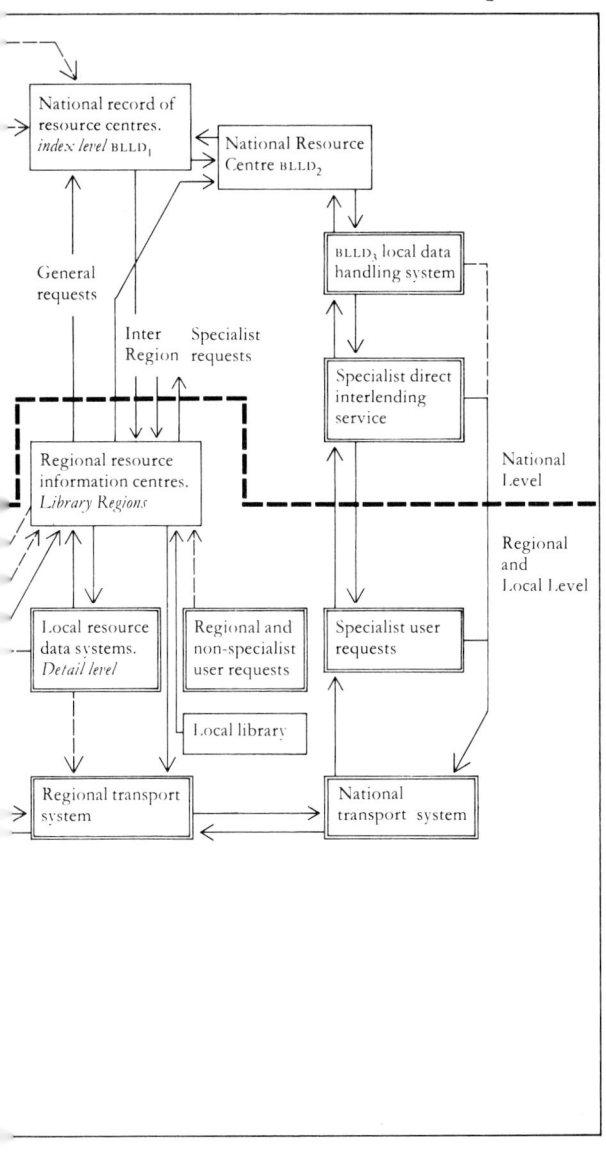

```
┌──────────────────────────────────────────────────────────────┐
│  National record of                                          │
│  resource centres. ◄──── National Resource                   │
│  index level BLLD₁  ────► Centre BLLD₂                       │
│         ▲                      ▲                             │
│         │                      │                             │
│  General│              BLLD₃ local data                      │
│  requests              handling system                       │
│                               ▲                              │
│         Inter    Specialist   │                              │
│         Region   requests                                    │
│                        Specialist direct                     │
│                        interlending                          │
│                        service                               │
│                                              National        │
│  Regional resource                           Level           │
│  information centres.                                        │
│  Library Regions                         ────────────        │
│                                              Regional        │
│                                              and             │
│                                              Local Level     │
│  Local resource   Regional and    Specialist user            │
│  data systems.    non-specialist  requests                   │
│  Detail level     user requests                              │
│                                                              │
│                   Local library                              │
│                                                              │
│  Regional transport           National                       │
│  system                       transport system               │
└──────────────────────────────────────────────────────────────┘
```

The Bibliographic Resource System would also offer a major opportunity for a shared cataloguing system, whereby libraries would input to the national data base entries for items not held on the national and international MARC files. This would provide a single source cataloguing subsystem by which co-operative automation would reduce the total cost of cataloguing by local re-use of central investment. This principle has been shown to work in the Ohio College Library Centre (OCLC)[10] in the United States, in LIBRIS in Sweden[11] and in FAUST in Denmark.[12]

The central co-ordination of major information retrieval services is probably also desirable. This is particularly true of automated services in view of the large hardware systems for storage and communication involved. The concept of a *regional* centre for information retrieval, subject resource information and other special services is not yet either clear or justified, and is a recurrent subject of discussion in several groups at present.

It would appear, however, that there is a need for a national referral centre for information retrieval and subject access which would be the centre of a network providing access to specialised bibliographic centres (Institute of Historical Research and the GLC Intelligence Unit for example) and local co-operative information centres such as SINTO, CICRIS and HULTIS, in addition to its own information retrieval services.

In the model this centre is referred to as the National Information Retrieval Service Centre, but logically one would assume that it should be part of the British Library Reference Division. The task of establishing even an index to information centres which in the model is referred to as the National Record of Resource Centres and the development of a network is enormous and it may well be that it could be begun by working out a methodology for identifying local and regional resources. Such a system is being developed at the regional centre (HBZ) in Cologne and is already providing a valuable service to libraries and information centres.

Again, while science and technology are fairly well served by abstracts and information retrieval systems, very little is available

Co-operation and the British Library

in the humanities and social sciences and pioneer work needs to be done in these fields if our readers are to be provided with adequate information. The indications are that there is an increasing demand for this information and although the 'old boy network' can help it is not a substitute for a properly organised service.

Whilst the Bibliographic Resources System can identify books and other library materials and provide by access to a national data base machine-readable entries for our catalogues, a great deal of library co-operation requires information on the actual physical whereabouts and movement of actual material.

In the Material Management System, the collection and handling of information for library co-operation purposes about actual material, the movement of material, and the (necessary) intimate knowledge of local practice and precedent, place the key functions of this system at *local* and *regional* level. This does not prevent a *region* being determined by other factors than geography; specialisation in serials is localised at the British Library Lending Division; patents and standards in the Science Reference Library.

These practical nuclei are likely points for library co-operation and some already exist in conventional form or in automative systems – BLCMP, SWALCAP and the library Regions, for example.

How these nuclei develop or new ones be established will depend on the willingness of librarians to co-operate in the fields of circulation, stock control and transport planning as well as interlending. Politics will also undoubtedly play a part, and may well determine how far and how well library co-operation can develop. Already, however, in some areas university, polytechnic, college and public libraries are co-ordinating the purchase of expensive books and specialised periodicals. In the South Western Region a co-operative system for acquisition and loan of sets of music scores based on Devon County Library has been established, and is paid for by the members of the Region.

The traditional pattern of inter-library lending has been radically changed by the establishment of the British Library Lending Division. The merger of the National Lending Library for Science and Technology which had dealt mainly with periodicals and reports in the fields of science and technology, and the National Central Library which had been more concerned with monographs, and with the humanities and social sciences, and operated mainly as a switching centre between libraries, has led to a much more comprehensive service. In 1973–74, 1,832,000 requests were received at the BLLD and Maurice Line estimated that the Division is now dealing with about three-quarters of inter-library loans traffic in the United Kingdom. Some 83% of valid requests were satisfied from BLLD stock and the acquisition of vast stocks of books and periodicals purely for inter-library lending purposes has added a new dimension to library co-operation.

The BLLD has also obtained the co-operation of libraries that had not previously co-operated in inter-lending. The most important of these libraries are the copyright deposit libraries (other than the British Library Reference Division) but other libraries with significant specialist collections such as the Royal Society of Medicine are also involved.

Another important contribution to library co-operation by the BLLD is the receipt of materials of which other libraries wish to dispose. It adds to its stock items which it lacks, and offers the remainder to other libraries. In this way valuable collections of little used materials are preserved for library use and, with the increasing pressure on space within libraries, this function is likely to grow in importance.

It is too easy, however, to say that the BLLD is the answer to all our inter-lending problems. Although the objective of the BLLD is to provide an efficient central lending and photocopying service in support of the other libraries and information systems of the country, the extent to which the Government will subsidise the acquisition of material for inter-library loans without some attempt to recover costs is debatable. In a period of inflation and economic stringency there may well be pressures on the British Library Lending Division to recover some of

Co-operation and the British Library

their costs; how far this would affect the total volume of requests is difficult to judge, but interlending within a local nuclei might well become more attractive.

It is also interesting to consider how far the establishment of BLLD has met a hitherto unsatisfied demand by readers for access to published information available through libraries. If the figures of inter-library loans within the London and South Eastern Library Region (LASER) are representative of other inter-library lending organisations, this must indeed be the case, as there has been no diminution of traffic within LASER. To what extent demand would have increased within LASER but for the establishment of BLLD is of course another matter.

It is attractive to envisage an automated network with each local or regional centre – and BLLD as a special centre – having a local data handling system to maintain lists of holdings, stock location files and so on, linked to a national centre. For technical and economic reasons a totally integrated system is unrealistic certainly for many years to come, but a national index to material, based on a national data base, pointing to centres holding each title is a more practical possibility and could link into the proposed British Library on-line data base. Regional and National Transport systems become integral with interlending in this model, and share access to the data systems for load planning and identification of physical location.

These developments are not likely to take place next week, but current trends and the present state of technology indicate these are perfectly feasible.

The establishment of the British Library has given librarianship in this country, for the first time, an organisation with the resources to provide services which can encourage the development of library co-operation. There is a general acceptance among librarians that the central bibliographic service provided by the British Library Bibliographic Services Division will continue as the leading source of bibliographic description of books published in the United Kingdom. Reservations on the central bibliographic service are principally concerned with the rate of implementation of the Cataloguing-in-Publication service to improve effective currency, and the volume of material which eludes copyright deposit or is excluded by internal rules.

It is generally accepted that part of the function of the British Library should be to provide leadership to the profession in many fields: guidance on library automation and strategic support for future developments to name but two.
The British Library cannot and in fact should not be the sole arbiter for the future. It is librarians and the users of their libraries who must ultimately decide what they want. Libraries are no longer just the custodians of collections of books; many readers demand and expect the librarian to exploit these resources and to provide services to the minor ethnic groups, to those learning to read as well as to the specialist. Library co-operation must be seen as a whole with the British Library as a part, albeit an important part. There must be a continuing process of consultation and development.

The need for co-operation may well be identified by a group of librarians in a particular area. For example, librarians are increasingly aware of the need to provide non-book materials for their readers. Many forms of recorded sounds on records and cassettes can be borrowed from public libraries, including poetry, drama, music, languages, sound effects, etc. To achieve full coverage of items issued in Britain and to make them available for interlending, the thirty-three London public libraries have established the Greater London Audio Subject Specialisation Scheme (GLASS). This scheme of co-operative purchase and storage highlights the need for adequate bibliographic records of this material.

The problems of improving information and cataloguing services for non-book materials in the United Kingdom have been under discussion for some time, and following the initiative of the Council for Educational Technology (CET),[13] a joint study into improved bibliographic service for audio-visual materials has been set up by the British Library and the Council for Educational Technology. The study is covering the following areas:

i   The needs of audio-visual cataloguing agencies and patterns of existing bibliographic provision
ii   The technical feasibility of creating a co-operative system built around computer based facilities
iii The operational and management options for such a system with costs

We must also consider the views and make use of the expertise of those who are not librarians. The Parry Report[14] recommended the sharing of resources in a local area to meet the needs of higher education, and the recent Department of Education and Science supported project in Sheffield is a welcome advance in this direction.

Advance in computer technology and telecommunications should be monitored and expert advice sought on their application to library operations. Detailed investigation and research may be required in these fields, and it would be wrong to omit from this study the contribution which research has made, and we hope will continue to make, to the future of library co-operation.

The credit for much of this research must be given to the Office for Scientific and Technical Information (OSTI) now the British Library Research and Development Department. Grants from OSTI provided the impetus for the development of the Birmingham Libraries Co-operative Mechanisation Project and for the development and evaluation of the SWALCAP system. It financed the *Study of computer assisted methods for the recording of book locations in regional library systems* by the South Eastern Regional Library System in 1968–69 which has led to the creation of a National ISBN interlending system.[15]
The London and South Eastern Library Region (LASER) received grants to carry out a study into the feasibility of converting a regional union catalogue into machine-readable form and its use as a basis for local catalogue conversion,[16] and a review of the potential for collaborative development in library automation (COLA).[17] It has also financed a feasibility study into a

national transport system for inter-library loans carried out by the Local Government Operational Research Unit of the Royal Institute of Public Administration.

These and many other studies into aspects of library and information systems provide a basis for future development. British initiative in library co-operation and in the promotion of bibliographic standards has been recognised and copied throughout the world. Long may it continue so to do.

References in text

1. McColvin, Lionel Roy. *The Public library system of Great Britain: a report on its present condition with proposals for post-war re-organisation.* London, Library Association, 1942.
2. Ministry of Education. *Standards of public library service in England and Wales: report of the Working Party appointed by the Minister of Education in March 1961.* London, HMSO, 1962.
3. Ministry of Education. *Inter-library co-operation in England and Wales: report of the Working Party appointed by the Minister of Education in March 1961.* London, HMSO, 1962.
4. National Libraries Committee. *Report of the National Libraries Committee.* London, HMSO, 1969 (Cmnd 4028).
5. Department of Education and Science. *The scope for automatic data processing in the British Library: report of a study into the feasibility of applying ADP to the operation and services of the British Library.* London, HMSO, 1972, 2 vol.
6. Great Britain. Parliament. *The British Library: presented to Parliament by the Paymaster-General by Command of Her Majesty* (Cmnd 4572). London, HMSO, January 1971.
7. Wilson, T. D. and Masterson, W. A. J. *Local library co-operation: final report on a project funded by the Department of Education and Science.* Sheffield, University of Sheffield Postgraduate School of Librarianship and Information Science, 1975. (Occasional Publications Series no. 4).

8. Buckle, David G. R. *et al.* The Birmingham Libraries Co-operative Mechanisation Project: progress report, January 1972 – June 1973. *Program,* 7 (4) October 1973, pp. 196–204.
9. Hudson, Richard F. B. *and* Ford, M. Geoffrey. *South West University Libraries System Co-operation Project: final report for the period July 1969 – December 1972.* Bristol, University of Bristol, 1973. (OSTI report 5151).
10. Kilgour, Frederick G. *et al.* The shared cataloguing system of the Ohio College Library Center. *J. Libr. Automn.* 5 (3) September 1972, 157–183.
11. Sandels, Marionne. *LIBRIS: a computerised Library Information System for Sweden: general information.* Stockholm, Swedish Council of Research Libraries, 1974.
12. FAUST: Folkebibliotekernes Automations System. *Scandinavian Publ. Libr. Q.* 5 (3) 1972, 62–67.
13. Gilbert, Leslie A. and Wright, J. W. *Non-book materials: their bibliographic control.* London, Councils and Education Press, 1971. (CET Working Paper 6).
14. University Grants Committee. *Report of the Committee on Libraries.* London, HMSO, 1967.
15. Christophers, Richard A. The LASER union catalogue and a national ISBN inter-lending system. *Program,* 7 (2), April 1973, 89–95.

16. Plaister, Jean *et al. Conversion of a regional union catalogue into machine-readable form and its use as a basis for local catalogue conversion: report on a feasibility study supported by a grant from the Office for Scientific and Technical Information of the Department of Education and Science.* London, LASER, 1973. (OSTI report 5164).

17. Ashford, John *et al. Co-operation in library automation: the COLA Project. Report of a research project undertaken by LASER and supported by a grant from the British Library Research and Development Department* ... London, LASER, 1975. (OSTI Report 5225).

Chapter Fifteen

The Academic Librarian of the Future

James Thompson

Setting
The rise of the academic librarian in Britain coincides very neatly with the founding and development of the Library Association. Before 1877 there were only four universities in England: Oxford, Cambridge, Durham and London; Scotland was content with its 'historic four' – St Andrews, Glasgow, Aberdeen and Edinburgh; whilst in Ireland there was only Trinity College, Dublin. From the 1880s though, there was a wave of foundations, beginning with the civic universities such as Manchester, Birmingham, Liverpool, Leeds, Sheffield and Bristol. A further and, for the meantime, final wave in the early 1960s – Sussex, York, East Anglia, Essex, Kent, Warwick and Lancaster – brought the number of universities in this country to just under fifty. In the academic year 1973–74, according to the University Grants Committee,[1] there were 244,728 full-time students attending universities in Great Britain, and the total number of full-time teaching and research staff paid wholly from university funds was 30,680.

The student numbers quoted in the previous paragraph represent eleven per cent of 'the age cohorts 18–21'.[2] By the 1980s another 11% will be attending other institutions of higher education, in particular the polytechnics. Since the 1960s, carrying on as it were the baton from the universities, no less than thirty polytechnics have been established. In addition, there are at present some one hundred and fifty colleges of education, though this number is expected to fall to a hundred or so in the near future as a result of closures or mergers. Along with these institutions of higher education must be counted those great research libraries, the national libraries, and in particular of course, the British Library. The British Library began operating as such in 1973, and within its three huge divisions – Reference, Lending and Bibliographic Services – employs and will continue to employ librarians who will maintain 'the traditions of scholarship set over the past 200 years by the British Museum'.[3]

It is principally in one of the foregoing settings that the academic librarian of the future will find him- or herself employed; and it can be predicted that whatever temporary falling-off there may be in the numbers of young people seeking degree courses, and however long any national economic recession may last, in the long-term the momentum for higher education will reassert itself, with an increased need for library services as a consequence.

Education and training
It would seem axiomatic that an academic librarian must be well-educated, and in the contemporary world it is ordinarily accepted that the formal means by which a good general education may be obtained is by pursuing a degree course. In academic librarianship, if not in other fields of librarianship, this view has never really been contested. The real development in academic librarianship over the past hundred years has been the growing acknowledgment that education and training in librarianship itself is a standard requirement for any librarian. As a result, it is the rule rather than the exception that academic librarians should possess a formal qualification in librarianship. The Library Association can take almost entire credit for the prevalence of this view.

The curious outcome of this conversion, however, has been a realisation that academic librarianship without scholarship is a nonsense. Education and training in librarianship is not sufficient on its own. The argument, simply stated, is that any individual who dedicates his life's work to the cause of higher education cannot logically withold himself personally from the ethos of the institution in which he works: he must necessarily wish to extend and deepen his own learning. Dr F. W. Ratcliffe, of the John Rylands University Library of Manchester, has commented on the current trend away from scholarship much more forcefully:

I do feel that the future of librarianship, given the growth of degrees in library science at undergraduate and post-graduate level, is likely to be much less scholarly than in the past. Already there is a dearth of librarians educated in those scholarly disciplines which have been and, to my mind, always will be the bread and butter of academic librarianship. This must produce a less scholarly profession, which will eventually be more orientated towards the body of librarianship in the country than to scholarship in its own environment.

The problem identified by Dr Ratcliffe is that though the academic librarian of the future will without difficulty associate himself with the discipline and ethic of librarianship as a whole – and this, of course, is an important step in itself – he may run the risk of alienating himself from the aims of his own institution.

It is, however, possible for the academic librarian of the future to maintain general professional links with all other librarians in all other contexts, yet still remain committed to the pursuit of scholarship which is the chief characteristic of all institutions of higher education. The current practical difficulty is that once a graduate has received state help to follow a postgraduate course in his subject, he finds it difficult to obtain further help to pursue a full-time course in librarianship. The result is that postgraduates do not readily find their way into librarianship (because of the insistence on professional qualifications), and librarians qualified by a postgraduate course are unlikely to return to scholarship within their own subject disciplines.

A resolution of this situation must be part of academic librarianship's future. To induce the scholar to enter upon librarianship as a career, it will be necessary for the Library Association either to persuade the Department of Education and Science that a reasonable proportion of postgraduate entrants should be enabled and permitted as of right to undertake full-time courses in librarianship, or alternatively, the Library Association and the schools of librarianship should organise – again as a matter of course and not in some limited or special

The Academic Librarian

way – a part-time route to a formal qualification in librarianship for postgraduate recruits. For the graduate who has chosen to pursue a postgraduate training in librarianship, it will be necessary to enable him to retain his first-degree connection with a particular subject discipline. The inevitable way here will be the further development of subject specialisation in academic libraries.

Functions

Subject-affiliated librarians have always existed in academic libraries. In colleges of art or technology or education, librarians have necessarily been or become specialists. We have had 'law librarians' and 'medical librarians' for many years. It is in one sense, at any rate, merely a logical extension that within large general academic libraries other subject specialists should emerge. It is also of course to do with the growth of libraries. When an academic library is first established it tends to be orientated primarily towards the undergraduate, and the functions of its librarians in turn tend towards the generalised and the technical. In the end this has to change, if only because, as J. W. Perry[4] has pointed out, 'a large university library must of necessity become more decentralised in character': the contents and the users become so diverse they cannot all be served from the same counter. Yet another reason for a conversion to subject specialisation by our libraries has been pinpointed by Dr R. S. Smith, the Librarian of Nottingham University:

Centralised services and standardisation will lead to a future diminution in the significance of housekeeping routines including cataloguing and classification. The emphasis will be on subject specialists and exploitation of collections.

There are of course some reservations about the steady movement towards subject specialisation in academic libraries; but these reservations have more to do with the form it should take rather than in regard to the principle itself. On the one hand we have the advocates of what has become known as the 'Germanic pattern' of individual subject specialists primarily concerned with book-selection – as exemplified in the views of

W. L. Guttsman, Librarian of the University of East Anglia[5] – and on the other, the advocates of the subject divisional arrangement of libraries, such as R. O. MacKenna, who favours 'subject orientated sectional libraries within a general library framework'. Subject specialisation is also winning the support of the new polytechnic libraries: in the words of K. G. E. Harris,[6] Librarian of Newcastle upon Tyne Polytechnic, 'it is a way of organising libraries in accordance with academic realities'. And of course those librarians such as Dr F. W. Ratcliffe who have aimed to retain and reinvigorate the longest and most scholarly traditions of academic librarianship have never departed from the concept of the well-experienced subject-affiliated librarian.

The functions of the academic librarian of the future will therefore be by and large those of a subject-affiliated librarian. I have analysed these elsewhere,[9] but in sum they are: collection building; organisation of materials; reference work, bibliographical assistance and information retrieval; and user instruction.

Numbers

If the academic librarian of the future is to devote himself to these functions rather than spreadeagle himself on the myriad tasks which constitute the total work of any library system, it follows that there will be some change in the number of academic librarians employed. My hypothesis is that the number of academic librarians per library will decrease, or at least remain constant whilst institutions only grow numerically in terms of student body. Where there are new subject developments in an institution – law or medicine, for example – then of course the number of specialist librarians will grow accordingly; and similarly the founding of new institutions will create new posts.

This hypothesis has been given some support by Dr R. S. Smith who sees one outcome of the current economic recession as being not that the demand for higher education will in the long-term slacken, but that 'the staff/student ratio will probably worsen' – and in his prediction must be included the 'library staff/student' ratio. More dramatically, C. E. N. Childs, the Librarian of Brunel University, has noted that if the two problems in British industry are overmanning and insufficient capital investment, the same is true of many university libraries in this country:

They spend too much on staff; too little on books, equipment and buildings. It is better, for example, to buy more copies of heavily used books than to employ staff to operate waiting lists for a small number of copies.[8]

And for those who subscribe to the theory that developments in the United States tend to presage what will happen within a few years in the United Kingdom, the following comment from I. R. Willison's report[7] on the American research library system in a period of economic restraint, is relevant:

The main strategy employed in holding down library budgets is to minimise duplication of professional staff, in the first instance between libraries themselves, by the use of local networks or consortia designed to exploit the potentialities of computer-based on-line shared processing (especially, to begin with, machine-readable cataloguing, MARC; the other element – shared acquisitions – envisaged by the National Program for Acquisitions and Cataloguing, does not seem to have got under way yet). In the second instance, it is hoped to minimize duplication of professional staff between libraries and the book trade, most noticeably by the use of specialist library catalogue publishers, such as G. K. Hall and Mansell Information, in connexion with retrospective recataloguing, and by the use of blanket approval arrangements with book-jobbers or, in the University of Toronto's more illuminating phrase, 'dealer selection' order systems, as an integral part of planned library collection development.[9]

It must be repeated that my hypothesis does not relate to the total numbers of personnel employed in libraries, but only to the number of academic librarians employed per library. In my book *Library power* which appeared in June 1974, before the real onset in academic libraries of economic restraint, I argued against the overstocking of libraries with academic librarians as opposed to other grades and types of personnel; and in the two years immediately subsequent, this argument began to take on a more than theoretical aspect as libraries began to suffer staff reductions. Because academic librarians as a group enjoy permanent tenure, staff reductions were mostly confined to junior and intermediate staff grades, and the result was that the previously-unrecognised imbalance between the number of chiefs and the number of red indians became all too obvious when the number of red indians was reduced still further. The situation was of course paralleled in university staffing as a whole: research scientists found themselves doing work formerly done by laboratory technicians, and academic librarians found themselves on the library's daily shelving rotas.

The fact which confronted both universities and university libraries was that in times of recession a permanent, expensive and perhaps too high complement of staff of academic status left them very little room for financial manoeuvre. One good long-term result of the economic ill-wind must be that in future the addition of an academic librarian to a library's staff will be more rigorously considered, and measured more critically against the appointment of a staff member or members at a lower grade. In very hard times two library assistants are worth more to a library than one assistant librarian.

Innovations
The American research library scene as viewed by Willison affords another clue to the future of the academic librarian in our own country. As can be seen from the comment of his quoted in the previous section, a feature of coming years must be a greater reliance by academic librarians on computer-based networks or consortia. The processing of library materials must become increasingly standardised, mechanised and centralised – or at least regionalised.

It is indeed about time that library technology underwent a radical change. One depressing aspect of reviewing the last hundred years of academic librarianship is the realisation that our profession is still by and large using the technology already available in the 1870s. Every academic librarian who takes his occupation seriously must be daily aware that most of our technical systems are in desperate need of an overhaul. Fortunately some innovations have crept on the scene and overtaken professional preconceptions and prejudices anyhow: the technology of photocopying, for example, has revolutionised interlending; computerisation has invalidated a whole range of manual, labour-intensive routines; and microforms have jostled many long-standing conceptions as to what an individual library can provide and store in the way of research materials.

As Dr R. S. Smith has pointed out, the main lines of technological development in libraries and their potentiality can already be seen: only the rate of development is in question. In his view, that rate is one of the determinants of the future of academic librarians; and his anxiety is that the library schools, manned by staff who have withdrawn from active librarianship, might not be able to handle adequately this aspect of professional education.

There will of course have to be other kinds of innovation. As academic libraries grow inevitably larger, our basically self-help open-access approach will surely break down. The standard schemes of book classification – in particular, Dewey and Library of Congress – are ramshackle even when judged by the most tolerant eye. Our cataloguing systems may have suited Panizzi, but they certainly do not suit the student of the 1970s; and the answer to this state of affairs must not be a condescending, 'so what?' In brief, we must rid ourselves of that virtuous feeling, dating from some decades ago, that by throwing open every shelf in our libraries to our poor bemused users we have necessarily done them such a good turn that we can then let them fend entirely for themselves.

Structure
It has long been held, no doubt with much truth, that the hierarchical structure of library staffing has blocked the introduction of many useful innovations: ideas come up from the bottom, but vetoes come down from above. But it is wrong to dismiss our traditional hierarchical structure too readily, if the only substitutes offered are either too exact an imitation of the structure of a teaching department – that is, a group of equal colleagues with the chief librarian as prima donna – or some ill-considered system copied from industry and commerce of

'man management' – a revolting concept even in less egalitarian times).

R. O. MacKenna has defended the hierarchical system as follows:

I don't see how a complex service organization such as a large library can operate effectively without clear lines of responsibility. (Its problems are quite different from those of a teaching department, and current trends of thought that seek to assimilate the two have me very worried indeed.) But there are great possibilities for increased meaningful consultation and improved communication (both upwards and downwards) – surely together the true essence of democracy – and both seem to me perfectly compatible with a hierarchical structure of ultimate responsibility.

And Dr Ratcliffe makes the practical point that 'the hierarchy works of course in two ways and one of them is the guarantee of promotional prospects', though he also acknowledges the current urge 'to involve all staff in library decisions and planning'.

Even so, it is very unlikely that the academic librarian of the future will find himself in a library staff structure arranged in an elaborate pecking-order. By virtue of being primarily a subject specialist, he should find, as I have noted in my book *Library power*, that he is instead one of a group of colleagues banded together by a common interest: and it is not really possible to have a pecking-order among specialists – an archivist cannot be thought of as being more senior than a maps librarian, nor a French literature specialist more senior than a local history librarian.

Promotional prospects do present a problem. Since without a multi-level hierarchy there is no distinct promotional ladder, the only solution can be the establishment of a distinct career grade, as in a teaching department. The further problem here, though, is that the translation from the equivalent of lecturer grade to senior lecturer grade still tends to depend on recommendation by the head of the department (or library): this is one of the reasons why heads can still get away with being prima donnas.

The Academic Librarian

Maybe this works no more unfairly and no more inefficiently than the hierarchical system, but academic librarians of the future would be well-advised to confront it in tandem with their teaching colleagues.

R. O. MacKenna's point about responsibility cannot be glossed over either. I have given one answer elsewhere:[10] namely, that a poor performance by a librarian in a functional area – cataloguing, for example – is much more amenable to a cover-up job than a poor performance in an entire subject area, which is obvious to all and in some ways is self-correcting since it will be the users who will identify and advertise inadequacies.

Chief librarian

In the last analysis though, ultimate responsibility for library services will continue to rest with an institution's chief librarian. It is another truth now universally acknowledged that, as J. W. Perry has observed, there has been and will continue to be a 'tremendous increase in the complexity of university library administration'; the same state of affairs pertains to some extent to every other kind of library in the field of higher education. Again those who look to the United States for some presentt clues as to future developments in this country will find much to ponder over in the major article by Arthur M. McAnally and Robert B. Downs[12] on the changing role of directors of university libraries.

The most surprising and disturbing discovery by McAnally and Downs is the declining status of chief librarians. Even in the United Kingdom this development has begun to make itself apparent. In the 1960s, stimulated no doubt by the excitement and high hopes engendered by the founding of several new university libraries, and the considerable expansion of those universities already in being, the university librarian had a relatively charmed life. He was, it can even be said, important and popular. But the disenchantment which has arisen because of his never-ending requirements for resources and accommodation, his increasing failure to meet staff and student needs, the worsening economic situation, and growing political resentment in regard to higher education generally, have altered this noticeably, and it would be a foolish chief librarian who did not now acknowledge the change. McAnally and Downs calculate that, if present trends in American university libraries continue, the average period for which a director of a university library will be able to hold down his job will only be five or six years. The pressures on him (or her) have grown too intense. It is to be doubted that such a situation will replicate itself so extravagantly in Britain, if only because our scale of operation is so much less, but nevertheless there are certain to be some parallels.

It is already observable that one of America's problems is happening here: namely, that direct communication between Vice-Chancellor and University Librarian is becoming less common. Such are the complexities of university administration that there is here, as in the States, a layer of administrative officers between these two individuals. The librarian has, *ergo*, less power and less influence.

Another parallel which we will certainly see, because most of the symptoms are already in evidence, is in the specific sources of pressure on the chief librarian. McAnally and Downs list these as follows: the president's office – that is, our Vice-Chancellors, the library staff – who are more articulate and egalitarian, the faculty, the students and state – in our case, governmental – agencies. Chief librarians who quite fancy a cosy, paternal image will be in for an extremely rough time. But McAnally and Downs also offer some solutions. In sum, they predict convincingly that the chief librarian of the future will have to be a person who is flexible and adaptable, must possess a stable and equable temperament, must have considerable qualities of endurance, and must be exceptionally persuasive. This is a tall order, but all the available evidence supports its validity.

Co-operation
The future of the chief librarian in an academic library has been summed up in a not essentially different way by R. S. Smith: 'The days of the autarchic university library with its idiosyncratic director are surely gone forever.' Dr Smith's point is that we shall in future witness a networking of library services, and cites

in particular the interest of the Department of Education and Science in this kind of development, exemplified by its 1975 circular on the possibilities of co-operation between local libraries of every kind.

In truth, most of the libraries in this country which are financed by the state now come, in one way or another, under the wing of the DES – not excluding university libraries, despite the existence of the University Grants Committee. The danger of this approach lies not so much in too ready an acceptance of the idea that because most libraries in higher education are financed from a common source, their books and services can easily be administered as a common pool, but from an intrusive and unpleasant element of anti-élitism such has already been threatened in the United States where (as I. R. Willison notes) one result has been a wrong-headed suggestion that mature libraries should lend indiscriminately from their rare book collections, and even that they should sell their rare books to help to cover their costs. Co-operation should mean neither jeopardising the future of existing centres of excellence, nor be an excuse to cut resources all round.

Nevertheless, there must indeed be far closer links between all types of library in the higher education sector. W. W. Dieneman has commented, for example, that universities 'will probably have to look beyond their own community, taking a positive lead in extra-mural activities and adult education within the environment'; and he adds that he personally has been disappointed that co-operation with other libraries has not been considered more positively by the Standing Conference of National and University Libraries, especially *vis-à-vis* polytechnic libraries. In the same vein, with regard to polytechnic libraries, K. G. E. Harris has written:

To cover what are temporary inadequacies, polytechnics depend heavily on inter-library co-operation and, having seen the benefits, are committed to co-operation as part of their basic philosophy. Apart from better exploitation of resources, the multiplicity of contacts developed with other libraries is most fruitful. Polytechnics are interested in joint action on periodical holdings, staff exchanges and other matters leading to meaningful library services. Where polytechnics find most difficulty is in their relationship with university libraries which do not want to be over-run by polytechnic students. That is what the universities fear but it is not the point at issue. Polytechnics need occasional access to specialist collections: the kind of assistance university libraries have been known to refuse. This is a blockage which will have to go if only because the potentialities are immense. That close co-operation is possible is shown by the excellent relationships built up between polytechnic and university libraries in cities like Sheffield. With the resources being ploughed into polytechnic libraries, anything other than the widest exploitation is wasteful. Maximum use will best be achieved by working in a regional context in co-operation with other libraries.[13]

Apart from the DES itself, two other bodies can play a major role in encouraging co-operation between libraries. The first is the British Library, forming as it does, the apex of our nation's library network. The British Library is, in the opinion of R. S. Smith, 'one of the best things we have done, second only to the Library of Congress, and the envy of all other library systems, both in its achievements and in its vision'. The other body, of course, is the Library Association itself.

In its one hundred years, the Library Association has achieved a true commonalty of librarians. The academic librarian of the future, whether he or she works for the British Library, or in a university, or in a polytechnic, or in a college, will share a more or less identical professional education and outlook. He or she will move more freely between kinds of library, not only because of a shared professional identity, but because the conditions of service and the financial rewards in each type of library will have been evened out also. Such free movement will be good for the libraries, good for the librarians, and good for our Association.

References in text

1. University Grants Committee. *Annual survey: academic year 1973-74.* HMSO, May 1975. Cmnd 6034.
2. *Commonwealth universities yearbook, 1974.* Association of Commonwealth Universities, 1974.
3. British Library. *First annual report, 1973-74.* British Library, [1975].

4. Perry, J. W. The problems and future development of the older and larger university libraries. *In Libraries and people: essays offered to R. F. M. Immelman.* Cape Town, C. Struik, [1970].
5. Guttsman, W. L. Subject specialisation in academic libraries. *J. Librarianship,* 5 (1) January 1973, 1–8.
6. Harris, K. G. E. Subject specialisation in polytechnic libraries. *Libri,* 24 (4) 1974, 302–309.
7. Thompson, James. *Library power.* Bingley, 1974.
8. Childs, C. E. N. Book figures give no clue to savings. *The Times higher education supplement,* 11 April 1974.
9. Willison, I. R. The American research library system in a period of constraint. *J. of Am. studies,* 9 (1) April 1975, 21–34.
10. Thompson, James. The argument against subject specialisation. *ARLIS newsletter,* 22, March 1975, 3–6.
11. Perry, J. W., *op, cit.*, p. 4.
12. McAnally, A. M. *and* Downs, R. B. The changing role of directors of university libraries. *Coll. and Res. Libr.,* 34(2) March 1973, 103–125.
13. Harris, K. G. E. The polytechnic library explosion. *New Libr. Wld.,* 73, September 1971, 83–85.

While the author accepts entire responsibility for the views expressed in this chapter he nevertheless wishes to acknowledge the helpful advice and criticism received from the following: W. W. Dieneman, Librarian, University College of Wales, Aberystwyth; R. O. MacKenna, Librarian, University of Glasgow; F. W. Ratcliffe, Librarian, John Rylands University Library of Manchester; R. S. Smith, Librarian, University of Nottingham; and D. H. Varley, Librarian, University of Liverpool.

Chapter Sixteen

The Special Librarian of the Future

M N Patten

Introduction
It was difficult in preparing this chapter to resist the temptation to write in the immediate future which one can do with a good degree of confidence or to write beyond the lifetime of our present undergraduates which will allow one to speculate without fear of rebuke. I shall prognosticate to the year 2000 by which time most of our undergraduates will be forty-five and at the height of their careers. If what is said helps them to plan their careers a little, I shall have achieved part of my aims.

What are these aims? Briefly to write continuously in the future tense with hardly a backward glance. Too much of what we do today is influenced by what happened yesterday. Further, to show that the so-called 'special librarian' needs a radical change in his training and outlook if he is to play a leading role in the new 'information society'. Because of their existing low status within their organisations many special librarians will be considered unworthy to fill the new exalted information management role. Finally, to show how we need to move away from our obsession with techniques and machines to consider the fundamental nature of information, what it means to different people and to co-ordinate the 'invisible city' – developed out of the invisible college.

The words 'special' and 'library' will have no significance in the year 2000. The Library Association will have joined hands with Aslib and the Institute of Information Scientists to form the Information Society. The British Library will have grown to full Departmental status and will be known as the Department of Information, entailing a senior Cabinet post. Information and 'resource' centres will abound, although their operation and development will be co-ordinated in a National Plan, a Regional Plan and a World Plan.

The realisation that information is power will extend from the boardroom across the whole community which will have been taught to appreciate its value, through the mass media, for decision making. The need for prediction will grow as the community's capacity to choose expands. The government will seek to control the information power of centres so as to control and influence decision interdependence. Information technology will become the centre of society's nervous system. It will need to be formed wisely if we are to fashion effective policies for the future of society.

The information barriers – terminology, foreign languages, receptivity, consciousness, comprehension and information transmission – will be overcome. Access will remain a problem as there will always be the information rich and poor. The gap between these will be narrowed by public funding and information subsidy – particularly in the case of key industries and young developing companies.

The ability and/or willingness to pay for information will mean that the activities of information centres will be extended to include many activities presently regarded as peripheral. Such centres will need to provide a 24-hour automated service to meet the needs of society. The investment in the information segment in the US is growing at the rate of 10%, equivalent to double that of the economy as a whole. The Japanese have announced in their 'Plan for Information Society, a National Goal Toward 2000' an investment in information over the next five years (to 1980) of 1000 billion yen. It will not be many years before this trend is fully reflected in this country. Matter, energy and information will be regarded as the three most important things to affect the quality of life, and in job categories most concerned with information technology, a 150% increase has been forecast for the next ten years.

Prospects for British Librarianship

It was stated earlier that this would be written with hardly a backward glance. We do not have to continually look back over our shoulders to acquire an understanding of our nature now or in the future. We are fully aware of our limitations, but prefer not to see the sty in our own eye and will spend our time designing systems which we think will correct the real or imagined faults of others. Carl Wait summed up this attitude in 1972 at the ASIS conference when he said 'The activation and proper use of information processes ... will not come by building more powerful computers, studding the sky with satellites or inventing higher level languages. This is looking in the wrong place, at things easy to see, but where there is nothing to find'.

The Man
Qualified and motivated manpower is the largest restraint on the evolution of successful information services in science and technology. – OECD

It has been calculated that four to five million people will be working in the 'information' field in OECD countries by 1985. This number could treble by the year 2000. Apart from the fact that there will be considerable numbers of people employed in what are now regarded as the separate fields of special librarianship, telecommunications and computers, within ten years there will be a much greater crossing of the old discipline lines with scientists, technologists and social scientists intermingling with information scientists and technologists for the whole of their careers or for up to five- or ten-year 'Fellowship' periods. The awareness of the need to attract outstanding workers in other fields to contribute to a balanced information society will grow rapidly with the guarantee of adequate renumeration and career security.

The need to monitor information on a vast scale in terms of collection, validation of primary data and analysis of both primary and processed data will require a whole new profession of intermediaries or 'interfacers' to control the flow of information between the automated information systems, the generators of information and the users. Beyond this level there

The Special Librarian

will emerge a new breed of analysers and synthesists capable of greater specialisation but operating in a much more flexible multidisciplinary environment. This means that the training programmes for new and existing staff need to be radically modified *now*. Job clearing houses will emerge with sponsorship by government and industry. In order to widen the range of expertise available, information specialists in industry as well as government establishments and universities will be encouraged to take secondments and sabbaticals.

The distinction between information scientist and special librarian will become even more blurred in the future as flexibility of approach becomes the keynote to success in the knowledge society. The Information Man will need to sell his services in the market place, competing with others in both public and private enterprise. He will need to be skilled in techniques of fund-raising, persuasion and, above all, continuing innovation. Finally yet another breed of interfacers will emerge: not the familiar information specialist/machine interface but one who can play an active lead role between the subject specialist who produces information but does not know how to – or does not want to know how to – disseminate and the information specialist who has the methods necessary to process and control the information but does not know *to whom* he should disseminate. This new type of information interfacer will give guidance and information on the effective use of all available systems.

Education

Educating the man to the full realisation of his future role will be the biggest problem. More and more developments, whether they are propagated by government, private industry, universities or societies, will begin to affect society as a whole. Users of information in all walks of life will judge the value of information given to them by making constant subjective appraisals of the quality of the decisions which they are required to take. Our students will be taught that information must be understood to mean different things to different people at different times, that the implied and unimplied relationships between information and people are the key to proper manipulation of the resources and resultant economic success.

To satisfy the needs of an information-dominated industrial society a modular training programme has been proposed by the OECD with a target audience of top management, information managers, information workers and information system designers. The twenty-five modules cover a number of topics not included in many college curricula at present, for example marketing techniques, network analysis and cybernetics. Future training programmes will need to go further and include subjects not covered in the proposal. The target audience net will also need to be widened to spread appreciation across existing discipline boundaries. Curricula content will be broadened to include control and decision theory, semiotics, value engineering/analysis and, above all, practical and theoretical communication. Courses on how to write and talk persuasively, how to amass facts to support arguments, how to adopt differing strategies in dealing with different groups of individuals will become fundamental to basic college training programmes. Degrees will be offered in Information or Communication Technology and degrees in Librarianship will become synonymous with Archival Studies. Emphasis in curricula will move from the existing overwhelming concern with the manipulation of information to explore more thoroughly its form, structure, content and overall significance. Communications will become, therefore, a major department in our universities and colleges, with a much greater co-ordination of activities in the three areas of communications technology, information technology and information proper.

Computer-assisted instruction will become commonplace with sophisticated programmes available for information management games. Students will use computer terminals over national and international networks to participate in learning games with their counterparts in other countries and other disciplines. Development of the learning game concept in many areas of information education and training will lead to flexible learning modules from which the student can choose in his own time without the hindrance of timetables. Face-to-face

The Special Librarian

communication by video will emphasise the reality of long-distance learning techniques and provide for informal dialogue within a particular learning module. Groups and individuals, whilst continuing to meet to discuss common problems at conferences and workshops, will increasingly use picture-phone techniques to facilitate group discussion and committee work. A national plan for continuing education in the information field will ensure refresher and up-dating course modules are available for the individual at all stages of his career.

It will not be sufficient for existing special librarians to upgrade their existing qualifications in the usual topping-up manner. They will be better occupied in learning new skills in, for instance, operations research, computers and systems management, enabling them to compete with those from other disciplines on a broader front. Information Man will become engrossed in cybernetics, bibliometrics and behavioural studies. Cybernetics will become a basic constituent in information science as we move towards the dynamic information centre concept. Adaptive control systems will be needed as man's realisation of the importance of the changing needs of society grows. Synergistics of systems will be another gloss put on by Information Man as he becomes aware of the need to study the behaviour of whole systems unpredicted by observation of behavioural patterns in separate parts of the system.

Information Overload
What of man himself? Alvin Toffler writing in his book *Future shock* instances the researches of Miller in the United States. His work has shown a strong correlation between schizophrenia and information overload. There is no doubt that as the volume of information continues to grow man needs to learn to manipulate it more effectively. It is evidently more important that he learns how to control it. Man is bombarded with unsolicited information whenever he walks down a street. Can we be sure that future SDI systems will be that much better than their contemporaries? Future systems will pay more attention to on-demand SDI with man the user interacting directly with automated data bases via simple-to-use visual display terminals using touch wire principles or oral communication. Because a

man expresses an interest in twenty subject areas it does not mean that he necessarily *needs* information to be sent him on all those subjects each and every week. Like an oscilloscope trace, his information needs will have peaks and troughs. Perhaps the decisions he has to take will result in four or five subject peaks in a week. Should not the user be able to interact with the system 'on-demand', as it were, with occasional sessions at a terminal to 'browse' in 'trough' areas? When a user's needs peak out in an area, he wants a synopsis, say, of activities in the past month, three months or even three years. Automatic analysis and synthesis techniques will provide him with a particular synopsis to meet his particular need from on-demand SDI systems. If we are to avoid the dangers of information overload, therefore, we have to modify our thinking on current awareness and 'unsolicited' information.

Materials
The information worker of the future will be applying himself to ways and means of rewriting the rules on who needs what and why. He will also be devoting considerably more effort to the form in which the information is required. This will hinge on two factors: **a** the physical desired form of the material – and this can be predicted with a good degree of certainty – and **b** the manner in which the data is assimilated, processed and extracted on demand.

Let us consider first, however, the information itself. There will be a much greater emphasis on smaller items of information gleaned from news sources. Ephemeral material will be looked at from new angles to investigate potential patterns of developments arising from its regular publication. The abstracting policies of the commercial and largely government – supported information data base companies will change to meet the demands of subscribers for an overall coverage of information in a particular field. There will be a much greater emphasis on numerical data and its analysis and synthesis to provide summaries for management decision-making. Computer software packages to automatically analyse information from differing points of view for different users will be commonplace in twenty-five years' time. By that time man's understanding of

The Special Librarian

and ability to control the constituents of industrial management information systems – i.e. internal, environmental and competitive information – through the interrelated networks of information services, computers and telecommunications, will enable him to devote his time to person-to-person communication and ideas transfer.

Scientific and technical books and journals are increasing in price each year by an average of 20% and the costs of printing and distributing are unlikely to show any tendency to decrease in the foreseeable future. Because of the ever-increasing twinning tendency of scientific and technological disciplines, journals will cease to have a significant value as current awareness devices and will become archival monuments or 'paper data banks' to particular specialists who because they are few in number will have to pay dearly for the privilege of retaining their own journal. What is likely to happen is that publishing houses will become clearing houses for information normally communicated through journals and will sell their information directly to commercial and/or government-backed data base services. Eventually, publishers' activity will diminish rapidly in this area as the individual learns that he can collect his royalties direct from a database organisation without the need of the services of a publisher/agent.

What about particular sources of information now regarded as everyday tools? We will no longer have to spend sums of money on copies of annual directories such as Kelly's. All company data will be available on-line along with trade literature and price-lists capable of instant on-line update. Sales and production activities of all companies will be available on-line to those entitled to such information: government, shareholders, customers and others.

In the past, special librarians developed niches for themselves through their wide knowledge of printed information sources. Gradually they have added to this the resources of their colleagues in the information field and their knowledge of the activities of experts in many other disciplines. In the future, it will be difficult if not impossible to train individuals in the exploitation of materials as we know them in their present forms. Rethinking of the whole information resource problem will reveal a new method of resource manipulation dependent on a thorough understanding of data and file structure and data base interrogation strategies.

The problems of translations will have been overcome with simultaneous translation at the time of automatic processing of all data of international interest. Regional and national translating agencies will cater for miscellaneous translating needs but eventually one will be able to key a message in English to a computer terminal and receive a reply in one or any number of languages or even submit the translated form direct to the intended recipient in whatever country via video. For a time there will be a surge in the need for simultaneous interpretation, particularly if international person-to-person communication via picturephone is to have its predicted success. It will be necessary eventually to have heuristic translating mechanisms to allow people of different languages to communicate in round-table conference on highly technical subjects from one side of the world to the other. These mechanisms will also be used in our schools and colleges to increase our ability to grasp the languages of others in an easier and more natural manner.

Information centres in government and industry, whilst relying heavily on centres of excellence for their basic information, will concentrate on collecting and processing material in fringe areas and will provide more tailoring and specialisation of products. Such centres will sell or exchange all or part of their resources to a clearinghouse which will be able to market such resources to others either by adding the data to its own data bases or by licensing others to do likewise. Much of the impetus will come from these centres for data compressing, file restructuring and automatic content analysis. Government policy will recognise the need to move outside the confines of college research in information science and technology to encourage experts from many disciplines in industry to make contributions in these areas, particularly in the early formative years. There will be growing interrelation between public and special or private sectors of the information community.

The Special Librarian

As authoritative government-backed centres of excellence emerge in essential areas such as energy, so the output of literature will be controlled so as to ensure that every piece of data of importance to the nation, region or single industry is screened and processed for use in a national data base. Competitors with these centres of excellence, unless receiving national funding because of some particular expertise, will fall by the wayside and the duplication of published material will diminish very quickly. More authors will publish summaries of their work with back-up microfilm files of their full work deposited at clearing-houses such as national or regional information centres or at the centres of excellence themselves. There will be little need for information users to purchase hard copy of these back-up files as video systems linked to microfilm data banks and computer data banks will allow individuals on a charge basis to call up files to CRT displays either at home or at their place of work. National and international directories of experts will provide access to vast stores of unpublished information which individuals will process on their own minicomputers with summaries and analyses stored on central processors for common use. An elaborate system of payment for information from experts' files will be established with highly sophisticated file security arrangements.

The growing use of audio-visual materials will take us rapidly into a non-book environment in the special library area in particular. The complaints about image quality and reproducibility will increase parallel with the growth in the use of audio-visual technology and within ten years there will be significant breakthroughs in the technology to overcome these complaints. Hard copy will still exist but the emphasis will be on audio-video records and magnetic records and the conversion processes and equipment necessary for these records. Many of these conversion processes such as COM (computer output on microfilm) microfilm reader-printers and tape and card conversion devices have been with us for some time but significant advances will be made in the development of optical scanning devices using laser technology, for instance, and in playback devices allowing one to hold data in local memory for repetitive use or referral purposes.

Prospects for British Librarianship

There are distinct signs that microfilm technology will be overtaken very quickly by video tape recording (VTR) technology and the emphasis will be on conversion processes to handle materials. Audio-video records and magnetic records will be standard material forms with the conversion processes invisible to the user. The much-predicted microfilm revolution, therefore, may never happen and future developments in this technology could well be determined by the path taken by VTR towards improved resolution capability.

Copyright will exist on all data, systems and software and an elaborate system of royalty payments designed to encourage innovation will be established. Requests for information whether in video or hard copy form will be chargeable and paid for like the conventional telephone account, with a regular crediting of the individual's or organisation's national account where royalties are to be accorded. All patent specifications will be processed automatically with on-line world search facilities available.

Machines
The need for data security is making governments concentrate on the development of indigenous computer industries. In the UK investment impetus in hardware will come from the government with bodies such as the British Library playing a leading role. The European Economic Community has stated that it wants to see a viable computer industry within the Common Market and one can foresee link-ups such as that of Siemens, Telefunken and Nixdorf being strengthened by the addition of their British and French counterparts.

Computer and communication technology will ensure the transmission of information both orally and visually without risk of ambiguity. Selective dissemination of information on demand is an exciting potential application for video-tape-recording and the recently announced Post Office system known as Viewdata will enable viewers to select from a large computer-held data bank and later use a two-way message service using a modified TV screen, connecting unit, telephone and keypad. This service, due to come onstream by 1978, will

The Special Librarian

form the basis for the national communications network to be established in the next decade. Computers will not only accept input in longhand – indeed Optical Character Recognition techniques are widely used already – but new technologies will enable information to be transmitted orally both for input and output. This prospect opens up immense possibilities for information users to interrogate data banks by voice alone and will remove the current need to master a keyboard before beginning interrogation. The most likely year of mass introduction of library access in the home in the USA is 1985. Mass introduction in the UK is likely to be five years later. Library access will provide an interactive browsing facility with a readers' advisory service via computer. Cost of hard copy or a slow-scan video transmission will be instantly available to the user.

Computer technology, by the time that fifth generation computers are with us, will have all the logical functions currently incorporated in software built into the hardware. Miniaturisation and heuristic systems will provide briefcase computers allowing man instant access to data. The dehumanisation concept currently associated by many with computers will have been replaced through wider, deeper education and training with a greater understanding of the role of the computer as the cornerstone of the information revolution. Individuals will replace their personal computers like washing machines and TV sets, and standard switching languages, allowing interfacing with any number of systems, will be supplied to suit the individual's needs.

The individual's ability and motivation to contribute to the knowledge society will be enhanced by the development of effective two-way communication systems. It will become increasingly important for man to be able to receive information in a partly or fully analysed form or as raw data, and record his judgement as to its pertinence, value and completeness in the form of feedback to the data base source. In such a way, researchers, for example, will be able to build theories on their own observations and those recorded in the same way by others. The importance of instant feedback will be recognised as a major constituent of a dynamic information-oriented society in government, industry and the community at large. The information will be self-generating to a degree beyond man's present appreciation of man-machine symbiosis, opening up prospects which are frightening to contemplate in the context of our existing world society. It has been shown that the unit cost of automatic processing of data has been diminishing at an annual rate of 30% for the past twenty years. This rate will drop as the software sophistication and machine usage increases to cope with the demands of man for more automated analysis of data and two-way communication. Nevertheless it has been confidently predicted that man will be able to process automatically the whole of human knowledge by the year 2000.

Networks
Railroads were to a mass production society what information networks will be to a knowledge society. There the analogy ends, for the information networks will feel government influence from their onset and they will not be allowed to spread haphazardly and be subjected to sudden closure with familiar social consequences. Long range planning by national and international groups should ensure that any obsolescence is immediately recognised and catered for within the overall network system. Developments such as 3-D television, laser communication, fully digitised telephone networks, home video-com_____ _____ udio-video tape cassette systems will assist hi_____ _____ and potentially one-to-one co_____ _____ access, availability and personal co_____ _____ s to information will become a part of our _____ _____ ginable by today's standards.

No p_____ ed communication networks will be economical for use by existing library/information services alone but the emergence of general purpose networks – by, for example, satellite and cable TV – will enhance the rapid growth of national information services sharing network costs. Telecommunication satellites are increasing in size and life expectancy constantly. They will be essential to the types of international networks envisaged by Unesco and other bodies. INIS and similar concepts were established more for political reasons than for any others. Future world systems will be based on the demand made by users exerting a high level of influence on governments or their agents. The ever-increasing cost of acquiring knowledge through research and development is speeding us to much more formalised forms of resource sharing. The present level of resource sharing between information centres will increase a hundredfold in the next fifteen years and telecommunications networks will take a large portion of the credit for this.

The problems facing information networks centre on their individual need to interface with each other to avoid overlap and inherent wastage in primary and secondary data content, and to standardise on both hardware and software used so as to allow users to interface freely on heuristic principles with one or more networks or data base constituents singly or simultaneously. At present there is a tendency to proceed down those lines which produce instant credit and the most inconclusiveness. Man will need to face and overcome the difficulties which are associated not so much with cost benefit – which will not be a predominant issue in a knowledge-dominated society – but with the 'one-time' value, stored value and future value of information to individuals, groups of people, institutions, countries and international networks. Other problems associated with data bases, computer utilities, data exchange, standardization, and internationalisation of computer controlled networks will be much more easily resolved by discussion and consultation than the 'value' problem and the linked question of what participation in a partial or total network is worth to the individual or the organisation.

The work of UNISIST will largely determine the future national and international networks for communication of information and the future internationally funded data bases serving world-wide groups of users. Full MIS implementation in industry and government will be speeded by the development of highly sophisticated data base management systems designed to take over all repetitive decision-making functions and to aid substantially in taking one-time decisions. Developing software for these data base management systems will necessarily require man to arrive at a much clearer understanding of the nature of the information he has to handle and, it has to be repeated, its meaning and value at different times to different people.

The existing special librarian in industry, government and organisation will become partially immersed by the data base management concept which will totally dominate the MIS scene in 1985. His total immersion will come with recognition of the whole information function as a main board responsibility. Information directors will control the corporate information resource and existing special librarians will become part of a resource team. Such directors will probably be accountants by training and very few special librarians will reach these heights without training in a much wider range of management sciences than those currently presented either in our colleges or professional course programmes.

Television has adequately demonstrated that it has the mass persuasion wherewithal to influence people in the use of future information systems and in the use of information itself. There is a need therefore to dominate the media and dispel the image created by the word librarian regardless of its qualifying adjective. Perhaps the following would be apt:

Epitaph
Special Librarian 1925–1985 OED n. obsolete. Replaced by Information resource specialist, officer, manager, controller, director. One who collects, analyses, synthesises and makes available information for the common good (of the company, country, community, etc.).

Relevant reading

1. Anderla, G. *Information in 1985: a forecasting study of information needs and resources*. OECD, 1973.
2. *Annual reviews of information science and technology*. American Society for Information Science. Annually.
3. Baran, P. *Potential market demand for two-way information services to the home 1970–1990*. Institute for the Future, 1971.
4. Coblans, H. *Librarianship and documentation: an international perspective*. Deutsch, 1974.
5. The Conference Board. *Information technology: some critical implications for decision makers*. Conference Board, 1972.
6. Debons, A. editor. *Information science: search for identity*. Dekker, 1974
7. *Proceedings of the American Society for Information Science*. ASIS, Annually.

Chapter Seventeen

The Public Librarian of the Future

Melvyn Barnes

In spite of the cliché about books being the life-blood of the public library service, it is generally accepted that a collection of books is a library only in terms of a dictionary definition. Librarians, perhaps regarded by the average ratepayer as under-employed and excessively remunerated, are vitally necessary if that collection is to do its work. They can, if properly trained and of the right calibre and attitudes, fully exploit even a deteriorating collection – possibly offering a service of a higher standard than one possessing a surfeit of books yet lacking staff.

The fact that approximately fifty per cent of public library expenditure is represented by staff costs does not, therefore, justify the condemnation generally heaped upon it. Nor is the rapid escalation in these costs, estimated at 40·2% by the Department of Education and Science in England and Wales between 1974–75 and 1975–76, a sign of over-indulgence or profligacy; that is, assuming the staff concerned are worth that degree of priority within the library's share of the public cake. What must concern us in the future is the inevitable deceleration in staffing costs, coupled with the familiar demand for increased and improved and more sophisticated services – our public wishes to receive more, and refuses to pay for it. This is the backcloth against which the public librarian of the future will have to operate.

The demand for better library services, which librarians themselves are eager to provide, will require staff of positive motivation rather than those who enter librarianship as a soft option, and they will need to be far more adaptable in their working methods than many librarians of the past and present. Schools of librarianship, in order to produce public librarians of the quality and in the numbers required, will pay less attention to our standing and reputation *vis-à-vis* other professions and increasing attention to the needs of the service for which their students are destined. Library educationists might become like architects who eschew the aesthetic considerations and begin to consider questions of practicality. This vision of the future is put forward in the spirit of optimism which so often pervades our profession, diluted by the pessimism occasioned by recent trends.

To prognosticate on the public librarian of the future is impossible without trespassing upon the preserves of other contributors to this volume. Staff will inevitably be influenced by developments in education and training, in management, in library design and in automation. A revolution in service patterns and personnel deployment, in order to function effectively, will require librarians of a revolutionary bent. In entering librarianship instead of a more supposedly exciting profession, they will run the risk of encountering supervisors who merely yearn for the good, solid, dependable staff of the past.

Irrespective of this, it may not be cynical to suggest that our own image of the new librarian will be irrelevant if our public image remains the same. Whatever librarians might think of themselves, objectives in the future will not be achieved if consumers fail to recognise the existence of this new breed. Perhaps it is too late to overcome the image of the public librarian which has been propagated by the media and devoured by the two-thirds of the population who never pass through our misjudged portals. We will still be caricatured as fussy old women of both sexes, the female variety with hair in a bun and the male variety who longs for the yesteryear of starched collars and pince-nez.

If more people came to see for themselves, today and increasingly so in the future, they would have the evidence of

The Public Librarian

their own eyes. The hair-in-bun librarian is more likely to be a young man than an elderly lady – and even the latter has ample reason to wear her hair in that style, as an industrial safety precaution necessitated by library automation.

But all this is general conjecture. To pass to specific conjecture, it seems reasonable to prophesy that the public librarian of the future will be influenced by a fresh emphasis upon particular aspects and concepts of the service; by developments within local government as a whole; by the expectations and needs of the profession itself, particularly in matters of paper qualifications, pay and prospects; and finally, by the possibility of erosion of the type casting which has affected entrants to the profession so far.

It is difficult to dogmatise upon the question of which areas of public library service will expand and develop in the future, one reason being the controversy surrounding some of them and the independent views discernible from one senior librarian to another. Two examples will suffice. Many librarians prefer the traditional departmental arrangement of central libraries to an integrated stock displayed in subject departments, while others prefer to give little thought to a service based on buildings and see librarians as community practitioners. Equally high feelings are displayed in the field of library automation, in which many senior librarians would reputedly find their barge-poles singularly under-employed.

It would be erroneous to assume that these sentiments will disappear as the chief librarians of today bow gracefully out into well-earned retirement, or the less deserved fate of injecting their wit and wisdom into the librarians of the future as visiting lecturers. On the contrary, it is their very welcome ability to think for themselves which might bring some of the newly fledged librarians to conclusions about such topics as subject departments and automation which might appear prematurely reactionary. Be that as it may, such decisions will affect in time the working methods and attitudes of other staff. It would be pleasant to be able to categorise the public librarian of the future in total accordance with the emergent concepts of today, but completely unrealistic. One even hears occasional talk of returning to closed access.

Having recognised our refreshing aversion to following trends slavishly, it is nonetheless necessary to mention a few areas which are likely to assume increasing importance and have a noticeable effect upon the type of librarian required.

First, one must not ignore the need for subject specialists. The question of the physical arrangement of a library building is totally irrelevant here. Even in a conventional reference or lending department, we shall see a movement away from librarians with cigarette-card minds – the amateurs, who know something about everything but really very little about anything. The public librarian of the future ought not to have instilled into him – and I use the gender for convenience, not to champion the minority – the divine right to select books and give bibliographical advice relating to every subject under the sun. Today it is unavoidable. In the future, careful selection and training and the much-maligned manpower planning must be employed to control not only the number of librarians, but also the subject coverage of public library staff. This does not necessarily imply a graduate profession, although it may be accepted as such if we can be sure of securing recruits with common sense and intelligence to supplement their academic accomplishments. We can also expect a greater representation of the sciences among graduate recruits, failing which we shall eventually have public libraries with a bias even less desirable than the present heterogeneous ragbag. The demands of the purposive library user, combined with the need to spend dwindling bookfunds ever more wisely, means that professional staff in the future will need to bring subject interests and knowledge to bear to an increasing extent.

Then there are the brainchildren of modern technology. All this will surely affect the staff of the future. No longer will the book oriented librarian be the norm, and the audio-visual specialist the whizz kid. The book will remain with us, whatever McLuhan may say, but will come rapidly to be regarded merely as one medium of communication. Discs and tapes, for example, still tend to be treated in libraries as something unique, bearing no relation to the book: separate collections, special regulations, and even differential rates of fines apply to them. It will not, one suspects, be many years before fully integrated collections become common and librarians – if not supplanted by media technologists – will cast off their bookish image.

There is also a clear trend towards the employment in public libraries of techniques from other fields. As libraries develop, mechanise, enhance their productivity and employ more staff, they will require expertise in such fields as systems analysis, accountancy, market research, organisation and methods, and the many facets of personnel management. It is possible that non-librarians will be increasingly introduced into public library staffs. Although it is generally considered wasteful for an individual department of a local authority to employ such experts separately, the alternative leaves much to be desired. At present, the librarian and the outsider from management services or the computer bureau have to argue it out, with the librarian appearing narrow-minded and the other failing to appreciate the most fundamental principles of librarianship. Perhaps techniques in such fields as management, finance and computer technology will become optional parts of library education, so that new entrants may choose to specialise and bring to the public library service the best of both worlds.

On the question of mechanising library procedures – which, despite some initial aversion, is gaining ground – we have already accepted it in place of traditional charging systems, accessioning and catalogue production. It is tempting to visualise a future without the need for non-professional staff to engage in mundane tasks, with self-service data capture devices for the issue and discharge of books, conveyor belts which automatically return books to the shelves, and robots continuously engaged upon keeping the books in perfect order. The abolition of the issue desk as the focal point would perhaps bring trained librarians into their own, and good non-professionals could be trusted to do work of a higher level which would ensure that fewer of them spend a brief and frustrated time in the public library service.

This frustration is by no means confined to junior staff. An increasing number of young professional staff display impatience with public library bureaucracy and – above all – our traditional methods. New concepts of service, and a new awareness of our social obligations, are permeating the profession and will bear fruit in years to come. The new librarian of the future is more likely to object to censorship and the restriction of free choice, and will have the courage to stand up and say so. He will probably play down the importance of prestige buildings created as memorials to chief librarians and architects, and display greater interest in the needs of community groups, the elderly, the disadvantaged members of society, and the two-thirds of the population who never come through our doors. The latter, he will feel, are better served by outreach programmes, taking disposable books into their own home ground and recognising that this is the only sort of library service that will raise a glimmer of interest.

And then, say the cynics, the purposeful visitor to the central and branch libraries will suffer as a consequence, if an increasing share of the financial cake goes on outreach programmes. If public libraries in the future are to serve the community to an extent never before achieved, we may need to have our cake and eat it too. This means there will be a place for librarians of traditional persuasion, as well as the new breed described above. Our unexciting image, that of a conventional and superficially unchallenging profession, has failed to bring this new breed into librarianship until comparatively recently. Response to urban change – even to rural change – may seem a hackneyed phrase, but it is only now that one can feel with confidence that new librarians are becoming aware of the need to respond.

When attempting to visualise the public librarian of tomorrow, one's definition depends not only upon the sorts of aspects and concepts of the service which will be freshly emphasised. There are also developments within local government generally – structural, managerial and financial – which will inevitably affect the issue.

One of these concerns the chief librarian's position in the

management structure of his authority. The job satisfaction of the chief librarian managing his own department and reporting to his own committee is being overshadowed by the inexorable movement toward larger departments and more comprehensive committees. Following the 1967 Maud Report on the management of local government, and accelerated by local government reorganisation seven years later, there has been total upheaval with barely a trace of uniformity. Public libraries in the United Kingdom are now controlled by amenities committees, arts committees, cultural committees, education committees, general purposes committees, leisure committees, and so on. There are at least thirty-six varieties, according to a recent Library Association survey – including, believe it or not, a small number of authorities which still maintain the sweet old-fashioned libraries committee. In addition to this, many chief librarians report to an overlord Director of Education, or of Amenities, or to an officer holding a far less likely title whose overall responsibilities embrace the library service.

This is all with us. It is inevitable that further reorganisation in individual local authorities will take the process even further. But will it affect the public librarian of the future, except at chief librarian level? Need we concern ourselves, in fact, with the discontent of a few chief librarians, with the ranting of those to whom overlord positions are bad principally because librarians are not normally appointed to them? If we view the new committees and management structures seriously, it is reasonable to suggest that they can perform the useful function of co-ordinating activities into total programme areas, be they educational or recreational, and represent the most effective use of resources by enabling a committee to determine its priorities. How can a metropolitan authority, for example, decide between a new library and a new swimming pool when the librarian and the baths manager insist upon making their separate bids, and it is left to lay councillors to sort it out? More libraries will be affected in the future by corporate management plans within local authorities, will be subject to more comprehensive committees, and will be controlled by overlord directors. If he is to survive and play a constructive part, the chief librarian will have to adapt himself to it. His senior staff, who represent him at meetings and interact with other council officers and write committee reports, will be similarly affected. We shall require librarians with wider horizons, and with a fuller picture of the local government scene. Above all, we shall require librarians with management skills – even, dare one say, a sufficient supply of managers who are not necessarily suited to pure librarianship?

Professional librarians do not all, of course, make good administrators or managers. We tend to attract and recruit those who have their own ideas concerning the attributes of a good librarian, and management skill and leadership potential are less important in an applicant's mind than is his love of literature. This is changing, will change even more in the future, and is inevitable if librarians are to assume a respected position in local government instead of perpetuating an isolated position surrounded by professional mystique. For those who do not aspire to the heights of management, we shall still need the dedicated bookman for subject work and the socially aware practitioner for community outreach.

The most effective development within local government at present, however, has not been created by the authorities themselves. It is, in fact, part of a much wider issue – inflation. Local authorities found themselves faced with a cutback in resources which depressingly coincided with the 1974 reorganisation, the climate worsened in 1975 and is likely to remain a significant factor for some time. In short, the scene within which the public librarian of the future will operate will be determined largely by financial rather than professional considerations.

If one discusses staffing requirements in purely numerical terms, it is bitterly disappointing that we shall be unable to achieve any sort of standards within the foreseeable future. But this is nothing new, as we failed to do so even when money was more plentiful. Those recommended by the Working Party on *Standards of public library service* in 1962 were not achieved generally in England and Wales until 1970–71 in respect of total non-manual staff, and the minimum standard for professional staff has still only been achieved generally in the London

The Public Librarian

boroughs. The 1962 recommendations were crude – some might even say unrealistic – and were calculated on a population basis with little or no consideration given to the sort of services provided.

At the time of writing, the 1962 standards are still all we have available. By the time this appears in print, the report of the 1972–74 project by LAMSAC on behalf of the Department of Education and Science will, hopefully, have been published. One says this more in hope than with any firm conviction, and the inexplicable delay in its publication surely justifies any cynicism. The LAMSAC project investigated the utilisation of staff of different types and qualifications in public libraries, and had the following objectives:

i   To create a methodology for the study of public library staff utilisation based on existing job analysis techniques
ii To produce models or formulae capable of widespread application in given situations and conditions
iii To determine categories of information required to enable accurate assessments to be made of local library authorities' actual staffing provision
iv If feasible to recommend revised standards of provision for all types of public library staff
v   To attempt to estimate the trained manpower requirements of a public library system, assuming the most effective utilisation of staff and to test the standard for general applicability

How effectively it succeeded, it is not possible to tell at the time of writing. It should, at least, assist us with the much-needed manpower plan which will enable the DES to bury that exaggerated problem of the early 1970s, the over-production of librarians, providing that new young librarians overcome their reluctance to move away from home and/or into the less salubrious industrial areas so as not to recreate the myth of more 'unemployed' librarians. At local level, public libraries will be able to use formulae to determine their staffing requirements.

All this is very nice. Joking apart, it is vital, and the LAMSAC project is one of the most important pieces of work undertaken in public libraries since the McColvin Report. The snag is that each local authority will take its own independent decisions on the subject, and will pay lip-service – any more constructive results will depend upon the enlightenment of the authority concerned and the financial situation. Manpower formulae might, some day, be mandatory in public libraries; until then the Secretary of State for Education and Science will remain as powerless as he was proved to be over the question of vicious cuts in various library services during 1975–76.

Be that as it may, we shall at last have something positive, the results of excellent research and job analysis, on which to base our future staffing plans. Up to now it has been hit and miss, combined with much publicity and gnashing of teeth about the schools inflicting more new librarians upon us than libraries can absorb – publicity which has done nothing to attract recruits of a high quality into a profession which apparently does not want them.

To return to the matter of finance, however, it is likely that for many years the average public library will be functioning with a staffing situation which is far from ideal. More important than the application of manpower formulae will be the question of the most effective deployment of existing staff. Formulae should nevertheless be useful as a means of identifying bias – perhaps a public library might find, for example, that some of its professional posts should be transferred from reference work to children's work, or vice versa. This may be a further reason why the public librarian of the future will need to be more flexible in his approach.

It is in this matter of the effective deployment of staff – particularly in a nil growth situation – that great changes have occurred in recent years. The need to make the best use of professional staff has given rise to new staffing patterns in an increasing number of library authorities: Leicestershire, Bedfordshire, Cornwall, Lambeth, Coventry, Rotherham, and so on. These new patterns, if they prove themselves effective, might well become the customary patterns, and this would indeed have a tremendous effect upon the public librarian of the future. If they involve the division of library authorities into zones, with a multi-purpose professional team serving the community throughout each zone without being confined to any one branch library, librarians will be required of abilities which are perhaps not too common. They will need to participate in the formulation of objectives and programmes, display considerable initiative without constant supervision, and be responsive to community needs.

Although a spin-off of the team approach is that it permits professional staff coverage in small branch libraries which would not justify full-time qualified staff, it must not be assumed that revolutionary methods of staff deployment will be witnessed only in rural counties or areas of social deprivation. Still with us, and gaining a new lease of life, is the question of allocating subject responsibilities to teams of staff in large central libraries or throughout urban systems. This will require librarians who are interested in applying such skills as stock selection, cataloguing, promotion and advisory work within a specified subject field; and they must be less interested in performing these individual technical processes in professional isolation. McClellan's ideas concerning service in depth, which have so much to offer, will not be forgotten and might actually emerge in public libraries to a greater degree than heretofore.

There are other facets of the deteriorating financial situation, quite distinct from questions of manpower planning and staff deployment, which will nonetheless affect the public librarian of the future in various ways. It is now necessary, rather than to attempt to spread the butter more thinly as each year passes, to scrutinise our services quite ruthlessly. As it is unrealistic to accept severe cuts in expenditure without cuts in actual services, it will be vital to decide where our priorities lie. No longer will it be possible to measure success purely in terms of growth; the easy success of the past, achieved by doing a little more this year of what one did last year, was not necessarily desirable. If there is a redeeming feature in the cutback of public expenditure, at least it forces us to review our options and decide where limited resources are best employed.

The future public librarian will not, one hopes, see reductions in expenditure purely in terms of a battle between the bookfund and the salaries estimate. Quite clearly a cutback in one will have repercussions on the other, possibly resulting even in further unnecessary expenditure. A significant reduction in the number of books purchased might not justify the continued use of so many staff on accessioning and cataloguing procedures; while a reduction in staff numbers, or even the freezing of vacant posts, can mean that a bookfund will be spent hastily and with insufficient care by the remaining staff under exceptional pressure within the financial year.

In such a situation, one hopes that more librarians will be prepared to examine the entire service rather than each component in isolation. They will have to ask themselves what they are trying to do. Is the middle ground, for example, any longer so important? Can we ignore the needs of the casual reader of ephemeral material, and refer such readers to the ample supply of paperbacks available from bookshops? Will we admit that the main satisfaction we obtain from work with these readers is derived from their effect on our issue statistics? Perhaps we shall no longer be all things to all men in the future, but will channel our resources more purposefully towards the student and researcher, the person who requires information and assistance on a variety of topics, and – at the other end of the scale – the challenging two-thirds of the population who currently have no use for libraries, some of whom suffer social deprivation or are less than literate.

Pressured by financial stringency, there are other questions which the public librarian of the future will need to ask himself. Is it, for example, necessary to concentrate so many professional staff into central library departments, making these services extremely expensive? Might we not overcome our antipathy to the use of senior non-professionals, thus releasing qualified librarians for missionary work in the community? Is it possible for more of our backroom processes to be performed by outside agencies? Perhaps the new librarians will be as conservative and idiosyncratic as we are today, reacting against the concept of nationally agreed forms of book processing, cataloguing, and so on. If so, their staffs will be condemned to a lifetime of unproductive work instead of being enabled to pursue more fruitful work with the public.

Future public librarians will also find a change from the climate of the fifties and sixties, where a local authority would proudly boast that it had a branch library on every street corner. It is coming to be appreciated that the butter-spreading operation results in an inadequate service being provided at all of the libraries, and raises the important question of concentrating resources into fewer and more comprehensive libraries. Recent trends in the reduction of bookfunds and the cutting of opening hours merely achieve a situation of equality for all, one in which all residents of a town can be uniformly dissatisfied because each is receiving as poor a service as his neighbour. Committees will perhaps be prepared to consider the theory that a library user is prepared to travel a little farther than the mile usually recommended, provided that he receives a comprehensive and efficient service at the end of his journey – this would be supplemented, of course, by special services for the elderly and infirm, and to schools.

There are two final points which need to be made on the subject of financial stringency. First, it is to be hoped that more of the new librarians will display less ignorance in money matters; ideas they must have in plenty, but they must also demonstrate the ability to put these into effect within the prevailing economic climate. They need not be inhibited by thoughts that new services or improvements are impossible, but they must realise that these might have to be measured against the continuation of existing services. A cost-consciousness and a willingness to consider options and determine priorities will be essential attributes of the public librarian in the future, and it will have to start in his library education rather than when he emerges into the cold, hard world.

Secondly, we shall increasingly need people who are able to develop ways in which public libraries can actually make money. Libraries are becoming regarded as a drain on the ratepayer, with little compensatory income. We shall require ideas to prove to the powers-that-be that public libraries are able to make money in ways more effective and less regressive than by merely raising the rate of fines or reservation fees. More commercial ventures in library publishing, particularly in the field of local studies, are likely developments. Bookshops within libraries might become commonplace features. Special consultancy services to researchers, authors, trade and industry could well be costed and offered for sale – do they, after all, get a free service from their solicitor, architect or accountant? And finally, new librarians will have to develop even more finely the art of raising money from our prime source, the local authority itself, which will only be favourably inclined if librarians have the ability to prove that they have put their own house in order and are offering something worth paying for.

The expectations and needs of the profession itself, particularly in the matter of paper qualifications, will also have an effect upon our hypothetical public librarian of the future. So too, and very naturally, will pay and prospects. Education for librarianship is a topic covered elsewhere in this volume, but the temptation to refer to it briefly in passing is not easy to resist, particularly as it will have such a significant influence.

A question of immense concern to everyone is the desirability or otherwise of establishing librarianship as a graduate profession. It is, in spite of the present welcome delay while discussion takes place, virtually inevitable. Providing it is not purely for reasons of prestige or comparability with other professions, it probably has as many advantages as disadvantages. It will not, however, be the *open sesame* to the highest positions in public libraries. This can be stated with confidence, in the firm knowledge that those responsible for making senior appointments in local government will always have sufficient common sense to recognise such factors as professional skill, management ability, and cumulated experience, and to regard these attributes as more important than the academic qualifications obtained before a candidate ever embarked upon his career.

Although the influx of graduates into public libraries is welcome, and degrees in librarianship are rapidly replacing the present type of Associateship, future entrants might well find that a better start to their careers would be achieved if they worked for a year or so in properly planned positions in libraries before attending library school. It appears that more are now being encouraged to do this. The direct entrant, it seems, is no longer necessarily preferred by the schools. Indeed the schools are likely to co-operate increasingly in the appointment of staff to trainee posts in public libraries, to ensure suitability both as a student and a prospective librarian, and this is to be applauded.

Then there is that other paper qualification, the Fellowship. The majority of future public librarians will be unlikely to proceed to this, and the decline in the number of Fellows was observed by the LA Working Party deliberating upon the future of professional qualifications. It is undesirable, but nonetheless true, that Fellowship will play a diminishing part in the profession; certainly it would be ludicrous to demand the Fellowship for the highest management positions in public libraries, when that qualification is obtainable by writing a thesis which in no way qualifies the person for the job. It must be repeated, however, that this diminishing role of the Fellowship is undesirable, because in days of yore it identified librarians of the highest professional competence. If it is to resume that function, the controversial proposal of Fellowships by attainment must be seriously considered. One of the deciding factors in the selection of senior public librarians in the future might then be that their professional association has recognised their advanced competence in the higher reaches of librarianship.

One further point needs to be made on the question of paper qualifications, particularly in view of the larger public library systems which have now come into being. Can it not be stated quite openly that the public librarian of the future will find it more valuable to pursue management studies of some kind rather than undertaking theses? His prospects in local authority librarianship will be affected by his ability to understand and solve management problems, and to cast off the narrow-mindedness which has sometimes been the hallmark of our profession. The amalgamation of departments, as described earlier, will require senior officers of broad horizons.

It is fully appreciated that there will still be many public librarians who will not seek the highest management positions, and an encouraging sign for the future is the likelihood that the bookman and the specialist will be able to continue doing their preferred work and be remunerated reasonably for it. The 1975 staff and grading census conducted by the Library Association reveals a sizeable increase in the number of posts graded at senior and principal officer level. Until comparatively recently, good salaries were normally restricted to the highest tiers in public libraries, and it was necessary for any ambitious entrant to have the chief librarian's proverbial baton in his knapsack. The inevitable result was the promotion to premier positions of some librarians who, if the truth be told, would have preferred to remain as reference librarians or bibliographers. In the future it is likely that those who are more interested in librarianship than in management will have their skills and knowledge more adequately recognised. They are not, after all, working purely for the love of it.

At the lower end of the scale, the situation is depressing. In fact, viewing the appalling lack of progress since 1966, it is extremely difficult to be optimistic. The insulting relegation of librarianship to the 'also rans' at the lower end of the trainee grade is something which perhaps will be corrected in time – but how much time NALGO needs, future librarians might find a perplexing question to answer. Similarly bad, in fact little short of scandalous, is the fact that the AP3 award for posts requiring chartered librarians was agreed in 1965, disastrously relinquished in 1966, and finally reinstated after resorting to arbitration in 1975. Having observed a decade of back-pedalling, one is tempted to warn prospective public librarians of the low regard evidently paid to our profession by national negotiators and employers. It can encourage them little to be told of the richer rewards at the top of the tree, if they have this sort of hurdle to scale at the outset.

It must be emphasised, however, that all the factors previously mentioned will merely be so much academic discussion if there is no change in our public image. The typical conception of a public librarian – studious, introvert, colourless, somewhat

The Public Librarian

eccentric, deficient in the social skills – has often attracted into the profession recruits who feel they match this specification. Doctors, parents and well-intentioned friends attempt to push into librarianship their protegées who are admirably suited to our calling, being shy and retiring, inveterate readers, or recovering from nervous illnesses. This image deters the extrovert, just as the impression that public libraries are middle class institutions may have deterred entrants from other than that class in the past.

If public libraries are to fulfil their important roles in the future, they will require staff with a wide range of personality types and from varied backgrounds. The extrovert and the working-class entrant – the latter perhaps becoming more prevalent as educational opportunities improve – will break through our middle class image to gain new ground in our work with non-readers and in community outreach programmes. They will need to demonstrate to the public that librarians are not a race apart, and that their services are not aimed solely at the academic minority. It is to be hoped, also, that the new generations of coloured residents in Britain will be attracted toward a career in public librarianship, particularly in view of the awakening interest in library work with minority groups. It is singular that our multi-racial society has never been reflected in the usage of the public library service; perhaps multi-racial librarians would go a long way towards rectifying this.

One has only to scan the pages of some of today's library journals to appreciate that a new style of public librarian is indeed already emerging. The creed of a librarian once described by D. J. Foskett as 'no politics, no religion, no morals' is unacceptable to the new breed. They cannot be all things to all men; they are committed to various ideals, and occasionally they display a degree of bias rather than tread the thin line of political and social neutrality. All this will be increasingly noticeable in the future, and hopefully we shall enter an era in which society will recognise the public librarian as a trained practitioner skilled in establishing fruitful communication with his fellow human beings – even if the mass media prefer to indulge in caricature, as doubtless they will.

Chapter Eighteen

The School & Youth Librarian of the Future

Jennifer Shepherd

'Human history' wrote H. G. Wells more than half a century ago 'becomes more and more a race between education and catastrophe'. A race which is likely to accelerate if, as has been prophesied, the changes of the next forty years are to equal in significance those of the last four hundred. To try to foretell the developments which will occur in libraries and education, and the consequent implications on the role of the school and youth librarian, must, to some extent, be like looking into a kaleidoscope. A pattern emerges, the pieces – existing and potential trends in education, sociology and technology. Shaken, the pieces will fall to form different patterns. Whatever the result, always there must be flexibility to allow for new factors or implications. Recession is one such example; had it been possible to see in advance the current economic position, it might well have been avoided. Inevitably it will halt development for a time, but it cannot put back the clock, and 'normal progress will be resumed as soon as possible'.

The library and change
It has been suggested by some pessimistic futurologists that libraries will eventually become obsolete. Facilities for access to data banks, and instant retrieval of information through home media may, in time, make some of our functions outmoded. Whether all homes will have access to these devices is questionable, but even so, information retrieval is only one aspect of our work. Libraries will still be needed, so will librarians.

The School and Youth Librarian

The librarian of the future must become a positive force in society, providing a necessary balance by supplementing the information given out by the media. He must work with educationalists to encourage the promotion of literacy, lifelong education and ensure that the individual is never denied his right to think for himself, to question, to understand and to use creatively the increased leisure that will come.

Specialisation and integration

What of school and youth libraries, have they a future? In the last decade the concept of integration has been fashionable. In public libraries this has resulted in open plan buildings, experiments with stock and more flexible patterns of staffing. In schools comprehensive education, team teaching, the integrated day, and the community school are examples of this. Increasingly the feeling is that over-separation in providing for children, youth, and adults is detrimental to community needs. Generally specialisation has become less respectable than in previous generations, perhaps because it can be in conflict with society's need for adaptable human beings, able to cope with change. Integration must be an acceptable concept, but there are dangers that without sufficient specialisation services will become superficial, and quality deteriorate.

Integration or specialisation will be one problem which will need to be solved in the future. But is this really a problem – are these concepts necessarily mutually exclusive? We have in the past tended to think that professional specialisations must be decided at the initial training stage. It has not been easy to change professions, or even within one profession to move from one branch to another. Would it not be more reasonable to decide first the staffing needs for particular services and then devise courses which cumulate to give the right blend of professional education?

In this connection there has been, in the past, some rather woolly thinking about the function of the school and youth library. Perhaps it has been assumed that since the user is the same, this overrides the purpose of use. But librarians and educationalists of the future will have to analyse the work more closely. It may be that public and school libraries will have different aims and objectives, and consequently be run on adjacent but parallel lines. It could mean more separation of identity, co-operation rather than duplication, mutual support rather than opposing proprietorship.

The needs of education
Deciding the type of librarian most suited to work in the school must start from the basis of understanding the educational process, its challenges and developments in the future. As education changes, so must the role of the school librarian. Librarian or teacher/librarian? In spite of the increase in resource based learning and the consequent implications on the school library, the proliferation of statements and standards and the increasing opportunities for dual training, still we have found no real answer to this question which has hung over both professions for forty years.

Currently education is in a state of transition. Still to be resolved is the dichotomy inherent in comprehensive ideals in a competitive society. Progressive education calls for non-selection, non-streaming and heuristic, resource based learning. This is the way of life in many schools today. The community school, *education permanente*, the open school where pupils are free to come and go as they choose, are further indications of the trend for flexibility and open endedness in education. The reasons are not hard to find – learner centred discovery methods of education can produce more perceptive students than formal and dicactic teaching. They may be more mentally active, socially adept, more resilient to cope with the fast moving pace of change. At the same time there are those who feel that already the pendulum has swung too far. Modern educational methods may not provide enough mental discipline. Too little competition can produce bored, soft students, and the needs of employers must be considered. Concerned that education for social change may have too much emphasis on social change and too little on education, they argue for a swing back to a more traditional approach. More recently there has come a movement for rationalisation – the emphasis on increased teaching of skills, literacy, numeracy, research techniques – basic training, without which self learning cannot take place. This does not confute heuristic learning; both can exist alongside, each supporting the other.

Educational technology could provide some of the answers here, defined as 'the development, application and evaluation of systems, techniques and aids to improve the process of human learning'.[1] It is also concerned with the relationship between different kinds of resources, the teacher, the book, the television film. It asks questions: 'What is the best means of creating an appropriate learning environment for a given task?' 'When is it that real learning takes place?'

Education in the future
What of the future? The scope for technology in education is tremendous: long distance xerography, inter-continental and multi-lingual transmission by satellite of educational programmes through television, teleprinter, and computer. On the nearer horizon, videodisc, holography, increasing use of microforms and audio-visual packages, are some of the more obvious implications.

It may be that more emphasis will be placed on the diagnostic approach to teaching, and the use of appropriate programmes to put right learning failures. Such emphasis would have to be viewed with caution, since it could be open to abuse by propagandists. Dial access, which has been styled the 'battery hen method' of education, is considered by some as a reversal of modern educational philosophy. Other changes may include more flexible timetabling and certainly more responsibility placed on the student himself, especially in secondary and higher education.

If students learn at different rates, couldn't some of them achieve the goal in three years or two, whilst others worked at it for five or six . . . ? Tell the student what is expected of him, what the end result of his liberal education should be . . . and then let the student decide, in the light of his own personality, interests, and ability, how best he can make use of the . . . resources to achieve that mastery.[2]

Whatever the outcome, it would seem unlikely that in the future there will be any complete return to the exam-orientated, subject-based approach.

The school library

How does this affect the school library? Without any doubt this must become increasingly supportive to the work of the school. It will seem less and less like a library in the traditional sense, rather a workshop, learning laboratory, the key to learning within the school. The school library will be stocked with multi-media, and it will also have extensive reprographic facilities and flexible arrangements of space to provide for different functions and groups of different sizes. Schools will have to spend more of their budgets on materials for the school library.

At the end of the last century a characteristic industrial plant had about 75% of its capital invested in the buildings and 25% in the tools and equipment. If you look at an educational budget you will see that this is roughly true... (today). In this century industry has reversed the proportions.[3]

The stock will have to be selected in relation to the curricula; and organised, indexed, disseminated, exploited, and educationally evaluated. Supplementary material will be published by educational bodies, national, local, or from an individual school.

With all this emphasis on reading or reserching for a purpose, it is still vitally important that students should be encouraged to read for pleasure, to browse, and to absorb. The Bullock Report[4] has emphasised the responsibility of both librarians and teachers in the promotion of literacy. It may be that in a future where there will be so much emphasis on technology this will be something which will have to be safeguarded.

The school librarian

If this is to be the pattern of the school and school library of the future – what of the school librarian? To fulfil these needs the role must become increasingly specialist – the post holder may be librarian-teacher or teacher-librarian, perhaps dual-trained, or a dual role filled by two people. It will probably become less important which profession is the base if adequate facilities exist for adding specialist training. However, the school library will certainly not be run by one person – adequate supporting staff, clerical and technical, will be essential. It will be necessary to ensure that a senior educationalist with responsibility for curricula development and educational evaluation is associated with the library.

It will be important for the school librarian to have adequate status, remuneration, and time to do the job, and also to ensure that he does not become isolated from the mainstream of *either* profession. One can see dangers if the school librarian is not fully recognised as teacher or librarian. If the right people are to be recruited, there must be the opportunities to advance in either career. This can only come by adequate training in both professions. The solution may be a graduate with basic training in library and/or education and postgraduate course work to boost as required. However the dose is administered the final result must include educational theory and practice, the teaching of reading, psychology, sociology, evaluation of materials, indexing, dissemination of information, knowledge of other libraries and library networks, and organisation and management. Personal attributes which will be welcomed include vision, energy, drive, confidence, adaptability, leadership and, overall, a belief in the positive role of the school library in education. The individual school library is never likely to be self-sufficient. It will need the support of a school library service or area resource centre staffed by specialist librarians with technical and clerical support. It may include librarian-teachers, some at high level to act as schools' advisers. As school libraries progress the demands on these central support services will become more technical and specialist; an increase in information, copying services, publication facilities, provision for the buying and servicing of materials and equipment will be required. Those working in this service must have an extensive knowledge of the materials and the needs of the schools.

The primary school

So far we have been thinking in terms of secondary education. For the majority of primary schools, if these continue to be based in small units, the 'librarian' is likely to remain essentially a teacher, though increasingly one with training adequate for this role. It will continue to be individual teachers who exploit and use the materials in the curriculum and encourage their pupils to read. Advice on selection and organisation of materials will be provided more systematically that at present, either through the centralised support services or its area branch, or the parent secondary school.

Teacher training

Inevitably, organisation of pre- and in-service courses for both primary and secondary teachers will make great demands on librarians. They will have to provide active, creative support in what will become recognised as an essential aspect of teacher education

> ... the division between librarian and teacher is one which has got to disappear. The librarian has got to become an active, creative guide in the learning process, just as much as the teacher ... the pattern that we are moving towards is one in which librarians and teachers join in the common enterprise as guides rather than teachers, assistants, promoters and motivators rather than direct informers.[3]

The Public Library and Youth

If, in fact, the school library is to become a special library, orientated towards the needs of education, the public library must continue to have responsibility for serving young people. Recently in some parts of the United States, public libraries have abdicated these services in favour of schools, and this seems tragically short sighted; a marriage of convenience caused by economic considerations, and without due regard to function. In Denmark, on the other hand, the school and public library have recently become totally divorced and decided 'to separate with little contact – the student doing the crossover'.[5] This seems equally unfortunate – the school library can all too easily become isolated, and the public library must have close involvement with community education if it is to survive. It

The School and Youth Librarian

should be possible to provide a means whereby there is mutual support, co-operation and involvement whilst not confusing co-operation with integration. The dual use library remains another unsolved problem of our time. The DES advises

> when the future location of public library service points is being determined, consideration should be given to the possible advantages of establishing dual-use libraries ... libraries of this kind should be considered only when the site is satisfactory from the point of view of both the general public and the educational establishment. Where these conditions can be met then dual-use can result in a significant improvement in both staffing and bookstock available to the School.[6]

No one would quarrel with that, but forced schemes for the sake of economy and without due regard to the separate needs of school and public have done great harm to this concept.

If the problems of siting are soluble, and the needs of the users and functions of the library are properly defined, there would seem to be nothing but advantages in dual-use; but it is in two libraries side by side, each supporting, but not encroaching on the other, that the real solution will lie.

The youth librarian

How best, then, can provision be made for young people by the public library? It is necessary to identify those elements which call for a specialist approach and then decide on the degree of integration with other services. The main reason for having specialists in this field has been that the developmental nature of the young user called for knowledge of his psychology, education, growth potential and detailed familiarity with relevant materials. The scope for exploitation and creative influence on reading habits has always been far greater than with adults, whose tastes are more formed and who are less likely to change. However, latterly the increasing sophistication of the young library user, and the widening curricula, have led to more integration between adult and children's services: this trend is likely to continue.

These days the youth librarian increasingly finds himself working in some sort of team situation perhaps as part-time specialist. Whilst this helps to keep a broadened outlook it can also be frustrating in lack of time, both for work and keeping up to date with the subject. Again, this should not be an insoluble problem. One answer might be the Youth Team, with librarians having particular specialisations: pre-school, primary, secondary. Adequately supported by clerical and technical staff, and working closely with the adult service team, it should be possible to counteract any tendency for an introverted attitude in either service.

The training needs for librarians working with youth partly overlap with those of the school librarian. There should be a greater emphasis on sociology and literature and rather less on education and information work. Ability to talk to large and small groups will be essential, and other attributes will include sensitivity to the needs of others, ability to adapt, lack of prejudice, 'open people, open to problems, open to themselves'.[7] The fact that the youth librarian is not in direct authority over children does not take away his responsibility for the induction of learning and creativity outside school.

The youth librarian is likely to be working in harness with other professions. Increasingly libraries will become part of corporate local government service. The youth librarian will find working with other community services, youth leaders, health educationalists, careers officers and teachers, ensures greater strength in planning for the overall needs of youth. The potential for work with young people is so great that even with increased numbers of specialist librarians it will never be possible to do more than skim the surface of what needs to be done. One answer may be in the use of volunteer workers – carefully selected, adequately trained and supervised. The youth librarian may find himself in this case more of a leader, adviser, and organiser than hitherto. The use of volunteers may also come, not only because in that way more work can be done, but because planning *with* the people rather than for them is essential, particularly in deprived areas. Might we see the return of the junior helper, for more considered reasons?

Central support in the services of a National Library Bureau may make available reviewing and bibliographical services. Some acceptance of national standards would be necessary in the interests of economy of effort.

The library – materials and activities
The stock of the library will obviously extend to include audio-visual materials, hardware, microforms and probably toys for young and disadvantaged children, games, and educational packages.

The arrangements of materials and the furnishing of libraries will become more attractive and informal. More viewing and listening facilities will be needed, and areas where young people can individually enjoy creative work with paint or clay, apart from any organised programmes. The library will become far more of a cultural centre with a schedule of events, 'happenings', folk music, creative art, drama, and book related activities – a lively centre of informal education. Opening hours may need to be extended if schools operate a more flexible timetable. The lending function may become less important. It could be more economically viable to copy an item, to either sell or give away. The sale of books and other materials in libraries and through library-organised projects will surely come. This would seem to be one way of ensuring an outlet for the less commercially viable items and providing people with the choice of buying their own materials – indeed the three aspects of loan, copying, and sale may become much more interlinked.

Publishing trends
Whilst the problem of adequate functional literacy will hopefully be a thing of the past, the promotion of reading for pleasure is likely to require more emphasis and better techniques. Whatever has been said by the prophets of doom, the book, inexpensive, portable, needing neither machinery nor power, available in infinite different varieties, suited to browsing, to skimming, reading or studying, must be preserved. Competition will come from other forms of media; some will be more suited to a particular purpose than the book, some will be attractive, but perhaps superficial. Librarians and educationalists will have

to work together to encourage young people to read. What is published will depend on what is wanted. Already visible on the horizon are increasing signs of large commercial publishers *marketing* their products and on the look-out for easy profit margins. Already the computer is being used to edit – could there be a danger of computer writing?

Librarians will not be alone in fighting to preserve the best: the original, the work of art, the stimulating rather than the stultifying. It is to be hoped that they will also be concerned to deter propaganda, if the library is to continue as a bastion of free thought.

Special groups
For some time much greater emphasis will be placed on the needs of special groups. It is difficult to foretell whether immigrants will remain a special group. Perhaps there will be a gradual progression to multi-racial integration, or the reverse could happen – ethnic separation. Either way, the library will have an important role in preserving or providing materials related to different cultures.

The needs of the gifted, the less able, the physically and mentally handicapped must not be forgotten. It should not be beyond the bounds of possibility to produce books or machinery more suited to their needs than those at present available.

The socially deprived will continue to be a particular challenge for librarians. The library building is off-putting to some people who may be easily inhibited by the need to fill in forms, find their way around, perhaps pay fines or fees. Much can be done to 'unfreeze' the library atmosphere. The logical extension of services must be to make books accessible in such places as supermarkets, playgroups and swimming baths. The provision of caravans, buses and playmobiles to lend or even to give away books, and to use as a base for folk music, drama, and film will enable librarians to go where the traditional library does not reach. The youth librarian must also venture into parks and playgrounds to encourage children to read. He must not be afraid to use some of the techniques of commerce to 'sell' reading and libraries.

The teenage library
It is notable that whilst the majority of libraries in this country have not provided facilities for teenagers, commercial enterprises have made millions out of such special provision. Today the young adult matures earlier and is more affluent than ever before. The result of a Finnish survey[8] concludes that '15–20 year olds require areas for their own use whilst the under-fifteens need contact with adults'. Perhaps future planning of buildings will provide separate areas for their use, and librarians will take more seriously their particular information needs and the wider selection of non-traditional materials for their use.

The need for an organiser for youth as well as for children is argued in some of the documentation from the States and recently adopted in at least one library in this country. In Canada and the USA Young Peoples' librarians bridge the gap between children and adults and perhaps here lies the answer – the special librarian rather than the special room.

As in education, cost-effectiveness and results will be called for, so the youth librarian will have to be more management conscious. Increasingly there will have to be some attempt at analysing and evaluating the results of promotional schemes, and it will be necessary for the youth librarian to be adaptable enough to change plans and programmes in response to the results. He will need, as will the school librarian, to keep abreast of new developments, methods and techniques.

Two patterns
And so it would seem that my kaleidoscope shakes down a pattern of school librarian and youth librarian. Each will have a slightly different professional education, but with a core essentially the same. The future school librarian will be working more closely with education, whilst the youth librarian will have the challenge and opportunity of bridging the gap between

formal and informal education. If each has a clear definition of purpose, a realisation of the challenge and responsibility to young people in and out of school, there will be more than enough for each of them to do.

References in text

1. *Educational technology: progress and promise.* NCET, 1973.
2. de Grazia, Alfred *and* Sohn, David A. *Revolution in teaching: new theory, technology and curricula.* Bantam, 1964.
3. MacKenzie, N. Educational communication. In *The shape of things to come.* London and Home Counties Branch of the Library Association. Library Association 1968.
4. Bullock, Sir A. *A language for life.* HMSO, 1975.
5. Thorsen L. *Public libraries in Denmark.* (Danish Information Handbooks). Det Danske Selskab, Copenhagen, 1972.
6. Department of Education and Science. Library Information Series No. 2. *Public library service: Reorganisation and after.* HMSO 1973 p 16. Para 75.
7. Bowen, E. Children *are* people *in* Library Association *Proceedings of the Public Libraries Conference,* 1973.
8. Nuotio, Samuli. Ongelmallinen nuoriso (The problematic young). *Kirjastolehti,* 66(1) 1973, 10–12.

Chapter Nineteen

Design of Library Buildings of the Future

J M Orr

To contemplate the future of library buildings in the present state of 'siege' and 'no-growth' economies which exist in the UK at the present time demands that kind of super-optimism which inspired the Library Association and Lionel McColvin to begin to construct a post-war reorganisation of public libraries in the dark days of the early 1940s when the country was in a war-created siege.

The building and equipping of libraries, however small, is a process which needs relatively large capital outlays and it follows, however regrettably, that reasonable economic savings can be made by delaying the start of new buildings and 'making-do' with the old. That this is what the near-future holds is perhaps the safest prognosis which can be made, but I take it that the purpose of this work is not to play safe but rather to live dangerously, making the presumption that the economy will revive and grow and that reasonable sums will be allocated to librarianship, notwithstanding the equally important demands which will come from other areas making demands upon the public purse, particularly those making contributions to social welfare.

Let the profession of librarianship remind itself that it is highly doubtful if any other group within society is as cost conscious as it has been forced to be. It deals with one of the cheapest manufactured commodities in a materialistic world, and one which takes a very considerable amount of wear and tear, allowing another 'make-do' situation whereby items which are in a state of physical deterioration may be retained because they are still used. Optimism for the future is justified if only by comparing the state of library buildings and their stocks in the pre-1945 era with their present state. If the advances made in the next thirty years equate with the advance made in the last thirty, there is hope.

To our profession it will be clear that many new buildings will be needed. At the summit, so to speak, is the much debated new accommodation for the Reference Division of the British Library. For something like twenty years it has been obvious to librarians that the need was imminent, but by the time the politicians who had to provide the finance became convinced, a new and highly emotional controversy arose concerning a site for the new building. After years of committee wrangling the issue is now settled and the BLRD moves to Euston Road. This unfortunate and seemingly interminable tangle serves to remind us of the difficulties of convincing political laymen of what may seem so obvious to us. Protracted negotiations lie ahead.

Shades of Carnegie
Many public libraries, especially in urban areas, are still operating services from buildings which, although they may still have architectural attractions, have an inflexibility which makes it difficult to promote the new services and the new image desired by many librarians. The patronage of Andrew Carnegie still casts shadows. Despite the very considerable increase in the provision of libraries in schools, with the rather sad change of name to 'resource centre', one still hears stories of the library rooms being taken over for basic teaching needs, an example of a very common failing of initial under-provision, always done with the needs of immediate economies in mind rather than future real needs. At the lower rung of the educational ladder the provision of books and learning resources is accepted as necessary, the need for the encouragement of the children to make individual use of them less so. Even if it is felt that it is better to store the books in the classroom, there is still a real need for the careful consideration of the method of display. The proposed continuing growth in higher education will continue to create increasing demands on their library services and it is no

Design of Library Buildings

great feat of crystal-ball gazing to realise that increase in the numbers of new buildings will also continue as has happened over the last ten to fifteen years. Accepting the optimism of future growth, what of the more detailed matters of concern?

I suggest that, more than anything else, the plea will be for the continuation and betterment of co-operation between librarian and architect. This much vexed question of yesteryear has seen a fairly dramatic recent improvement. Continual financial pressure on architects to design buildings on limited budgets has seen the last of Gothic intricacies and the last of expensive prestige materials. Added to this is the pressure from clients to listen to their needs which, together with over-increasing specialisation, has seen the emergence of the corporate management concept of the design team. It may be that the architect has to play the role of leader of the team and as such has had to be the final arbiter if this has proved necessary, but the idea of the corporate approach has taken much of his autocracy away. No longer can the librarian claim that the architect acted unilaterally, nor the architect that the librarian did not know what he wanted. As part of a working design team they must communicate with one another and with other specialists on the team. Much of the communication will be informal talk, but the formalities of the librarian's brief to the architect, possibly on pro-formas for simplicity and standardisation, the architects' sketches and plans, and written memos and letters will all help to achieve the desired objective. The signs are good for the future and it may be unfortunate to introduce a somewhat discordant note, but it seems reasonable to speculate that society may at some time decide that the method of percentage payment of professional architectural services is disproportionate to professional expertise supplied by the client, and a more equitable method found to further equate the different yet compatible roles. Progress in design of functional buildings as libraries will only be achieved by such close liaison, with sympathy and empathy being shown by both.

Having said that, let us look at the architect's problems: in many instances it will be found that librarians can offer encouragement to him, the only proviso being that in achieving his objective he gives a very high priority to his design in terms of the activities which it is anticipated will be required to take place.

The trouble with the over-zealous, cost-conscious, functionally-orientated client is that his insistence on these principles being applied severely restricts the architect to multi-storey square boxes (or rectangles) at least in high-density areas where libraries are most likely to be built. His chances of producing a prestige building like the cathedrals of old being built to the glory of God, are next door to nil. Yet librarians would like prestige buildings, built, if you like, to the glory of civilisation which would now be indubitably different but for the existence of libraries. Is this too much to hope for? It is if we expect this for all libraries, but perhaps for one or two. If Australia can see its way to finance its Sydney Opera House, despite the fact that the whole venture was fraught with difficulties of all kinds, is it too much to hope for some similar prestige library buildings? It may be that the UK has a golden opportunity with the new BLRD. The change of site for this building offers a chance for a rethink of the plans. This is the finest and most prestigious library in the UK. As the British Museum Library, it gained international recognition of the highest order and many of its features were copied elsewhere, though in the twentieth century it was overshadowed by others with more outgoing philosophies. Part of the intention of the creation of the new British Library was to give a new lease of life to the Museum Library. Let the new building proclaim this, let it be symbolic of the importance and necessity of libraries, let it be prestigious, and it could be one of the greatest architectural challenges of the century. If this is achieved it could well be that others will follow.

Restraints and opportunities
Even if architects are allowed aesthetic freedom to achieve prestige buildings they will be subjected to other constraints. One of these is being pressed now, and the pressure is likely to increase. The immediate power shortage in the UK will to some extent be alleviated by the full utilisation of North Sea oil, but current shortages have alerted the world that fossilised fuels are not inexhaustible. The need for energy conservation places a responsibility on architects to design buildings which are

sufficiently well insulated to minimise the production of heat and to install systems which conserve and recycle what is produced. This is advantageous to libraries, as insulation to keep heat in means that noise is kept out and good recycling systems means better air-conditioning and therefore better environmental condition for readers, staff and stocks. One major criticism most often levied at recent new library buildings concerns the heating and ventilation. Even where full air-conditioning systems are installed, localised hot or cool spots seem to develop. Any advances made to overcome these problems will be most welcome and completely compatible with a librarian's aim. It is possible that energy conservation may mean a reduction of lighting standards but provided the reduction is sensible this may be turned to advantage. These standards have risen throughout the century to such a level that one wonders how anyone ever read anything after sundown before the advent of electric light. Why, in any case, should the standards have always been higher in the USA than the UK? There is no evidence that the Americans are more myopic; there is evidence that they are more affluent and in a better position to squander light. To some a high level of artificial illumination only adds to the already harsh and clinical lines of many modern libraries. A more judicious use of lighting can be more aesthetically pleasing.

The architect, no less than any other artist, is dependent on, and to some extent dictated to, by the materials available to him. The differences between stone, red-brick and glass-and-concrete buildings are less than subtle, and the latest era of glass, concrete and chrome has contributed largely to the clinicism mentioned above. A few years ago it was thought that a new materials-era was imminent – plastics. In 1955 the first all-plastic house was manufactured and many more experimental prototypes have been produced, apparently with considerable success. At its strongest, plastic is almost indestructible, its strength-to-weight ratio is excellent, it is water- and vapour-proof, it can be produced in a wide range of textures and colours, and it can be moulded to almost any shape. An almost ideal building material, but of course there is a catch.

Injection-moulding equipment is highly capital intensive, and must therefore produce long runs to reduce unit costs, and to the regret of many architects the building industry is not organised for mass production on the scale necessary, though the factory prefabrication of building units by such systems as SCOLA and CLASP may be the foundation for future plastics manufacture. This high cost is the reason why present plastics are mainly used for long-run items such as piping, wiring, and equipment such as chairs, tables and light fittings. The extension of its use to major building components could see some fairly radical changes.

The mass production of building units should reduce the cost of buildings, but it would lead to more standardisation and further reduction of the architect's scope in designing something special, but this will be no different from the dilemma he has been in throughout history. The problem to be solved is how to mass-produce units cheaply, yet have a sufficient variety of them to afford the architect's scope. The other alternative is to research for cheaper production methods to make short-run moulding economic. We should not leave this point without commenting that costs saved are mainly in labour for building and that if prefabricated massproduction leads to unemployment then this may be unacceptable to society. In this instance we must hope that society does not take a 'Luddite' attitude to the problem, but that the money saved in building costs is used for increased library staff-establishments.

The multiplying of building units may lead to an increase in the flexibility of building design. This is one principle of design upon which every writer on the subject is agreed. In an age of constant and rapid change it is a brave man who is prepared to be adamant on what will be required of a building in ten years' time and it needs a prophet to look fifty years ahead. Methods of modular construction of large buildings allow much scope for future alteration of room sizes, and a minimum of fixed furniture and equipment means that it is relatively easy to alter the configuration of rooms – it is much more difficult to increase the total size of buildings. Given a site on which expansion is possible, the construction of the building should be such that a future increase of square metreage is possible with a minimum of

Design of Library Buildings

fuss. A meccano-set method of building may seem to put severe constraints on the concept of symbolic prestige, but there is an aesthetic argument that there can be great beauty in simplicity. When an architect finds a fairly recent university library 'credible only as a disinterred bunker with Gothic hood moulds', it is obvious that simplicity has its apostles.

However convenient building flexibility is to a librarian, it is no substitute for complacency with regard to the functions the design of the building has to achieve. Economic pressures are applied to current as well as capital expenditure and librarians – as always, some will say – will have to scrutinise their services very thoroughly. Cost-benefit analyses of library activities need not lead to cheese-paring savings, but should force librarians to reconsider the basic philosophies of their services in order to achieve some order of priority.

The needs of non-book media
One important area in which this continual evaluation will take place is the use of audio-visual media of communication in all types of library. The obvious benefits of the spoken word and the visual picture, movie or still, has to be balanced against the expense of the software which carries the message and the hardware which is necessary to transmit it. The reality of readers' resistance to the technology, coupled with the expense of providing appropriate consultation situations and areas, will demand a very close market appraisal. At the present time there are examples of under-provision and over-provision. Gramophone records are now commonplace public library provision, audio-cassettes less so, and the provision of listening facilities in the libraries for those who do not possess play-back equipment is lamentable. At the same time in many a school, polytechnic, and university library, batteries of machines are made available on the glib assumption that readers are queuing to use the new media. There is going to be a continuing need for objective research on the use and value of the new media, if libraries of the future are to make proper provision in their design. A time-honoured method of estimating requirements has always been to relate the concept of your new building to the

practicalities of similar buildings at present in operation, and what is often of most value is an honest appraisal of what has gone wrong rather than what is right. May we be protected from people who cannot make mistakes.

Evaluation of objectives, aims, targets, organisations, function, services, techniques and activities at all levels is a prerequisite of good design. The more certain a librarian is about these concepts the more sure he will be in briefing his architect, and the more likely the physical building will help in achieving the fundamental philosophies.

At national level the new building for the BLRD has to achieve two major aims. It has to act as a great storage library and offer a modern-day service to advanced research workers. Major decisions will be required relating to storage methods including possible outhousing. The trend towards subject departmentalisation, started by the insistence that there should be a separate National Reference Library of Science and Invention – now called the Science Reference Library – will be of utmost importance. The decisions taken, and the reasons for these decisions, will be scrutinised with great care by the whole profession of librarianship and it is probable that this new building, like that of its predecessor, will act as a prototype for many future designs.

Equally so, it is probable that the new BLRD building will reflect much of present-day design, and it is likely that the standardisation of design so prevalent in new university library buildings will reappear. This standardisation takes the form of a rectangular, multi-storeyed building, of modular construction with open-plan floors on which are mixed various proportions of staff offices, display shelving, stack shelving, seating and study areas, all with appropriate circulation aisles. Many will hope that there may be possibilities of breaking this pattern, yet in the rapidly expanding and ever-changing institutions of higher education flexibility is of the utmost importance and the pattern achieves that. The more practical proposition is that within the general pattern more subtle changes of direction are made in terms of more attention being paid to details of design.

Design of Library Buildings

School and public library design
The evangelists of librarianship are the school and public library services. A major part of their role is to attract users to the fascination and excitement of using the communications stored within them. To this end their premises must have the best possible site, must clearly proclaim its purpose, and should encourage a sense of adventure with all who use its services. It could be claimed that the clinicism of present design, manifold in the regimentation of ranges of book-cases, tiered with plasticated books, is contrary to a spirit of adventure. There is scope for much imagination here if only at the level of designing special exhibition areas with a real impact. In a modern society in which the control of mass-media is vested in fewer and fewer people it may be considered vital that there is at least one channel through which the individual John Citizen has unrestricted freedom of choice of communications. That channel must be the library network of the country, and to the majority the initial introduction to the network is the school library, and the continued use of the network is via the public library. By their design both types should loudly proclaim this ideal.

The occasions on which special libraries are purpose built will remain few and far between, forcing the special librarian to join his other colleagues in concentrating on the level of design concerned with the detailed activities of users.

The previous plea for an objective assessment of the uses of audio-visual materials can be extended to all other library activities. Many of these, like the basic activity of reader consulting book, have not changed much throughout the years, yet this is no reason for complacency in thinking that all the answers have been found. There must always be room for new experimentation with old problems. Undoubtedly many new ideas will founder on the rock of practicality; nevertheless this is the methodology of progress. The failure of the expanding-sided, mobile library did not herald the demise of the mobile library, nor for that matter the end of the idea. The challenge of designing a mobile to have the necessary compactness for mobility yet a reasonable area to operate from will always be a fascinating one.

It is not particularly difficult to think up new possibilities of design if, in the first instance, practicalities are ignored. A useful psychological game can be played in this process of the creation of new ideas. Based on a concept of corporate thinking the game may be called 'Brain-Storming' and the rules are simple. A group of interested and reasonably knowledgeable people meet to discuss problems, which are put to the group, each member being invited to comment in an uninhibited way. The discussion is unstructured in that remarks are made to the group as a whole and not to individuals so that structured dialogue is avoided. All discussion is recorded and later analysed in the hope that the interaction of ideas in the corporate mind may reveal new possible approaches. An inter-disciplinary approach can provide additional stimulation and reminds us of the team approach. Invariably the leisurely and objective analysis of ideas highlights the extremes and indicates the areas where practical compromise and balance has to be found.

Two possible areas of discussion which seem obvious are the problems connected with the storage of books and other graphics, and the provision of study facilities for readers. In the first instance it will be found that an extreme storage situation which may be cost saving must be balanced against an objective of displaying materials to allow free and easy access to the stock. Periodical literature is a good example. A full, face-on, vertical display of current issues can be attractive and encourages use, but it is expensive in lateral space. At the other extreme horizontal storage saves a great deal of space but provides no eye-catching display. There are a number of compromise, intermediate situations, but the necessary furniture is expensive. It may be that all alternatives have not been explored and let those who think that they have been be reminded that it is not so very long ago that the LTP box was produced as a result of an American research project. That simple, cheap yet effective little box in one form or another is now found in a very large number of libraries as it has proved to be a really practical method of dealing with fugitive pamphlet, leaflet, and broadside literature. It may be that other similarly simple solutions are to be found in solving problems of storage and display of the many other new media now prevalent. The problems, old and new, must continue to be reviewed in the future.

Tailor made for users
For those who feel, as I do, that library services should be tailored to meet the needs of an individual user, the challenge of examining and re-examining design problems with this objective in mind should have some priority. It can clearly be held that the design concept of how readers meet and interface with professional staff is sadly lacking in many libraries. How do you design furniture which does not present a barrier-like appearance? The creation of study facilities also needs examination. Open-plan flexibility makes it difficult to provide privacy, yet this is often desirable. But how often? There is some evidence that some undergraduate readers opt for communal reading-tables, whilst others opt out of the library when this becomes over-crowded at peak periods. It would seem that there is a need for provision of a variety of study situations with different levels of privacy thus allowing individual choice. The balance of casual, open-table, open carrel, and closed carrel situations needs investigating if appropriate provision is to be made in the future. Some would also hold that a more detailed survey of the ergonomics of reader and study tables is badly needed if advances in design have to be made. Time-lapse camera studies are needed.

So, if the future may seem bleak for the higher levels of design problems, there must still be many thousands of relatively minor, yet important, practicalities which can be looked at. As one example – and it would be very surprising if a 'brain-storm' did not produce many more – a Director of Libraries recently told me of how he disliked card-catalogue drawers with handles and he therefore specifically ordered a design with concealed finger-pulls. After a short period of use female staff were complaining of broken finger-nails.

The revision of library standards will continue. Those which are promulgated as building standards will have to be rigidly adhered to as they come in the form of legislation framed in the best interests of safety and it is possible we may be faced with some relating to energy conservation. No doubt professional bodies will also produce more in the hope that they may be used to upgrade allowances of space requirements, but these will be subjected to much local variation and certainly to cost-pressures as they prevail at a particular time and place.

Which brings us back to the rather pessimistic beginning, somewhat frantically searching for an optimistic end-note. For this, it is necessary to take a flight of near-fancy into the realms of near-technology if not science fiction. Paradoxically this could mean the end of library buildings as we know them. If the ultimate objective of librarianship is to meet the needs of the individual as and when he requires access to graphically recorded communications, it must be conceded that this can only be finally achieved by direct and immediate access to a store of the totality of the world's libraries. Advances in communication systems technology may eventually be able to provide individual consoles, perhaps portable, by means of which a central 'data-bank' may be 'tuned' into. The technological problems are immense, the social implications no less so, and the ever-present major problem of librarianship to retrieve to meet individuals' requirements will require even more detailed study. If society can embark on the research necessary for a space age, it may be that it will one day face up to this challenge.

Index

ABLISS *see* Association of British Librarianship and Information Science Schools
AGRIS, 175
ASIS *see* American Society for Information Science
Aberdeen University, 216
academic libraries *see* university libraries
acquisitions, 38, 98
Adams, Professor W. G. S., 72
Africa: school libraries, 110
agents – blbliothecaires x, 59–61
Algermissen, Virginia. *Biomedical librarians in a patient care setting*. . . . 191
Allende, Salvador, 131
Allred, John, 84
  The purpose of the public library, 142
American Society for Information Science, 232
Anglo-American cataloguing rules 1908, 202
Anglo-American cataloguing rules 1967, 116
architects:
  libraries, 59
  of library buildings, 277 *et seq.*
archive studies, 31 *et seq.*
Arnold, Brian C., vii
art galleries, 175
art libraries: staff, 13
Art Libraries Society, 13
Asia: school libraries, 110
Asian immigrants, 129
Aslib, 13, 43, 60, 124, 230
Assistant Librarian The, 24
Association of Assistant Librarians, 20, 21, 23–24, 25
Association of British Librarianship and Information Science Schools, 4
Association of London Chief Librarians, 82
Association of Special Libraries and Information Bureaux *see* Aslib
Association of Teachers in Colleges and Departments of Education, 114
  audio-visual communications section, 115
Association of Teachers in Technical Institutions, 114, 115
Audiovisual Librarian, 124
audio-visual media xi, 13, 17, 29, 42, 55, 92, 108–124, 193–194, 212–213, 239–240, 242, 248–249, 265, 271, 281
Australia: library services, 169
Axford, H. William. *The interrelations of structure, governance and effective resource utilization in academic libraries*, 46, 50

BLCMP *see* Birmingham Libraries Cooperative Mechanisation Project
Bains Committee, 55
Baker Report, 80

287

Index

Barbour indexes, 59
Barnes, Melvyn, vii, xii
Baumfield, Brian H., vii, xii, 152–168
Bedfordshire County Library, 254
Berman, Sandford, 137
Beswick, Norman W., vii, xi
bibliographic references, 28, 56, 70, 86–88, 106–107, 124–125, 151, 184–185, 201, 214–215, 228–229, 244, 274
bibliographic services, 35 *et seq.*, 52, 205
Bibliothèque Nationale, 177
bibliotherapy, 198–199
Bingley, Clive vii, xii, 152–168
Bird, J. *see* Totterdell, Barry *and* Bird, J.
Birmingham Libraries Co-operative Mechanization Project, 98, 204, 209, 213
Birmingham University, 216
Blyton, Enid, 135
Board of Education. *Report on public libraries in England and Wales*, 73
Bodleian Library, 101
Bond, Edward, 131
book trade, xii, 40–41, 74, 152–168, 258, 271–272
Books in English, 93, 98
Bourdillon Report, 76, 78
Bristol University, 216
  library co-operation, 204
British Broadcasting Corporation, 94
  film and videotape library, 114
  record library, 114
  sound archive, 114
British Film Institute, 114
British Institute of Recorded Sound, 114
British Library, xi, xiii, 11, 15, 16, 61, 62, 64, 73, 75, 80, 99, 116–117, 127, 184, 228, 230–231, 240
  formation, 203–204, 217
  relations with Library Association, 17–18, 56
  research, 56, 212–213
British Library Bibliographic Services Division, 211–212, 217
British Library Board, 205
British Library Lending Division, 62, 80–81, 207, 210, 211, 217
British Library Reference Division, 208, 210, 217
  accommodation, 64, 276, 278, 282
  Science Reference Library, 282
British Library Research and Development Department, 72, 73, 82–84, 213–214
British Museum Library *see* British Library Reference Division
British national bibliography, 98, 116
British Rail, 64
Brodman, Estelle. *Users of health science libraries*, 195
Brown, Eleanor F. *Bibliotherapy and its widening applications*, 199
Bruce, Lenny, 134
Brunel University, 221
Buckinghamshire County Library, 84
Bullock, Sir A. *A language for life*, 268
Bush, Vannevar. *As we may think*, 103–104

CANCERLINE, 190
CATV *see* community antenna or cable television
CICRIS, 208
CIM *see* computer input from microfilm
CLASP system, 280
COLA *see* collaborative development in library automation
COM *see* computer output microfilm
Cabinet of Dr Caligari, 130
California, 29
Cambridge University, 216
  Library Management Research Unit, 77, 82, 83, 144

Index

Campbell, A. *and* Metzner, C. A. *Public use of the library and of other sources of information*, 143
Canada:
  library education, 34
  library services, 169, 273
Cardiff University: library co-operation, 204
Carnegie, Andrew, 61, 276
Carnegie United Kingdom Trust. *A report on library provision and policy* 72–73
cataloguing, 8, 13, 14, 38, 52, 89, 98–101, 115–117, 204 *et seq.*, 221, 225
Ceefax, xi, 94
Census of staff in librarianship and information work in the UK, 79
Certain, C. C., 109
Chaplin, A. H. *Basic bibliographic control*, 177
Chartered Institute of Public Finance and Accountancy, 149 *and* Society of County Treasurers. *Public library statistics*, 81–82
Chicago, 29
Childs, C. E. N. *Book figures give no clue to savings*, 221
Chile, 131
Christophers, Richard A. *The LASER union catalogue and a national ISBN inter-lending system*, 213
Chronically Sick and Disabled Persons Act, 1970, 200
Circle of State Librarians, 13
circulations, 89, 97
classification, 14, 89, 202, 223
Classification Research Group, 29
Cleveland County Library: factory loans scheme, 133
Clough, Eric, 43
Cockburn, R. *Science, defence and society*, 62
collaborative development in library automation, 213
college libraries, 26, 64, 109 *et seq.*, 216
  co-operation, 209
  finance, 75
  staff, 17
College of Librarianship Wales, 30, 31, 32, 83
colleges of education, 80
Cologne: library co-operation, 208
community antenna or cable television, 92
computer applications, 13, 18, 29, 35, 40, 42, 44, 47, 53, 55, 73, 89–106, 108 *et seq.*, 173 *et seq.*, 190–191, 203 *et seq.*, 221, 223, 234 *et seq.*
computer input from microfilm, 95
computer output microfilm, 239
Conference of librarians held in London October 1877 *see* International conference, 1877
Conservative Party: involvement with libraries, 73–74
Cooper, Brian, vii
co-operation:
  international, 14, 61, 63, 243
  local, 80–81, 119, 205 *et seq.*, 227, 242–244
  national, 14, 63, 80–81, 202–214, 227–228
  regional, 204 *et seq.*
Corbett, E. V., 43–44
  1965–1975: a decade to remember, 76
Cornwall County Library, 84, 254
Council for Educational Technology, 113, 114, 115, 116, 119, 212–213
Council for National Academic Awards, 30, 31, 34
Coventry public libraries, 254
Coward, Bruce, ix
Croghan, A. *A code of rules for, with an exposition of, integrated cataloguing of non-book media*, 116
Crosland, Anthony, 63
Cutter's expansive classification, 202
Czechoslovakia: libraries, 132

289

Index

DEVSIS, 175
Dainton Report, 73, 203
data-banks, 40, 240, 262
Davis, Bette, 132
de Grazia, Alfred *and* Sohn,
   David A. *Revolution in teaching*, 265
Denmark:
   library co-operation, 208
   public libraries, 268
   school libraries, 268
Department of Education and
   Science, xi, 18, 71 *et seq.*, 144, 218, 253
   inspectors, xi, 76
   library co-operation, 203, 204, 213, 227
   library information series, 76
   organisation, 73
   Secretary of State, 11, 254
   Public libraries and their use, 82
   Public library service, 269
   The scope for automatic data processing in the British Library, 203
Department of Health and Social
   Security, 85
Devon County Library, 84, 209
Dewey Decimal Classification, 202, 223
Dieneman, W. W., 227, 229*n*
disadvantaged: library services, 32, 135–136, 143, 196, 200, 250, 272
displays, 13
Downs, Robert B. *see* McAnally,
   Arthur M. *and* Downs, Robert B.
Dudley, Edward, ix
Durham University, 216

East Anglia University, 216, 220
Eatough, C. L., 108
Eccles, Lord, 73
economic recession, 1, 5, 28, 72, 75–76, 112, 145, 152, 217, 220, 221, 252, 262, 275
Edinburgh University, 216
Edison, Thomas Alva, 108

education and examinations:
   dual qualifications for
      librarianship and teaching, 17, 267–268, 270
   for librarianship, xi, xii, 1, 3, 4, 6–7, 11, 15–16, 17, 18–19, 24, 25, 29–42, 44 *et seq.*, 78, 79, 115, 192, 217–219, 233–235, 246, 258–259
Educational Foundation for Visual
   Aids, 113
Eliot, T. S. *Notes towards the definition of culture*, 126–127
Ellis, C. D. *see* Talbot, J. R. *and* Ellis, C. D.
Emery, R. *Staff communication in libraries*, 48
English Stage Company, 127
Enright, Dr., 123
Essex University, 216
European Economic Commission, 25, 90, 240
Exeter University: library
   co-operation, 204
Exeter University Institute of
   Education: regional resource
   centre experimental project, 118–119
Eynon, G. B., vii, x

FAUST *see* Foklebibliotekernes
   Automations System
FID *see* International Federation for
   Documentation
Ferrybridge cooling towers, 71
film librarians, 13
finance, 1–2, 5, 17, 28, 47, 61, 64, 72, 75–78, 152–153, 245, 252, 254–258
Finland: youth libraries, 273
Folkebibliotekernes Automations
   System, 208
Foskett, D. J. 261
Fothergill, Richard, 119
France: school libraries, 110

GLASS *see* Greater London Audio
   Subject Specialisation Scheme

Index

Gans, Herbert. *People and plans*, 142
Garrison, Guy, 45
General strike, 153
Gilchrist, Alan, 60
Glasgow University, 216
Goebbels, Dr., 126, 130
Gordon Walker, Patrick, *see* Walker, Patrick Gordon
government:
  involvement with libraries, x, xi, 2, 5, 14, 18, 61, 64, 71–86, 129, 152
  libraries, 63, 64, 75
Gramophone, The, 114
Greater London Audio Subject Specialisation Scheme, 212
Greater London Council Intelligence Unit, 208
Greene, Graham, 154
Groombridge, B. *The Londoner and his library*, 143
Grosz, George, 130
Guttsman, W. L. *Subject specialisation in academic libraries*, 220

HELPIS *see* Higher Education Learning Programmes Information Service
HULTIS, 208
Haas, Warren. *Scholarly communication*, 90–91
Hall, G. K., 221
Hamming, R. W. *Computers and society*, 101–102
Harris, K. G. E.
  The polytechnic library explosion, 227–228
  Subject specialisation in polytechnic libraries, 220
Harris, Michael. *The purpose of the American public library*, 142
Harrison, K. C., vii
Harty, Sir Hamilton, 128
Havard-Williams, Professor P. *see* Williams, Professor P. Havard-
health sciences libraries *see* medical libraries

Henderson, R. P., 108
Henry, Florence, 109
Herbert, A. P., 167
Herzberg, F. *Work and the nature of man*, 46, 48
Higher Education Learning Programmes Information Service, 113
Hilliard, R. P., vii
Hillingdon Project, 144, 147
Hindemith, Paul, 130
Holroyd, Gileon, vii, x, xi
Home Office, 85
Hookway, Dr Harry T., 68
hospital libraries *see* medical libraries

ICA *see* United States: International Cooperation Administration
IFLA *see* International Federation of Library Associations
INIS, 242
ISBN *see* International Standard Book Numbers
ISDS *see* International Serials Data System
Illinois, 29
Imperial Chemical Industries Ltd, 64
Imperial War Museum, 114
Independent Broadcasting Authority, 94
indexing, 35, 37, 59, 115
induction training *see* training, in-service
information handling, xi, 7, 12, 14, 29 *et seq.*, 57 *et seq.*, 89–106, 172 *et seq.*, 186–191, 206 *et seq.*, 231 *et seq.*
information scientists, 13, 34, 36, 41, 184, 233
information services, xi, 11, 12, 27, 60–61, 71 *et seq.*, 172, 186, 231 *et seq.*
Inland Revenue, 61
Inner London Education Authority, 113
  media resources officer, 119–120

291

Index

in-service training *see* training, in-service
Institute of Historical Research, 208
Institute of Information Scientists, 13, 230
Institute of Municipal Treasurers and Accountants *see* Chartered Institute for Public Finance and Accountancy
Intergovernmental conference on the overall planning of national documentation, library and archives infrastructures, 33
interlibrary loans, 14, 80-81, 204 *et seq.*
International Bureau of Education, 110
International conference, 1877, 169
International Federation for Documentation, 179
International Federation of Library Associations, 34, 77, 116, 169 *et seq.*
international librarianship, 24-26, 169-184
International Library and Bibliographical Committee *see* International Federation of Library Associations
International Serials Data System, 177
international standard bibliographic description for non-book materials, 116
International Standard Book Numbers, 99, 213

Japan: investment in information, 231
Jara, Victor, 131
Jast, Louis Stanley, 140-141
Jessup report, 78
John Rylands University Library, Manchester, 218
Johns, Capt. W. E. *Biggles*, 135
Johnson, I. M. *see* Taylor, J. N. *and* Johnson, I. M.

Johnson, J. *A survey of construction industry libraries*, 59
Jones, Arthur C., 78
Jordan, Peter, 45

Kalamazoo (Michigan), 109
Kelly's directories, 237
Kemeny, J. G. *A library for 2000 AD*, 104
Kent University, 216
Kenyon report, 73, 169, 184
King's Fund Centre. *A library service for the mentally handicapped*, 198
Knapp, Patricia, 52

LAMSAC *see* Local Authorities Management Services and Computer Committee
LASER *see* London and South Eastern Library Region
LIBRIS *see* Library Information System for Sweden
Labour Party:
  involvement with libraries, 73-75
  The arts: a discussion document for the Labour movement, 74
Lambeth: public libraries, 254
Lancaster University, 216
  library, 144
  Library Management Research Unit, 82, 83
law libraries: staff, 13
learned journals, xi
Lee, Jennie, 86
Leeds Polytechnic:
  Public Libraries Management Research Unit, 84
  School of Librarianship, 17, 31, 38, 83
Leeds University, 216
legislation, 15
  see also individual acts
Leicestershire County Library, 74, 118, 254
Lenny, 134
Leverhulme Trustees, 30
Lewis, Sinclair. *Dodsworth*, 168

Index

Librarians for Social Change, 13
libraries:
  buildings, xii, 74, 77, 82–83, 275–286
  rôle in society, 126–139
  standards, 14, 15, 84–85, 285–286
  statistics, xi, 81–82
Library Advisers, 18, 71, 76, 77, 80, 84
Library Advisory Council for England, 123–124
Libraries and their finance, 72, 75
Library Advisory Councils, 18, 78, 85–86
Library Assistants' Certificate, 15, 66
Library Association, 114, 129, 228
  Audio-visual Group, 124
  branches and groups, xi, 6–10, 20–24
  Cataloguing and Indexing Group, 21
  centenary, ix, xiii, 3, 184
  Centenary Celebrations Sub-committee, ix
  Centenary Celebrations Working Party *see* Centenary Celebrations Sub-committee
  conferences, 43, 86, 129, 169–170, 184
  Council, ix, 9, 10, 19, 21–22, 25, 135
  education and examinations, 1, 3, 4, 6–7, 11, 15–16, 18–19, 24, 25, 29 *et seq.*, 217–219
  Executive Committee, ix
  finance, 8
  future rôle, ix, xi, xiii, 1–12, 27–28
  history, ix, 73, 202, 216, 275
  information service, xi, 27
  in-service training, 46, 52, 55–56
  international activities, 24–26, 169, 182–184
  International and Comparative librarianship Group, 25, 182–183
  Library History Group, 10
  lobbying of Ministers and MPS, 5, 14
  membership, 1, 2, 12, 13–28, 135
  Public Libraries Group, 21, 22
  publications, 24
  relations with British Library, 17–18, 56
  research, 1, 2, 4, 14
  Royal Charter, 26
  salaries and conditions of service of members, 4, 25, 26–27
  secretariat, 6–11, 19–20, 21, 25
  staff and grading census, 260
  standards, 3–4, 10–11, 14, 15
  statistics, 81
  unification with other professional bodies, 11–12, 28, 230
  voting membership, 4–5, 16
  Working Party on Association services, 3, 10, 20, 21–22
  Working Party on future of professional qualifications, 259
Non-book materials cataloguing rules, 116
Professional and non-professional duties in libraries, 46, 66
Library Association Record, 24
Library Information System for Sweden, 208
library management, x–xi, 32, 35, 38, 40–41, 43–55, 57–69, 223–226, 249, 251–252, 259–260
Library of Congress, 99, 228
  Classification, 223
library schools, xi, 3–4, 11, 14, 17, 29–42, 43 *et seq.*, 78, 79–80, 83–84, 122–123, 218, 223, 246, 254, 259
library science: standards, xi
Library service in a multi-racial community (conference), 129
library suppliers, 157–159
Likert, R. *New patterns of management*, 65
Lincoln: public libraries, 144
Line, Maurice, 203, 210
Liverpool University, 216

Index

Local Authorities Management Services and Computer Committee, 78–79, 82, 253–254
local government reorganisation, xii, 47, 55, 63, 64, 78, 80, 81, 153, 165, 251, 252
Local Government Operational Research Unit *see* Royal Institute of Public Administration
local history:
 librarians, 13
 societies, 118
Locke, Dr W. N. *Computer costs for large libraries*, 91
London and South Eastern Library Region, 80, 211, 213
London Festival Ballet, 128
London Symphony Orchestra, 128
London Union Catalogue *see* London and South Eastern Library Region
London University, 216
Los Angeles Free Press, 137
Loughborough Technical College School of Librarianship, 31
Loughborough University of Technology, 17, 31, 32, 38
Luckham, B. *The library in society*, 143

MARC *see* Machine Readable Cataloguing
MEDLARS *see* Medical Literature Analysis and Retrieval System
MEDLINE, 190–191
McAnally, Arthur M. *and* Downs, Robert B. *The changing role of directors of university libraries*, 225–226
McCarthy, Senator Joe, 132
McClellan, A. W. *The reader, the library and the book*, 141, 255
McColvin, Lionel R. *The public library system of Great Britain*, 73, 141, 203, 254, 275

McGregor, D. M. *The human side of enterprise*, 49
Machine Readable Cataloguing, 99–100, 117, 204, 208, 221
Mack, Elizabeth, 43
MacKenna, R. O., 220, 224, 225, 229n
MacKenzie, N. *Educational communication*, 266
McLuhan, Marshall, 248
Malmo City Library, 133
management *see* library management
management review analysis programmes, 49, 53
Manchester University, 216
Mansell Information, 221
Mant, A. *The manager as professional*, 69
Marsh, Richard. *In place of profit*, 64
Martin, Lowell A. *Adults and the Pratt library*, 146
Martin, W. J. *The Highfield Community Library, Belfast*, 148
Marxism: newspapers, 61
Maslow, A. H., 48
Massachusetts Institute of Technology, 91
Masterson, W. A. J. *see* Wilson, T. D. *and* Masterson, W. A. J.
Mathis der Maler, 130
Maud Report, 251
M'Bow, Amadou Mahtar, 179
media centres *see* resource centres
medical libraries, xii, 7, 85, 186–201
 staff, 13, 191–192
Medical Literature Analysis and Retrieval System, 190
Members of Parliament, 71
memex, 103–104
Merrison Report, 192
Metzner, C. A. *see* Campbell, A. *and* Metzner, C. A.
microfilms and reprographic processes, 32, 39, 41, 93, 189–190, 223, 239–240, 265, 271
Middlesex County Library, 109

294

Index

Ministry of Agriculture, Fisheries and Food, 60
Ministry of Education:
  Standards of public library service in England and Wales, 73, 203, 252–253
  Working party on inter-library cooperation in England and Wales, 73, 203
mobile librarians, 13
Monroe, Margaret. *Reader services and bibliotherapy*, 199
Morrison, P. D., 43
Munford, Dr W. A. *A history of the Library Association 1877–1977*, ix, x
Murison, W. J. *Images and real people*, 51
museums, 175
  charges, 74
music libraries: staff, 13

NALGO *see* National and Local Government Officers Association
NATIS *see* National Information Systems
NUPE *see* National Union of Public Employees
National and Local Government Officers Association, 68, 260
National Central Library *see* British Library Lending Division
National Council for Educational Technology, 116
National Educational Closed Circuit Television Association, 115
National Health Service, 68–69, 194, 195
National Information Systems, 33, 34, 40, 90, 173 *et seq.*
National Lending Library for Science and Technology *see* British Library Lending Division
national libraries, 80, 82, 217
  cooperation, 14, 203
  finance, 75
  staff, 13
National Library of Medicine. *Clinical librarians accompany physicians on ward rounds*, 191
National Reference Library of Science and Invention *see* British Library Reference Division: Science Reference Library
National Union of Public Employees, 68
net book agreement, 155–156
The New Chilean Song, 131
New Library World, 166
New Zealand: library services, 169
Newcastle upon Tyne Polytechnic, 220
Nixdorf, 240
North America:
  bibliotherapy, 198–199
  college libraries, 121
  public libraries, 117
  university libraries, 49
North Staffordshire: public libraries, 144
North Western Polytechnic, London *see* Polytechnic of North London
North Western Region, 80
Northern Ireland: public libraries, 148
Nottingham University, 219
Nuffield Foundation, 118

OCLC *see* Ohio College Library Centre
OECD *see* Organisation for Economic Co-operation and Development
OSTI *see* British Library Research and Development Department
Ohio College Library Centre, 98, 100, 208
Ontario College Bibliocentre, 101
Open University, 68, 92, 118, 193
Oracle, 94
Organisation for Economic Co-operation and Development, 72, 232, 234

295

Index

Orr, J. M., vii, xii
Oxford University, 216

PCMI *see* photochromic micro-image system
PRF *see* potential requirements file
Panizzi, Antonio, 223
Paris conference on cataloguing principles, 29
Parker, J. Stephen, viii
  International librarianship – a reconnaissance, 171, 183
Parra, Violetta, 131
Parry Report, 15, 73, 81, 213
Patent Office, 61
Patten, M. N., viii, xii
Paulin, Lorna
  In-service training, 49
  The work of the library advisory councils for England and Wales, 76
Peace News, 131
Perry, J. W., 225
  The problems and future development of the older and larger university libraries, 219
photochromic micro-image system, 93
Plaister, Jean M., viii
Pluse, J. M. *The AAL's working parties and the future*, 28
Poland: libraries, 132, 133
polytechnic libraries:
  co-operation, xii, 209, 227–228
  finance, 75, 77
  resources, 119, 281
  staff, 17, 67
  subject specialisation, 220
Polytechnic of North London, 31, 32, 83
Post Office, 94, 104, 240
Postfax, xi, 104
potential requirements file, 98
Powell, Lawrence Clark, 50
Previn, Andre, 128
prison libraries, xii, 85, 196, 199–200
Public Lending Right, 73, 74, 154, 166–168

public libraries, xii, 26, 41, 58, 60, 62, 64, 71 *et seq.*, 173
  automation, 247, 249
  buildings, 263, 283–285
  charges, 74, 258
  co-operation, xii, 14, 209 *et seq.*
  finance, 75 *et seq.*, 152–153, 245, 252, 254–258
  resources, 78, 109 *et seq.*, 194, 203, 247 *et seq.*
  services for the disadvantaged, 32, 135–136, 143, 250, 272
  staff, 13, 15–16, 43 *et seq.*, 45, 48, 55, 66, 78–80, 82, 153, 245–261, 263
  statistics, 80–81
  user needs, 140 *et seq.*
  youth work, xii, xii–xiii, 7, 13, 74, 268–274
Public Libraries and Museums Act, 1964, 15, 73, 76, 81, 84, 117
Public Libraries Research Group, 145–146, 149
public relations, 5, 13, 18–19, 41, 51
publishing *see* book trade

Queen's University Belfast School of Library Studies, 30, 31

Raeburn, Anna, 135
Ranganathan, S. R. *Five laws of library science*, 141
Ratcliffe, Dr F. W. 217–218, 220, 224, 229*n*.
rate support grants, 77
Ravilious, C. P., 110, 116
reference librarians, 13
regional library bureaux, 80
report literature, 41, 42
Report of the departmental committee on libraries, 169, 184
research and development:
  bibliographical, xi, 1, 2, 4, 13, 18, 31, 33, 82–84
  industrial, 62, 173
  medical, 192–193
research monographs, xi

Index

resource centres, 16–17, 33, 108–124, 198, 208, 231, 264, 276
managers, 13
Roberts report, 73
Ronan Point flats, 71
Rotherham: public libraries, 254
Royal Canadian Institute, 108
Royal Institute of Public Administration, Local Government Operational Research Unit, 80, 214
Royal Opera House Covent Garden, 128
Royal Shakespeare Theatre Company, 132
Royal Society of Medicine, 210

SCOLA system, 280
SCONUL *see* Standing Conference on National and University Libraries
SDI *see* selective dissemination of information
SINTO, 208
SPINES, 175
SWALCAP, 204, 209, 213
Sadler's Wells, 128
St Andrews University, 216
Sargent, Sir Malcolm, 128
Saunders, Wilfred L., 43
British librarianship today, ix, x
see also Schur, Herbert *and* Saunders, W. L.
Savage, Ernest A.
The librarian and his committee, 57
A librarian's memories, 14, 21
Sayers, W. C. Berwick, 109
Scandinavia: public libraries, 117
Schofield, J. L. *Job evaluation, job analysis, job satisfaction and resistance to change*, 48
school libraries, xii, 7, 16–17, 32, 64, 74, 75, 82, 85, 173, 266, 276
buildings, 283–285
resources, 109 *et seq.*, 281
staff, xii, 13, 17, 262–268, 273–274
School Library Association, 114
Schools Council, 113, 118

Schur, Herbert
Education and training of information specialists for the 1970s, 45, 47,
and Saunders, W. L. *Education and training for scientific and technological library and information work*, 78
scientific and technical information, 72, 90, 172, 208, 237
scientific reports, xi
Scotland, 63
Scottish Educational Film Association, 113
Scottish Opera, 128
Select committee on public libraries, 1849, 72
selective dissemination of information, 60, 164, 235–236, 240
serial librarians, 13
Sewell, Philip H., 80
Government concern for libraries and information services, 71
Shakespeare, William, 63
Sharp, H. A., 109
Sheffield, 81
local library co-operation, 204, 213, 228
Sheffield University, 216
Centre for Research in User Studies, 83, 148
Postgraduate School of Librarianship and Information Science, 30, 31, 32, 38, 83, 204, 213
Shepherd, Jennifer, viii, xii
Shera, Jesse, 51
Shimmon, Ross, viii, xi
Siemens, 240
Simpson, Neil A., viii, xi
Simsova, Sylva. *Comparative librarianship: the next ten years*, 182–183
Slade Film History Register, 114
Smith, Dr R. S., 219, 220–221, 223, 226–227, 228, 229 *n*
Society of County Treasurers *see* Chartered Institute for Public Finance and Accountancy

297

Index

Sohn, David A. *see* de Grazia, Alfred *and* Sohn, David A.
Somerset County Library, 118
South Africa: library services, 169
South America: school libraries, 110
South East Region *see* London and South Eastern Library Region
South Cheshire: public libraries, 144
Soviet Union:
  libraries, 132
  school libraries, 110
special libraries, 26, 60, 80, 109 *et seq.*, 147, 164
  co-operation, 14
  resources, 236–240
  staff, 13, 15–16, 48, 230–244
staff *see* library management *and* under particular types of library
staff training *see* training, in-service
Standards for libraries in colleges of education, 15
Standing Conference on National and University Libraries, 227
Stewart, Charles C. *Your hospital library – an awakening giant*, 193
stock editors, 13
Strathclyde University School of Librarianship, 31, 32
students:
  at British universities, 216
  grants, 79
subject specialisation, 5, 18, 46, 53, 67, 80, 219–220, 248, 263–264, 282
Sussex tapes, 118
Sussex University, 216
Sweden:
  library co-operation, 208
  school libraries, 110
  workers' libraries, 133
Switzerland: school libraries, 110
Sydney Opera House, 278

Talbot, J. R. *and* Ellis, C. D. *Analysis and costing of company training*, 48, 54

Taylor, J. N. *and* Johnson, I. M. *Public libraries and their use*, 144
teacher-librarians, 17, 264, 267–268
teachers, 79
  salaries, 74
Telefunken, 240
Teleview, 104
Thomas, P. *and* Ward, V. *Where the time goes*, 65
Thompson, James, viii, xii
  The argument against subject specialisation, 225
  Library power, 43, 45, 220, 221, 224
The Times Educational Supplement, 44–45
The Times Literary Supplement, 92
Toffler, Alvin. *Future shock*, 45, 235
Toronto University, 221
Totterdell, Barry, viii, xi
  and Bird, J. *The effective library*, 144, 147
trade literature, 42
trade union for librarians, 26
training, in-service, xii, 13, 43–55
translations, 238
Trinity College, Dublin, 216
Tynan, Kenneth, 134

UBC *see* Universal Bibliographic Control
UNIDO *see* United Nations Industrial Development Organisation
UNISIST *see* United Nations Information System in Science and Technology
Ulster *see* Northern Ireland
Unesco, 33, 34, 110, 242
  see also National Information Systems; United Nations Information System in Science and Technology
United Nations general assembly, 171–172
United Nations Industrial Development Organisation, 172

Index

United Nations Information System in Science and Technology, 33, 173 *et seq.*, 243 *see also* AGRIS; DEVSIS; SPINES
United States, 169, 172
 Apollo project, 71
 college libraries, 109
 computer applications, 122, 221, 241
 co-operation, 63, 208, 227
 International Co-operation Administration, 179
 investment in information, 231
 library buildings, 279
 library education, 29, 34, 39
 national conference of professors of educational administration, 123
 national program for acquisitions and cataloguing, 221
 national technical information service, 102
 public libraries, 109, 142–143, 268, 273
 school libraries, 109 *et seq.*, 268
 university and research libraries, 221, 222, 225
Universal Bibliographic Control, 174 *et seq.*
University College London School of Library, Archive and Information Studies, 17, 29, 30, 38
University Grants Committee, 73, 77–78, 126, 227
university libraries, 7, 26, 32, 41, 49, 58, 64, 67, 75 *et seq.*, 97, 109 *et seq.*, 147, 173, 281
 buildings, 282
 co-operation, 14, 209, 226–228
 finance, 75, 77–78
 staff, 13, 15–16, 17, 45, 47, 48, 216–228
 subject specialisation, 219–220
University of Buckingham, 64
University of Wisconsin Library School, 199

user needs, xi, xii, 35, 41, 44, 140–150, 202, 285
Usherwood, R. C., viii

VTR *see* video tape recording
Vanderbilt University, 92
Varley, D. H., 229 *n*
Ventris, Michael, 91
Verne, Jules, xiii
video tape recording, 240
Viewdata, xi, 94, 240–241

Wade, J. R., viii
Wait, Carl, 232
Walker, M. *Subject specialisation*, 67
Walker, Patrick Gordon, 64
Ward, V. *see* Thomas, P. and Ward, V.
Warwick University, 216
Watkinson, H., *and others. Managing to survive*, 64
Wells, H. G., xiii, 262
Welsh National Opera, 128
West Indian immigrants, 129
West Indies: library services, 169
Williams, Professor P. Havard, vii, 34
 Planning information manpower, 34
Williams, Raymond, 130
Williams, Shirley, 90
Wilson, T. D. *and* Masterson, W. A. J. *Local library co-operation*, 204
Wiltshire County Library, 118, 119
Woman, 135
Wood, Sir Henry, 128
Woods, R. G., viii, xi

YLG News, 24
York University, 216
Yorkshire: library co-operation, 80, 204

Ziman, Professor J. M. *The light of knowledge*, 105